Global Software Development Handbook

Titles in the
Auerbach Series on Applied Software Engineering
Phillip A. Laplante, Pennsylvania State University, Series Editor

Antipatterns: Identification, Refactoring, and Management
Phillip A. Laplante and Colin J. Neill
0-8493-2994-9

Global Software Development Handbook
Raghvinder Sangwan, Matthew Bass, Neel Mullick, Daniel J. Paulish,
and Juergen Kazmeier
0-8493-9384-1

Software Engineering Quality Practices
Ronald Kirk Kandt
0-8493-4633-9

Global Software Development Handbook

Raghvinder Sangwan · Matthew Bass
Neel Mullick · Daniel J. Paulish
Juergen Kazmeier

CRC Press
Taylor & Francis Group
Boca Raton London New York

CRC Press is an imprint of the
Taylor & Francis Group, an **informa** business
AN AUERBACH BOOK

CRC Press
Taylor & Francis Group
6000 Broken Sound Parkway NW, Suite 300
Boca Raton, FL 33487-2742

First issued in paperback 2019

© 2007 by Taylor & Francis Group, LLC
CRC Press is an imprint of Taylor & Francis Group, an Informa business

No claim to original U.S. Government works

ISBN-13: 978-0-8493-9384-6 (hbk)
ISBN-13: 978-0-367-39025-9 (pbk)

Library of Congress Cataloging-in-Publication Data

Global software development handbook / Raghvinder Sangwan ... [et al.].
        p. cm.
    Includes bibliographical references and index.
    ISBN 0-8493-9384-1 (alk. paper)
    1. Computer software--Development. 2. Software localization. I. Sangwan, Raghvinder.

QA76.76.D47G587 2006
005.1--dc22   2006047730

Visit the Taylor & Francis Web site at
http://www.taylorandfrancis.com

and the CRC Press Web site at
http://www.crcpress.com

Contents

SECTION II: PLANNING

SECTION III: ORGANIZATION STRUCTURE

SECTION IV: MONITORING AND CONTROL

Section V: Case Studies

Foreword by Manfred Broy

Development of large software systems has been and will continue to be a challenging engineering task, in particular as projects become more interdisciplinary and distributed. Fritz Bauer coined the term software engineering in a conference in Garmisch in the late sixties. In the 40 years since then we have seen much progress in making software engineering tasks more systematic, better manageable, and more predictable. This was achieved by enormous advances in software life cycle models, better techniques to plan and control projects, sophisticated architectures, more adequate methodologies, superior modeling techniques, and improved tooling. Today we have gained a better understanding and deeper insights into the rules, principles, and success factors of software development. But still, we find numerous challenges in engineering large software systems.

At a time when companies and networks of companies are becoming distributed and are cooperating all over the world, offshoring is one of the most popular ideas in management but is controversial in software engineering. The development of software in internationally distributed projects, where software is developed in many distant places, is one of today's big challenges. We still must face and master the challenges of global software development (GSD). Although many ambitious industrial projects are ongoing using global software development approaches, so far not enough experiences have been systematically collected, properly analyzed, and published about the heuristics, principles, and rules of distributed global software development.

Software engineering is a difficult task in any case. However, in global software development we have to deal with additional challenges. Some are obvious and well known like different time zones or difficulties in the communications among team members with different cultural backgrounds. Others are subtler such as building up trust between the teams and taking care of the general key success factors of software development, many of which are not so easy to achieve in global software development.

So far, our systematic know-how in GSD is relatively poor. Questions to be answered for GSD comprise among others the following themes:

- Software life cycle models
- Project planning, estimation, and risk management
- Implications of GSD on the phases of software development such as requirements engineering, design, implementation, integration, and testing
- Quality assurance
- Team organization
- Team skills and special training
- Division of labor and responsibilities
- Communication organization
- Implications on the software product, especially the architecture
- Infrastructure and tool support.

In addition to these more detailed technical and methodological issues, from a management point of view we are interested in questions like:

- What are overall success factors and principles?
- What is the economical impact?
- Which kinds of projects are best suited for GSD?

Therefore it is highly appreciated and a value in itself that Siemens Corporate Research in Princeton started experiments in global software development in 2003 within the Global Studio Project (GSP). Two one-year experiments have been carried out since then. Several universities around the world were involved in this first experiment in the academic years 2004/05 and the second experiment was undertaken one year later.

The goals of these experiments were clear. The project was aimed at the collection of empirical data in global software development as well as to find appropriate processes, tools, and forms of collaboration. It supports increasing our understanding of how one has to organize global software development projects to be sure that they are successful. The ways to plan and run the experiments were less clear during its initial planning in 2003.

In fact, it is important that such experimentation can be done without running into enormous economic risks for companies when they take the first steps in global software development on real-life projects. Therefore, the value of a project experiment of this kind cannot be estimated high enough. It is particularly important that in a project like this, all the data can be made publicly available — in contrast to real-life software development projects where there are problems with keeping failures secret and not talking about confidential details.

Being involved in GSP in many ways and seeing my research group at the Technical University of Munich taking part in the experiment for two years, I can only say that it was a highly interesting and valuable experience. It was also very encouraging to see how the researchers and students involved in the projects learned much about GSD and finally understood much better many of the issues of software development.

This book presents a good collection of the findings and conclusions of two years of the GSP. It provides a first data basis for GSD. However, this book not only reports on the GSP. Perhaps even more important, it gives several hints and tips on how to organize GSD projects, what to do and keep in mind to be able to do successful GSD. This advice is based both on experience from the GSP and on the deep analysis and background knowledge of the researchers involved. Here the expertise and long-term training of the project team and the researchers at Siemens Corporate Research at Princeton in business aspects, requirements engineering, architecture, methodology, and tool support proved to be essential.

What I like about this book is its lightweight presentation of a number of complicated and intricate themes. It is of value for one interested in software development as such, but it is, in particular, of high value to researchers, developers, and project managers interested and involved in GSD.

It is a pleasure to thank especially the team at Siemens Corporate Research for their efforts in making the experiments available to the research community, making sure that their interesting results are published, and seeing this as a contribution to the body of knowledge of software engineering. Being involved myself in the experiments with a team at the Technical University of Munich, it is a pleasure for me to see this book coming out. It is a valuable document and contribution on topics of growing interest and general importance for our world's economy and our engineering skills.

Manfred Broy
Chair of Software & Systems Engineering
Fakultät für Informatik
Technische Universität München

Foreword
by James D. Herbsleb

Particle physicists invest an awful lot of time, energy, and money in blasting particles into each other. They have good reason, of course — it's generally not possible to observe all the behaviors of interest when particles are in their natural habitat, so tightly are they bound to each other. Violent collisions serve to scatter these bits of matter and energy in all directions, and by observing them in this highly dispersed and kinetic state, one is actually in a much better position to infer the unobserved forces that were at work all along.

Geographically distributed projects serve an analogous — if unintended — function in software development. As practitioners and researchers, we are continuing to learn about the surprisingly critical and diverse functions served by physical collocation, the opportunities for communication and collaboration it affords, and the shared context it provides. Until we all began observing the trajectories of distributed teams as they flew off in unexpected directions, we weren't fully aware of how much "coordination work" a project requires, and how invisibly much of it is handled when people simply occupy the same space.

All of this is not just to provide the reader with a grandiose and possibly entertaining metaphor, but it is to say that there are at least two ways of reading this excellent new book. One is to read it as the authors intended, as a guide to managing the particular difficulties of distributed projects, based on extensive experience, and combining many sound, well-established techniques, and innovating when there are no existing tools already on hand. They describe a way — not *the* way, as they are at pains to point out — *a* way of approaching distributed projects, with particular attention to the difficult early stages. It combines elements from methodologies that one would not expect to peacefully coexist, such as the Rational Unified Process (RUP) and Scrum. It calls for moving in directions that appear at first contradictory — be more agile *and* more rigid? But as you dig into the material, and as you see the ideas applied in the well-documented case studies, you begin to realize that the wisdom in the book is deeper than "be agile" or "define your process." It engages the reader in thinking about *when* to be agile about *what*, and *which* processes require discipline and *why*. While many readers will no doubt be tempted to apply it in cookbook fashion, it is not intended as a recipe to be followed by rote, but it's rather more like the suggestion of a path that has worked for them, along with thoughtful descriptions of the lay of the land and the locations of nasty traps along the way. Whether you follow that particular path or not, you will benefit from the geography lesson.

Which leads me to the second way of reading this book: as a source of insights about the forces at work in software development more generally. As one of the group of researchers participating in the Global Studio Project (GSP), I have come to believe that many of the ideas we have developed and tried out in this "laboratory" could benefit collocated teams nearly as much as geographically dispersed teams. Our experiments with social network analysis, for example, have shown this to be a valuable and practical tool for monitoring coordination problems, which can occur in any project of significant size, collocated or otherwise. Techniques for achieving clarity in work assignments are critical for dispersed teams, but are likely to be very helpful in other cases as well. This project has helped me come around to the view that coordination is the central problem, and collocation is just one — albeit a very powerful one — of the many solutions. When collocation is not possible, the authors describe how to substitute the other solutions to manage a project effectively.

This book represents a well-thought-out synthesis of the authors' experiences, the published literature, and the research performed by the GSP research team. The reader will find it to be a highly useful, practical, and well-informed guide to the current state-of-the-art. There are still many problems to solve in this area, but reading this book makes me realize how far we have come.

James D. Herbsleb
Institute for Software Research
International School of Computer Science
Carnegie Mellon University

Preface

The idea for this book started with the involvement of Siemens Corporate Research (SCR) with many global software development (GSD) projects at Siemens, a multinational organization employing more than 30,000 software engineers with offices in most countries around the globe. Working on these projects, we found that, collectively, Siemens companies around the world had gems of information on GSD that would be of tremendous benefit if synthesized into a structured body of knowledge. We wanted to, however, first validate and vet this body of knowledge and broaden our base with the research community. Consequently, SCR launched a research program on GSD in 2003 in close collaboration with Carnegie Mellon University, Harvard Business School, International Institute of Information Technology Bangalore, Monmouth University, Penn State University, Technical University of Munich, Pontifical Catholic University of Rio Grande de Sul, and the University of Limerick. This book is a result of the collective wisdom harnessed from the many GSD projects from Siemens and the experiments conducted by this research community from eight schools in five nations across four continents. The wisdom has three main pillars: (1) the best practices of project experience that made this book concrete, (2) an intensive literature analysis that broadened the base of the experience, and (3) the experimental research that was never done before in global software development and which gave us extraordinary insights.

Based on this collective wisdom, we have identified a number of factors critical to the success of GSD projects. While these factors are useful for all projects, the business case and necessity is much greater when projects are geographically distributed across several time zones, with many remote teams having no history of ever working together and compounded by language and culture differences. For each of these factors we have codified best practices and defined a process framework that leverages these best practices, providing guidance on how the best practices can be operationalized within a given project.

While working on the book, we also observed a desire among engineers working on GSD projects to adopt agile software development practices that favor lightweight processes with minimal documentation that can be dynamically adapted to the demands of a project. One would think, however, that distributed development would require lots of documentation due to its high communication needs. Although seemingly counterintuitive, these observations led us to think of combining the two trends.

This book offers a unique perspective on global agility, a concept that describes the convergence of two movements — globally distributed and agile software development. We recognize that many of the agile practices work best in a collocated environment, and therefore we have attempted to augment agile practices where needed so that we can maintain much of their benefit yet scale the approach to a GSD context. We have done this by developing and defining infrastructural configurations, processes, mechanisms, and best practices that allow for optimal trade-offs between agility and process discipline. The emphasis is especially on product developments that require a new or modified software architecture. Our emphasis is also on the early phases of a project because of its importance to GSD projects.

This book is for both software engineering practitioners and students of project management focused on distributed development of software. It should be particularly useful to project managers who are planning a distributed project, but those currently involved with such projects may also find useful advice and a fresh perspective on this subject. It can be used as a supplement to an undergraduate- or graduate-level course in software project management, especially when discussing issues surrounding globally distributed software development.

We have organized this book into five major sections. The Introduction section, consisting of Chapters 1 and 2, puts forth our motivation for this work and describes a process framework for GSD. We introduce a number of critical success factors key to the success of GSD projects.

Chapters 3 through 8 form the Planning section. We start with the modeling of the business requirements that are progressively refined from the product features to system requirements. Concurrent with the requirements engineering effort, we identify the architecturally significant requirements that influence the architecture of the system under consideration. We then take into account the structure and characteristics of the distributed teams to gauge their ability to create a system with the given architecture. This information is used to derive system modules and their specifications. A long-term build and release plan is developed from the feature and module requirements specification. A development plan that estimates schedule, resources, and costs is finally put in place, and an iterative time-boxed approach is used to achieve synchronous development of components among the various geographically distributed teams around the world.

A number of factors achieve greater significance when projects are globally distributed. Coordination and control become difficult due to distance among geographically distributed teams. While there are technologies and tools available to facilitate remote communication, our research and experience suggest they may not be as effective as face-to-face meetings. One way to tackle this problem, therefore, is to minimize excessive communication by optimizing the amount of collaboration between teams. Collaboration can be optimized by breaking the system into loosely coupled subsystems and components. Each team can then work relatively independently of one another on a given subsystem or component. There must, however, be a central organization responsible for the specification of these components, their shared architecture, and coordinating their distributed development through regular builds of a testable application. Members are also needed to straddle the central and the geographically distributed teams to (1) overcome issues related to teams not knowing each other, each other's language and culture, and the absence of a project's daily processes to be followed by the members at different sites; (2) create a shared project vision; and (3) build cooperation and trust. Chapters 9 and 10 discuss an organization structure that not only fosters team building, but also achieves effective collaboration among the central and the geographically distributed teams.

The Monitoring and Control section describes issues surrounding the quality of the product and process in a distributed environment. We also realize that when the central organization is the product owner that distributes the development of its constituent components to the distributed teams, it must consider fostering cordial, long-term relationships with these teams, treating them as its partner and competence center for the component(s) it delivers. Establishing such relationships is especially useful considering the ongoing support and maintenance needs of the product under development. Because communication is a big challenge between the central organization and the distributed teams — especially ones separated by several time zones — special attention is given to the tool infrastructure and discovering patterns of communication among these teams to determine effective strategies for managing such communication.

Chapters 14 through 17 present case studies that capture our experiences (both good and bad) from various distributed projects that we were involved with at Siemens. The names of the projects in these case studies have been coded to isolate the identity of products and people involved. The projects vary in size, keeping in mind that small-scale projects will be more relevant to smaller companies and large ones would benefit larger organizations. The relevant parts of these case studies are threaded through all the chapters in the book, giving readers a perspective on how the theory is put into practice.

Chapter 18 concludes the book, highlighting issues surrounding globally distributed software development projects. We analyze both successful and failed projects and summarize our beliefs described throughout the book on how to run a successful project with distributed teams.

The accompanying CD provides a video overview of the Global Studio Project (GSP) described in Chapter 14. In addition, the GSP Wiki is provided as an example of the knowledge management infrastructure used for the experimental global software development project.

Acknowledgments

This book is a result of the experiences many of our friends and colleagues have undergone while engaged in large-scale, geographically distributed software development projects. We are indebted to them for sharing their wisdom.

We wish to acknowledge the excellent work that was done by the students involved in the Global Studio Project, most notably Zakaria El Houda, Stefan Gersmann, Lutz Kuederli, Alan Malone, Brian Casey, and Sean Eade.

Many thanks to the reviewers, known and unknown, for their critical comments; we are especially grateful to Patrick Keil, Robert Schwanke, Stephen Masticola, George Phoenix, Scott Carney, and William Sherman.

It has been a pleasure working with Auerbach Publications in the development of this text. Special thanks to our editor, John Wyzalek, for his continued guidance and encouragement throughout the entire process.

Finally, we thank our families for their love, patience, and support during the writing of this book. We affectionately dedicate this book to them.

About the Authors

Raghvinder S. Sangwan is an Assistant Professor of Information Science and a member of the Graduate Faculty at The Pennsylvania State University. Prior to joining The Pennsylvania State University, he worked as a lead architect for Siemens Medical Solutions on geographically distributed development projects, building information systems for large Integrated Health Networks. He continues to serve as a consulting technical staff member for Siemens Corporate Research in Princeton, New Jersey, where he has been performing research on global software development. Dr. Sangwan is a member of the IEEE and ACM, and holds a Ph.D. in Computer and Information Sciences from Temple University in Philadelphia, Pennsylvania.

Matthew Bass is a Software Architect for Siemens Corporate Research. In this role, he has participated in domains such as Train Control, Building Automation, Medical Engineering, and Automation. Prior to coming to Siemens, he worked for the Software Engineering Institute at Carnegie Mellon University. Bass has a Masters of Software Engineering from Carnegie Mellon University and an undergraduate degree in Computer Science from the University of Pittsburgh.

Neel Mullick has a Masters degree in Business Administration from the Indian Institute of Management and a Masters degree in Software Engineering from Carnegie Mellon University. He has experience in both the development and management ends of the spectrum of software engineering and is currently Project Manager at Siemens Corporate Research for the Global Studio Project — an experimental research and development project aimed at testing, instrumenting, and codifying the best practices for globally distributed software development.

Daniel J. Paulish is a Distinguished Member of Technical Staff at Siemens Corporate Research with more than 20 years of experience in software engineering management. He is currently doing research on global software development practices, processes, organizations, and tools, and he is the leader of the Siemens Software Initiative in the Americas. He has been an international lecturer on software project management, software process improvement methods, and measurement. He is the author of *Architecture-Centric Software Project Management* and a co-author of *Software Metrics: A Practitioner's Guide to Improved Product Development.* Dr. Paulish was formerly an industrial resident affiliate at the Software Engineering Institute of Carnegie Mellon University, and he holds a Ph.D. in Electrical Engineering from the Polytechnic Institute of New York.

Juergen Kazmeier holds a major degree in Mathematics and a Ph.D. in Computer Science from the Technical University of Munich. He has worked at Siemens AG on software development processes, methods, and tools, and has been a researcher and consultant on modeling languages and visualization methods. As a member of the corporate development audit unit, he analyzed and supported large product developments and information technology projects. Within the Intelligent Transportation System Division, he headed a global development group, as Vice President of R&D. Since 2003, Dr. Kazmeier has been responsible for the Software Engineering Research Department at Siemens Corporate Research, where he started the Siemens research initiative on global software development.

Glossary

Build plan: *See* Integration and test plan.

Component: An independently deployable runtime entity.

Coordination: The act of managing dependencies among activities.

Coordination capability: The ability of an organization to manage dependency among activities.

Development plan: A plan estimating development schedule, resources, and cost.

Engineering release: An incremental delivery of a work package at the end of a monthly sprint of an iteration; at the end of an iteration, several engineering releases make up an executable release of a fraction of a product.

Feature release specification: A bundling of features into releases that can be sold in the market.

Integration and test plan: A plan that shows how features of a product are integrated and tested based on the order in which they are realized.

Iteration: A period spanning a number of monthly sprints that lead to an executable release of a fraction of a product.

Module: A static software implementation unit.

Product manager: A role that owns a product primarily determining market needs for the product and doing feature release planning identifying bundles of features that comprise a saleable solution.

Project manager: A role responsible for planning the entire life cycle of a product, primarily creating project plans for implementing the product, performing risk analysis, and proposing strategies for mitigating those risks.

Project plan: A document that contains the feature release specification, the development plan, the integration and test plan, and the release plan.

Release plan: A high-level marketing description of the various product releases planned to be sold.

Schedule: A plan for performing development tasks specifying the order and time allocation for each task.

Sprint: One month duration within an iteration that in the construction phase leads to an engineering release.

Supplier manager: A role at the central site that helps manage the relationship and projects with remote sites or suppliers of the modules to be developed.

Abbreviation List

ACM: Association of Computing Machinery
ACSPP: Architectural Center Software Project Planning
ADD: Attribute Driven Design
ANSI: American National Standards Institute
API: Application Programming Interface
ASAP: As Soon As Possible
ASCII: American Standard Code for Information Exchange
ASP: Application Service Provider
ASR: Architecturally Significant Requirement
ATAM^{SM}: Architecture Tradeoff Analysis Method^{SM}
BAS: Building Automation System
BCS: British Computer Society
C&C: Component & Connector
CASE: Computer-Aided Software Engineering
CD: Compact Disc
CDC: Connected Device Configuration
CDR: Critical Design Review
CM: Configuration Management
CMM: Capability Maturity Model
CMMI: CMM Integration
CMU: Carnegie Mellon University
COCOMO: Constructive Cost Model
CORBA™: Common Object Request Broker Architecture
COTS: Commercial Off-the-Shelf
COV: Change-of-Value
CPM: Critical Path Method
CPU: Central Processing Unit
CRS: Component Release Specification
CSA: Computing Services Association or Canadian Standards Association

DB: Data Base
DBMS: Data Base Management System
DCOM: Distributed Component Object Model
DDD: Detailed Design Document
DLL: Dynamic Link Library
DLOC: Delta Lines of Code
DMA: Direct Memory Access
DPS: Data Processing System
DRM: Defect Removal Model
DSM: Design Structure Matrix
DSP: Digital Signal Processor
ECO: Engineering Change Order
ECR: Engineering Change Request
EDP: Electronic Data Processing
EEPROM: Electrically Erasable Programmable Read-Only Memory
ER: Engineering Release
ERB: Engineering Review Board
ESPRIT: European Strategic Programme for Research and Development in Information Technology
FDA: Food & Drug Administration
FP: Function Points
FPA: Function Point Analysis
FRS: Feature Release Specification
FS: Financial System
FSS: Field System Simulator
G/Q/M: Goals/Questions/Metrics
GA: Global Analysis
GSD: Global Software Development
GSP: Global Studio Project
GUI: Graphical User Interface
HIS: Health Information System
HLD: High-Level Design
HLDD: High-Level Design Document
HTTP: Hypertext Transfer Protocol
HW: Hardware
HVAC: Heating, Ventilation, & Air Conditioning
I&C: Instrumentation & Control or Industrial & Commercial
IDE: Integrated Development Environment
IEEE: Institute of Electrical and Electronics Engineers
IHN: Integrated Health Network
IPC: Interprocess Communication
ISDN: Integrated Services Data Network
ISO: International Standards Organization

IT: Information Technology
J2EE™: Java 2 Platform, Enterprise Edition
KLOC: Thousand Lines of Code
KPA: Key Process Area
KPR: Known Problem Report
LAN: Local Area Network
LOC: Lines of Code
LTIP: Long-Term Incentive Program
MBO: Management by Objectives
MBWA: Manage by Walking Around
MLOC: Million Lines of Code
MR: Modification Request
MRS: Marketing Requirements Specification
MTBF: Mean-Time-Between-Failures
MTS: Microsoft Transaction Manager
MTTF: Mean-Time-To-Failure
MTTR: Mean-Time-To-Repair
MS: Microsoft
MSLite: Management Station Light
MU: Monmouth University
NASA: National Aeronautics and Space Administration
NLOC: Net Lines of Code
OMG: Object Management Group
PBX: Private Branch Exchange
PC: Personal Computer
PCG: Product Control Group
PCS: Project Control System
PERT: Program Evaluation & Review Technique
PLA: Product Line Architecture
PLC: Programmable Logic Controller or Power Line Communications
PMW: Project Manager Workbench
POIM: Planning, Organizing, Implementing, Measuring
PPP: Product Planning Process
PR: Problem Report
PROM: Programmable Read-Only Memory
PUCRS: Pontifical Catholic University of Rio Grande de Sul
QA: Quality Assurance
QAW: Quality Attribute Workshop
QFD: Quality Function Deployment
QM: Quality Management
R: Release
R&D: Research & Development
RAM: Random Access Memory

RCS: Revision Control System
RE: Requirements Engineering
RMI: Remote Method Invocation
ROOM: Real-time Object-Oriented Modeling
RPC: Remote Procedure Call
RUP®: Rational Unified Process
SCCS: Source Code Control System
SCM: Software Configuration Management
SCR: Siemens Corporate Research, Inc.
SDLC: Software Development Life Cycle
SDP: Software Development Plan
SEI: Software Engineering Institute
SEL: Software Engineering Laboratory
SEPG^{SM}: Software Engineering Process Group
SNA: Social Network Analysis
SOAP: Simple Open Access Protocol
SPR: Software Problem Report
SQE: Software Quality Engineering
SRE: Software Risk Evaluation
SRS: System Requirements Specification
SW: Software
SWAG: Scientific Wild-Assed Guess or Silly Wild-Assed Guess
TQM: Total Quality Management
TR: Test Release
TUM: Technical University of Munich
UI: User Interface
UL: University of Limerick
UML™: Unified Modeling Language
URL: Universal Record Locator
V&V: Verification & Validation
VAR: Value-Added Reseller
VP: Vice President
WWW: World Wide Web
XML: eXtensible Markup Language

Section I

INTRODUCTION

Chapter 1

Motivation

The movement toward globally distributed software development has gathered pace in recent years. The geographic distribution of software development projects at Siemens and across other software development organizations, both big and small, reflects this trend. To date, Siemens has executed many software development efforts using distributed teams and understands that there is a large impact of distributing software development on the entire development life cycle, including the management practices (Herbsleb et al., 2005). Globally distributed software development or global software development (GSD) brings with it many pros and cons that if not managed carefully can easily turn any GSD venture into a loss-making enterprise. One of the more important trade-offs in the course of any GSD project is that between agility and process discipline. This chapter provides a background on GSD, presents some of its challenges, and introduces the need for managing its complexities in an efficient and structured manner so as to better reap the rewards inherent in GSD.

1.1 What is Global Software Development (GSD)?

In short, one can define global software development (GSD) as software development that uses teams from multiple geographic locations. In some cases, these teams may be from the same organization; in other cases, there may be collaborations or outsourcing that involve different organizations. These teams could be within one country (in fact, evidence suggests that once teams are separated by more than 50 meters, further distance is immaterial) or on other sides of the world (Allen, 1984). In any case, introducing physical distance between teams that are working together to develop a software system introduces complex and interesting challenges that are only beginning to be understood.

Many technological, organizational, and economic factors have led to the increased globalization of development projects. Although this has been happening for the past decade or so, it is closer now to becoming the norm rather than the exception. Some of the more common and well-established motivators for globally distributed software development include (Carmel, 1999; Herbsleb et al., 2005):

- ■ Limited trained workforce in technologies that are required to build today's complex systems
- ■ Differences in development costs favoring dispersing team geographically
- ■ A "shift"-based work system facilitated by time zone differentials allowing for shorter times to market
- ■ Advances in infrastructure (e.g., Internet bandwidth available and software development and integration tools)
- ■ A desire to be "close" to a local market

While the profile and motivations behind GSD projects often differ, one characteristic remains constant. It is inherently more difficult to coordinate projects where teams are separated by physical distance. While in traditional collocated software development projects there are often standard practices with defined milestones and artifact templates, much of the coordination ends up occurring in an ad hoc way. Engineers seem to gain an intuitive understanding of the requirements by osmosis. The "real" system design largely lives in the collective heads of the designers and developers rather than on paper. Evidence suggests that much of this "shared understanding" derives from working closely together. The ability to be able to talk around the water cooler or over lunch aids greatly in the development of such a shared understanding. Jim gets to know how Sue thinks about the project and can easily interpret her comments and communications. Agile practices have recognized and explicitly attempted to foster these kinds of interactions through practices such as pair programming, daily stand-up meetings, and having customers collocated with developers.

1.2 Challenges to Global Software Development

As mentioned, GSD projects come in many shapes and sizes. It is not uncommon to have multiple divisions, organizations, cultures, and languages represented on a project. Often, many of the participants have never met before; they may have different levels of domain experience and may have motivations that conflict with the goals of the project. All these factors conspire to make it increasingly difficult to coordinate across teams, manage evolution, and monitor progress (Herbsleb and Moitra, 2001; Mockus and Herbsleb, 2001). Past studies have shown that tasks take about 2.5 times longer to complete in a distributed setting versus a collocated setting (Herbsleb and Mockus, 2003).

It has been well established that until people meet face-to-face they may have a very difficult time coordinating on complex tasks remotely and our experience supports this. When an issue or question arises, it often is quite difficult to know who to go to. An individual at a remote site often does not have visibility into the activities of other people who are not at their same site. Because of this, much time can be spent trying to find someone who can help. The other thing that often happens is that in the absence of available information, assumptions will be made. These assumptions may conflict with the requirements or assumptions made elsewhere in the project and result in problems being introduced into the software.

Likewise, when engineers get inquiries or reports of problems from people they do not personally know, they are less likely to be responsive. Perhaps they interpret the problem report as a criticism of their work, or they do not feel the same sense of urgency regarding the problem with which their remote colleague is dealing. They may not respond at all to e-mails or, if they do, the responses may not be crafted with the same care that responses to known individuals would be. Furthermore, they may be unavailable due to a local holiday that is not celebrated at the requester's location. It is also not uncommon for the motivations to differ drastically from one team to another. One location may fear that the current project, if successful, will replace a legacy product for which they have been responsible. Fear of job loss may prevent people in that location from sharing information openly.

Cultural and language differences also come into play. For example, we have experienced reluctance from some non-native English speakers to participate actively in teleconferences. They prefer to address concerns and questions via e-mail. We (at the time a group of Americans) found e-mail slow and frustrating. It was only after a significant time on this project that the reason for this was discovered and explicit protocols put in place to deal with the concerns. Likewise, the local culture and style can often cause confusion and frustration. One example that we well know involves a culture that tends to be very direct when interacting with another that is much less so (we avoid mentioning any specifics). In phone and e-mail correspondence, the direct culture reported frustration that their counterparts never seemed to get to the point. They would call and ask about unrelated issues before getting to the point. The less direct culture, however, viewed their counterparts as being rude. These misconceptions were resolved when a series of personnel exchanges was arranged, and the dedication and seriousness with which all were attacking problems became evident and personal relationships were formed over beers in the evening.

Many other logistical issues end up taking much more time than often anticipated. Figuring out how to align technical infrastructures, dealing with connectivity issues imposed by a particular network topology, figuring out how to align management practices and organization processes where required, etc., are all difficult and time-consuming concerns that take valuable resources and time from the project. If the factors mentioned above are not considered and addressed, the likelihood of producing a quality product, within schedule and budget, are greatly diminished (in fact, paying attention to these factors does not guarantee success by any stretch of the imagination).

1.3 Managing Global Software Development

Through much pain, trial and error, we have developed a set of practices that we use on projects that are geographically distributed. While these practices are not a silver bullet, we have attempted to capture experiences good and bad, and codify them into a framework that provides a more structured way of organizing and executing GSD projects.

Through this collective experience, we have identified factors critical to the success of GSD projects and codified best practices for these factors to enable a successful outcome. We have developed a process framework that leverages the best practices codified in the critical success factors and is based on global agility that combines the trend of globally distributed software development with that of agile software practices. When thinking of agile practices, the reader would be expected to conjure up an image of software development that essentially is in a collocated environment. We have recognized that many of the practices in the agile manifesto (Cockburn, 2002) have gone a long way toward addressing problems of shared understanding and project evolution. These practices fall short, however, when operating in a global context. We have attempted to augment agile practices where needed so that we can maintain most of the benefits yet scale the approach to a GSD context. This can happen only by developing and defining infrastructural configurations, processes, mechanisms, and best practices that allow for the optimal trade-off between agility and process discipline (Boehm and Turner, 2004).

Our process framework is based on an iterative model of development with a clear definition of roles and responsibilities, a well-defined infrastructure to facilitate coordination and collaboration and many other aspects tying the notions of process discipline for GSD with agility. Understanding the basic tenets of working effectively in a distributed environment — such as optimally splitting work across sites, increasing and enhancing communication across sites, facilitating ready access to experts, using tools and practices to enhance awareness across sites — is what forms the basis of our approach.

1.6 Summary and Conclusions

GSD is inherently difficult. Problems with coordination, motivation, and aligning of technologies, infrastructure, and processes often cause projects to grind to a halt. GSD is, however, a reality that is here to stay and so we must learn how to execute such projects efficiently and successfully. This book has codified many years of experience in GSD projects into a set of practices that can be applied to projects large and small that are using geographically distributed teams.

1.7 Discussion Questions

1. Why are GSD projects more difficult to manage than collocated projects?
2. Which agile practices would be easier to adopt, and which would be challenging in GSD projects?

References

Allen, T. et al., *Managing the Flow of Technology: Technology Transfer and the Dissemination of Technological Information within the R&D Organization*, MIT Press, Cambridge, MA, 1984.

Boehm, B. and Turner, R., *Balancing Agility and Discipline: A Guide for the Perplexed*, Addison-Wesley, Boston, MA, 2004.

Carmel, E., *Global Software Teams: Collaborating across Borders and Time Zones*, Prentice Hall, Upper Saddle River, NJ, 1999.

Cockburn, A., *Agile Software Development*, Addison-Wesley, Boston, MA, 2002.

Herbsleb, D., and Mockus, A., "An empirical study of speed and communication in globally distributed software development," *IEEE Transactions on Software Engineering*, 29(6), 481–494, June 2003.

Herbsleb, J. and Moitra, D., "Global software development," *IEEE Software*, 18(2), 16–20, March/April 2001.

Herbsleb, J., Paulish, D., and Bass, M., "Global Software Development at Siemens: Experience from Nine Projects," *Proceedings of the 27th International Conference on Software Engineering*, St. Louis, MO, 2005, pp. 524–533.

Mockus, A. and Herbsleb, J., "Challenges of global software development," *Proceedings of the Seventh International Software Metrics Symposium*, April 4–6, 2001, London, England, pp. 182–184.

Chapter 2

Critical Success Factors for Global Software Development

John works for BAS Corporation, which grew over years through mergers and acquisitions of companies around the world. BAS Corporation wants to consolidate the disparate products from its different companies into a single product line to simplify new product development and achieve economies of scale. John is asked to spearhead this effort. Although he has managed many challenging projects successfully, John has never worked on one that involved coordinating the efforts of development teams from multiple sites around the world. He begins to wonder how his approach to this project would be different from managing a single-site collocated project.

In the age of global economy, many of us are finding ourselves in a similar situation for perhaps a different reason. Labor rates are currently low in Eastern European nations, Brazil, India, and China, and there could be cost savings if development is outsourced to these regions. A company may have expertise in a set of technologies or a domain, thus making it attractive for partnership. Shortage of staff and time-to-market pressures may force an organization to carry out parallel development using a workforce from around the world.

This chapter looks at issues of concern in global software development (GSD) projects and provides factors that are critical to the success of such projects. In addition, it begins to describe a process framework for how one might realize these critical success factors. The overview in this chapter serves as a road map for the details that follow in subsequent chapters.

2.1 Issues

When organizations initially get involved with GSD, they often drastically underestimate the impact of using geographically distributed teams. One reason for this is that the extent to which people in collocated environments rely on ad hoc and informal communications to develop software is under-recognized. The impact of not having this informal communication and not accounting for its absence is often quite disastrous. The authors have seen this play out time and time again in failed projects from many different organizations.

Based on these experiences, a number of factors critical to the success of a GSD project have been identified. These factors are admittedly high-level and do not in and of themselves adequately convey the intuition born of years of experience. To help explain how these critical success factors can be operationalized, we have developed a process framework to illustrate a process that embodies these factors. This is not meant to suggest that this process framework is a solution for everybody. A one-size-fits-all solution does not exist. Rather, it is meant to further explain and demonstrate how these critical success factors can be realized in a GSD project.

2.2 Critical Success Factors

This section discusses the critical success factors for GSD projects. While these factors are useful for all projects, the business case and necessity is much greater when projects are geographically distributed across several time zones with many remote teams having no history of ever working together, compounded by language and culture differences. These factors are meant to embody experience from many such projects (and thus very abstract). How these factors are realized in any given project depends on many things, such as the organizational processes, the characteristics of the teams, the organizational structures, and the system to be built. Implementing these success factors must be seen as an investment that pays off in risk mitigation and quality. In the remainder of this book we give examples and guidance for how to account for these factors in your projects.

2.2.1 *Reduce Ambiguity*

While it is desirable to reduce ambiguity for all aspects of any project, a lot of uncertainty and ambiguity gets addressed in collocated projects through informal communication. GSD projects do not have the same luxury. Ambiguity leads to assumptions. These assumptions are not readily apparent to the powers that be, and therefore conflicting assumptions can exist for quite some time before they manifest themselves as problems. These problems lead to re-planning, redesign, and rework. All of these are difficult to execute in a distributed environment. Coordination can be slow, arduous, and ineffective. The impact of having to do these coordination-intensive activities can cause long delays, leave teams idle and frustrated, cause quality problems, and have (on more than one occasion) caused a project to be stopped.

These ambiguities can be with respect to the organizational processes, the management practices, the requirements, or the design. Combined with a lack of experience and domain knowledge in the teams, the situation can get even more complex. Therefore, much thought and work should go into establishing conventions for how different teams work together to ensure that they extract the intended meaning from project artifacts. Processes should have clearly defined rules of engagement, requirements should be modeled so they are easily understood, architecture should be elaborated with dependencies among modules identified and components specified with well-defined interfaces, work packages should be created for individual teams with clearly stipulated task assignments, and, above all when communication occurs between teams to seek some clarification, one must ensure that answers to questions are correctly understood.

What is a clear articulation to one team with a particular background and culture may very well not be clear to another. Mechanisms for verifying that particular aspects of the project are understood, training programs, or personnel swapping may be required. Staffing should be done carefully to balance technology experience and domain knowledge. The particular characteristics of a project are going to govern the amount of ambiguity that the project can deal with as well as the appropriate mechanism for addressing this ambiguity. For example, if a sponsoring organization has been involved with a long-term relationship with remote teams, likely there is an established working culture that makes it easier to communicate particular aspects of the project, versus two teams that have never before met or worked together.

2.2.2 Maximize Stability

Instability has an influence on many aspects of a project. Agile processes, for example, are a response to unclear and unstable requirements. Some of the major tenets of agility strive to create an environment that optimizes the amount of ad hoc and informal communication (e.g., pair programming, working in a collocated space, on-site customer representatives, short iterations, daily stand-up meetings, etc.). It makes sense then that in distributed projects, where these types of communications are difficult, stability is a factor. The impact of having unstable aspects of the project is similar to that of having ambiguous areas in your project.

What does this mean, however? Well, again, it largely depends on the particulars of the project, but it may mean that one must delay initiation of the development phase beyond that of typical collocated projects to allow the specification of requirements and design to further stabilize. Change requests are a major risk to GSD projects as they need 2.4 times longer to resolve in distributed environments as compared to collocated projects (Herbsleb and Mockus, 2003). Therefore, the need for excellent requirements engineering and architecture cannot be underemphasized. It may mean that additional prototypes are developed, UI mock-ups are designed, frameworks are developed, or development environments are customized. There are many ways in which the stability of various aspects of the project could be increased. We will give examples and talk more about how this can be done later in the book.

2.2.3 *Understand Dependencies*

The interdependencies between tasks imply the volume, frequency, and type of coordination needed among the participants in a GSD project. It is critical for planning and execution of the project to have a handle on what coordination needs are likely. Typically, the dependencies are thought of as a "calls relationship" among the subsystems that are to be distributed. While such a relationship does imply a dependency, there are many other aspects to consider as well. From a technical perspective there are many factors that may imply coordination. For example, if there is a hard latency requirement, that could imply some coordination between all the teams involved in developing code that could execute concurrently; or, if one team is responsible for developing a subsystem that requires a complex image processing algorithm, there may be an increased need for coordination.

The technical aspects of the project are not the only sources of dependencies, however. There are many temporal dependencies that stem from the planning or staging of the implementation. For example, implementation might be distributed by development phases or by complete modules or subsystems allocated to different development sites. The latter can be much more advantageous than the former. We go into some detail about how to identify these dependencies and how to account for them in your project.

2.2.4 Facilitate Coordination

The complement to understanding the interdependent nature of the tasks is to facilitate the corresponding coordination. It must be the case that the teams that need to coordinate are able to do so in a way that is commensurate with the need. There are many different ways in which teams can coordinate. While this is usually thought of strictly in terms of communication, it is much broader than that. Communication is one way in which teams can coordinate, but they can also coordinate via processes, management practices, and product line architectures, to name a few. These choices can be seen as a trade-off between overhead and risk. For example, if an organization were to design and develop a framework that would constrain the design and implementation choices of a remote team, while enforcing the remote team's compliance with the original intent of the team, the cost of building such a framework, however, is quite high. The framework would also eliminate the need to communicate the embodied design decisions in other ways.

In our experience, it is often the case that GSD projects put too much emphasis on cost reduction by moving some of their development to low-cost sites. Little attention, if any, is given to investing in improving the process and development environment that could automate to some degree and guide to a great extent the coordination efforts of the collaborating teams.

It is not always clear up-front, however, what the need is or how well a given solution would work in a given environment, so it is often wise to have back-up strategies in place if things go awry.

2.2.5 Balance Flexibility and Rigidity

In many ways the practices of GSD projects should be both more flexible and more rigid than their collocated counterparts. Remote teams often have different backgrounds, different development processes, different experience levels, different domain knowledge, different cultures, and in some cases different organizational practices. The overall development process should be flexible enough to accommodate these differences. This may mean giving the remote teams some freedom in adopting a more agile internal development process. The process, however, also should be more structured and rigid in a particular way. It must be rigid enough to ensure that particular aspects of the project are well defined and the processes followed as the normal safety nets are in place, for things such as instructions are understood, architectures are complied with, requirements are achieved, configuration management (CM) processes are adequately defined, integration and test procedures are appropriate, etc. This is necessary to monitor progress, ensure that deadlines are met, and guarantee quality.

2.3 A Process Framework

Figure 2.1 shows a process framework for GSD. It is not the intent here to describe a rigorous process that every project should follow. Rather, to more easily introduce the concepts found within this book and demonstrate how the critical success factors can be realized, a high-level process framework with steps that project teams are likely to follow is described. This is not intended to be a one-size-fits-all process. While we have used this process in practice, it usually requires tailoring and adoption for the given context. The activities within this framework are shown as sequential steps covering the areas of requirements, architecture, project planning, and product development, but in practice these steps will be highly iterative.

The goal of the requirements engineering step of the process is to gain a good understanding of the requirements so one knows what is it that one is trying to build, and to identify the driving requirements — those that are architecturally significant and have the most value to the business for which the system is being built. We use model-driven requirements engineering (Berenbach, 2003, 2004a, 2004b) that uses the Unified Modeling Language (UML) to specify the requirements. UML as a specification does not provide any guidance on how it must be used; we have, through our research, developed approaches that leverage UML's ability to add meaning to the links among the requirements, thus making them easier to analyze for completeness, consistency, and quality as well as allow for automated tracing to design models and tests.

While model-driven requirements engineering is a systematic development and maintenance of detailed product requirements that begins when

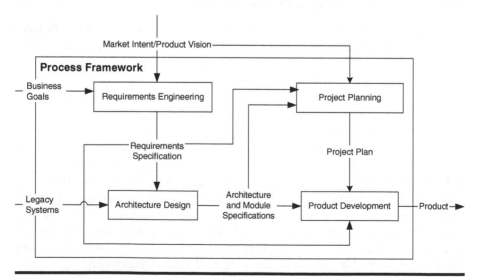

Figure 2.1   A process framework for GSD.

a project has gained enough momentum, there is a need early in the project to develop a business case, define a product, and gather customer requirements. This can be accomplished through prototyping and story-boarding (Song et al., 2005). To discover key architecture-relevant requirements, their interactions with other project requirements, and formulate strategies to address any resulting conflicts, we use a technique called Global Analysis (Hofmeister et al., 2000).

For globally distributed software development projects, model-driven requirements engineering offers several benefits that help overcome some of the issues related to communication, coordination, and control. Visual modeling aids comprehension and communication among distributed teams. Tool support for evaluating the models gives on demand a measure of size, progress, consistency, completeness, and quality. Most significantly, however, UML models can support automated traceability; modeled requirements can be traced forward to their corresponding design and tests, and backward to the market intent, stakeholder requests, and business goals. This can help with requirements coverage (i.e., what requirements have been implemented in a given release) and impact analysis (i.e., what is the impact of a requirement change).

The focus of the architecture design step is to get a detailed understanding of the architecturally significant requirements and create an executable architecture. Many software development methodologies treat architecture only indirectly or implicitly. The quality of systems developed using such methodologies thus depends largely on the skill level and experience of its architect. We use architecture-centric methods (Bass et al., 2003) such as the Quality Attribute Workshop (QAW), Attribute Driven Design (ADD), and the Architecture Tradeoff Analysis Method (ATAM), which provide explicit and methodical guidance to an architect in creating systems with desirable qualities. The QAW uses stakeholders early in the software development life cycle to discover the quality attribute requirements that drive the structure of a system; ADD uses these requirements to design the architecture; and the ATAM helps stakeholders understand the consequences once an architecture for a system has been determined.

The project manager uses the requirements specification and the architecture and module specifications to generate a project plan to implement the new product (Paulish, 2002). The project manager performs risk analyses, defines proposed project strategies, does incremental release planning, and generates a proposed development plan describing how and when the product should be developed. Estimation methods are used to determine the effort and schedule to implement the product.

In the product development step, the application modules are designed, implemented, tested, and integrated to produce intermediate product releases, some of which are beta tested at the customer site. This eventually produces a product baseline mature enough to be deployed in the user community.

The organization of product solution development is optimized using small, distributed module development teams synchronized by a central organization. The development teams worldwide receive module specifications from the central team. Each team, led by a supplier manager, is responsible for the design, implementation, and testing of the assigned module. In our experience, the role of the supplier manager is often not sufficiently defined and implemented but is a key role in our approach (see Chapter 10).

In keeping with the best practices of agile methodologies, these teams carry out iterative implementation of their modules in small increments using test-first development. Tests to exercise module interfaces are provided by the architecture team because these tests not only help verify the modules, but also help developers understand the semantics of the interfaces much more clearly (Simons, 2002). The modules are designed using known design patterns and refactored on a continuous basis to maintain their quality (Fowler, 2004).

2.4 Development Phases and Decision Points

We use a phased product planning process. Like the standard Rational Unified Process (RUP), it has four significant stages in the software development life cycle (Arlow and Neustadt, 2002; Larman, 2005). The *inception phase* is the visionary milestone phase wherein the problem to be solved and its potential solutions are investigated to determine the feasibility of the project. Once considered feasible, the project enters into the *elaboration phase*. This is the core architecture milestone phase wherein requirements are prioritized and those deemed architecturally significant are implemented first. At the end of the elaboration phase, a more reliable software development plan is put into place and the *construction phase* of the software begins. This phase is the operational capability milestone phase because at the end of this phase the software is deployed in the production environment of one or more beta customers to demonstrate its operational capability. Once operational, the software moves to the *transition phase*. This is the product release milestone phase, as the software product is now generally available in the market.

Tip: Make offshore members a part of the central team in the early phases of the project.

A number of requirements and architecture related activities require collaboration to impart domain and architecture expertise to the offshore teams. It is advisable in the inception and elaboration phases to involve members of the offshore teams so they begin to gain an understanding of the domain and the architectural vision. These members can then be relocated to their home sites when the construction phase begins and act as local experts. Furthermore, we suggest that these key members of the offshore teams be relocated to the central site with their families. This minimizes home-sickness, and provides local support as "culture shock" issues arise.

These phases span over multiple iterations, each iteration leading to an executable release of a fraction of the complete product. The number of iterations in the phases and their duration will depend on the size of the project. We use Scrum techniques (Schwaber, 2004; Schwaber and Beedle, 2001), and therefore our iterations for large projects are further subdivided into monthly *sprints*. Teams are assigned work packages for an iteration that are completed incrementally on a monthly boundary. We call these increments *Engineering Releases*. At the end of an iteration, several engineering releases make up an executable release of a fraction of a product. For smaller projects, the duration for an iteration may well be the same as that for a sprint and, therefore, this type of planning may not be necessary.

These phases often have management decision points separating them. A decision point review is conducted to evaluate the results of the current phase, the proposed plans for the next phase, and authorize the resource investment required for the next phase.

A phased product planning process is used to achieve the following benefits:

■ Product development is viewed as an innovation funnel of new ideas. Many ideas are researched, but a smaller number of the best ideas are invested in to become products.

■ Early phases typically require fewer resources than later phases, where potentially large development teams are required to implement and test the new product.

■ Communications from development to the field sales force are controlled during early phases. The sales force is discouraged from selling new ideas rather than existing or very soon-to-be-developed products. Product research ideas, if communicated too early, can increase customer expectations and sometimes negatively impact the sales of current products.

- Quality targets can be better identified, measured, and controlled. The decision point reviews can be used as gates by which a project must meet certain quality criteria before proceeding to the next phase of development.
- Decision point reviews allow management to view and control proposed budgets by project, by phase. If a particular potential product looks promising in the market, but its development requires an unanticipated investment, fiscal-year budgets can be modified or trade-offs can be made among projects.
- Less promising projects can be stopped. Phases and decision points help management decide how to best invest in future products and balance their portfolio of products.

New product development can consist of some incremental improvements to a current product as a new version or release, a new product within an existing market segment, or an entirely new product line. The focus of this book is on new initiatives where a new or modified software architecture is required to implement the product. Thus, situations where relatively minor new features are added to an existing product with an existing architecture are not addressed. In this situation, organizations usually define an incremental release plan, and enhancements are made until the new version is released to the field. Phased approaches can also be used for major functionality additions, where investments are being made in parallel for requirements definition for the next or future releases of the product currently being developed.

This book puts special emphasis on the early phases of software product development. If requirements analysis, architecture design, and project planning are done well during the early phases of development, the product is much more likely to be developed per scope, schedule, and budget than if these activities are skipped or done poorly. On the other hand, these activities are never fully completed, and issues are often left open until the very end of development. Thus, a set of guidelines, rules of thumb, and tips are provided for effectively managing the early phases of software product development.

An example phased product planning process is given in Figure 2.2. The types of management decisions (*D*) that are made for our example phased product planning process are:

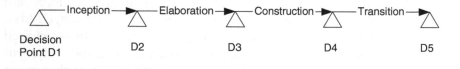

Decision Point D1   D2   D3   D4   D5

Figure 2.2 Example phased product planning process.

- *D1*: decision to initiate research (product, technology, or market) for a new product or products.
- *D2*: decision to initiate requirements definition and analysis and high-level architecture design.
- *D3*: decision to develop the product. A proposed project plan is reviewed at this meeting identifying the scope, schedule, and investment required to develop the product per the requirements and architecture defined within the elaboration phase.
- *D4*: decision to release the product to the market for customer use. Some organizations can also add an intermediate decision point where the new product is announced to the field prior to the completion of its development.
- *D5*: decision to sunset or remove the product from the market. Intermediate decision points can also be added to distinguish when the product will no longer be sold to new customers versus when the product will no longer be maintained with current customers.

2.5 Summary and Conclusions

This chapter identified issues of concern in GSD projects and provided factors that are critical to the success of such projects. A process framework for software development with geographically distributed teams that leverages the critical success factors in addressing some of the issues in GSD projects was described. A management framework for evaluating current phase and initiating the next phase was discussed.

2.6 Discussion Questions

1. List some of the significant differences between single-site collocated and multi-site distributed software development projects. What are some strategies to manage these differences?
2. Justify why model-driven requirements engineering is superior to text-based requirements engineering. Why do you think it is particularly important to global software development projects?
3. What is the significance of architecture-centric methods to the architecture of a system and to project planning?
4. The various decision points at the beginning and end of the software development phases act as quality gates. What do you understand by this statement?

References

Arlow, J. and Neustadt, I., *UML and the Unified Process: Practical Object-Oriented Analysis and Design*, Addison-Wesley, Boston, MA, 2002.

Bass, L., Clements, P., and Kazman, R., *Software Architecture in Practice, second edition*, Addison-Wesley, Boston, MA, 2003.

Berenbach, B., "The automated extraction of requirements from UML models," *Proceedings of the 11th Annual IEEE International Requirements Engineering Conference (RE'03)*, Monterey Bay, CA, September 8–12, 2003, pp 287–288.

Berenbach, B., "Towards a Unified Model for Requirements Engineering," *Fourth International Workshop on Adoption-Centric Software Engineering (ACSE 2004)*, Edinburgh, Scotland, U.K., May 23–28, 2004a, pp. 26–29.

Berenbach, B., "The evaluation of large, complex UML analysis and design models," *Proceedings of the 26th International Conference on Software Engineering (ICSE 2004)*, Edinburgh, Scotland, U.K., May 23–28, 2004b, pp. 232–241.

Fowler, M., "Using an Agile Software Process with Offshore Development," April 2004, retrieved on November 6, 2005, from Martin Fowler Web site: http://www.martinfowler.com/articles/agileOffshore.html

Herbsleb, D., Mockus, A., "An empirical study of speed and communication in globally distributed software development," *IEEE Transactions on Software Engineering*, 29(6), 481–494, June 2003.

Hofmeister, C., Nord, R., and Soni, D., *Applied Software Architecture*, Addison-Wesley, Boston, MA, 2000.

Larman, C., *Applying UML and Patterns: An Introduction to Object-Oriented Analysis and Design and Iterative Development, third edition*, Prentice Hall, Upper Saddle River, NJ, 2005.

Paulish, D., *Architecture-Centric Software Project Management*, Addison-Wesley, Boston, MA, 2002.

Schwaber, K., *Agile Project Management with Scrum*, Microsoft Press, Redmond, WA, 2004.

Schwaber, K. and Beedle, M., *Agile Software Development with Scrum, 1st edition*, Prentice Hall PTR, Upper Saddle River, NJ, 2001.

Simons, M., "Internationally Agile," *InformIT*, March 15, 2002, retrieved on November 6, 2005, from InformIT Web site: http://www.informit.com/articles/article.asp?p=25929

Song, X., Rudorfer, A., Hwong, B., Matos, G., and Nelson, C., "S-RaP: A Concurrent, Evolutionary Software Prototyping Process," *Proceedings of the Software Process Workshop*, May 25–27, 2005, Beijing, China.

Section II

PLANNING

Chapter 3

Requirements Engineering

Alberto, the project manager for the BAS project, found his project in dire straits. His testing team was getting monthly deliveries without knowing what functionality had been implemented, it was not clear to him (or to anyone else from what he could tell) what the individual development teams were going to deliver in any given iteration, and the overall project was getting further and further behind schedule. Furthermore, his colleague Subu, working in the requirements engineering (RE) team, was becoming overwhelmed with the large number of existing requirements residing in the Caliber database, but even more overwhelmed with the rate that new requirements were being added. Because the product development had been ongoing for six years, with no end in sight, it was difficult to trace how the system design had changed over time to accommodate all the evolving and new requirements.

While the root cause of Alberto and Subu's predicaments could have been the combination of many activities gone awry, without a requirements engineering process suitable for GSD it would be difficult to avoid such a situation. In this and the next chapter we focus on requirements engineering in one form or another. This chapter focuses on the functional requirements engineering process, what the issues are as they relate to GSD, and our approach for dealing with those issues. In support of the critical success factor "Reduce Ambiguity," our approach puts significant emphasis on clear specification of requirements and adequate traceability for determining requirements coverage and impact of change. Chapter 4 discusses how we identify and manage architecturally significant requirements, how they relate to functional requirements, and what the implications are in a GSD context.

3.1 Background

As with other aspects of software development, the requirements engineering related issues that GSD projects experience can also be found in collocated projects. The likelihood and impact of these issues, however, is not the same in GSD and collocated projects. For example, change management can be problematic in all projects; in GSD, however, it is very difficult to do an accurate impact analysis of a requirements change because of limited visibility into the detailed activities of distributed development teams. For the same reason, it is also more difficult to ensure adequate quality of the delivered code.

As in all projects, other activities (i.e., the design, testing, and planning processes) depend on the requirements engineering process. Because these processes are also more complex in a GSD project, an extra burden is placed on the requirements engineering effort to allow for a suitable execution of these activities. This section discusses these issues in more detail and then the chapter goes on to describe our approach for dealing with these problems.

3.1.1 Change Management

Change management is an area that can be difficult under the best of circumstances. By change management (at least in this instance) we are talking about managing the ripple effect of a requirements change. Managing the change includes:

- *Impact analysis*: What is the cost of the change? We would need to have an accurate understanding of what activities (and the assignment of these tasks to resources) would be involved.
- *Updating the associated artifacts*: Both the requirements and associated design must be updated.
- *Replanning*: If the change is accepted, we need to work the modifications into the schedule.

As mentioned, with GSD projects it can be quite difficult to have transparency into the details of the activities of the various teams. Without clear traceability between the requirements and the design, it can be difficult to determine the teams impacted by a requirements change. In a GSD project, design or review meetings are not as easily executed or as effective as when team members are located at one site.

There also should be clear traceability between the requirements and the project plan. In a traditional agile environment, the relationship between the requirements and the plan is very dynamic. While we do adjust the plan regularly, we have clear tracing between the requirements and the plan to facilitate both the impact analysis and the replanning activities. We discuss how we do this in an upcoming section.

3.1.2   Quality Assurance (QA)

QA-related activities are also quite significant for GSD projects. It is important to get regular accurate feedback on the progress of the various teams as well as the overall project. One of the things that can be difficult for many projects is to have test plans that have sufficient coverage and are executed in parallel (or virtually in parallel) with the construction of the system. Agile approaches advocate that the development teams conduct unit tests as part of the development processes (e.g., as in a test-driven development approach). We advocate this as well, but agile approaches do not usually address integration or system tests across teams. We have found that this is a critical aspect of development for GSD projects. To be able to do this level of testing, the requirements must be specified in sufficient detail so that it is clear what deliveries are expected from the development teams for each iteration. This helps to ensure that the development teams are on the same page, are being productive, and have the support they need to be able to iteratively build the system.

3.1.3   Impact on Related Processes

For us to be able to conduct the design, planning, and testing activities in a way that is suitable for GSD, we need to have a requirements engineering process that supports tight coupling with these efforts. That is, the outputs of these activities must maintain a clear traceability; any change in one of the outputs should easily carry over as updates to the other. In Alberto's case, having such a process would have solved most of his problems. While this implies more up-front rigor (as one might expect in a waterfall approach), this is not true. We will discuss this in more detail in the project planning process chapter (Chapter 7).

3.2   Requirements Engineering Process

The previous section discussed the importance of traceability for GSD projects. Our approach to maintaining traceability is based on creating models of requirements and design in UML. In addition, we decompose

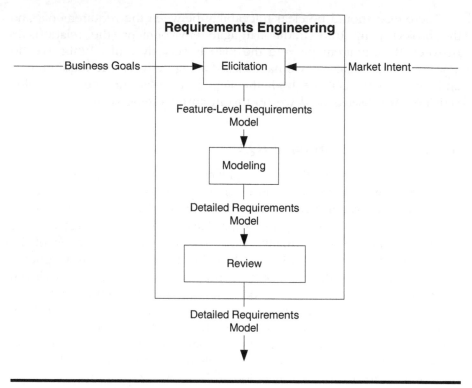

Figure 3.1   Requirements engineering workflow.

requirements hierarchically from features to detailed requirements to facilitate mapping between requirements and the project plan. We also generate test cases directly from the requirements model (see Figure 3.1).

This section describes our approach for eliciting, documenting, analyzing, and reviewing the requirements. We identify the activities, participants, inputs, and outputs involved with the process. We also discuss how we generally execute this process across the phases of the software life cycle.

3.2.1   Elicitation

Before this activity begins, the product vision or market intent should be created. There must be a reasonable definition of why the company is building the product, what the system will be used for, and what the target markets are. Without a concrete road map defining the specific target markets (it can be surprising how often there is only a vague notion of what specific markets and regions are intended), it can be difficult to concretely define the users, and items will be overlooked, assumptions will be made, and much effort spent in areas that are ultimately not needed or desired.

We conduct the requirements elicitation activity as part of a structured meeting. The goal of the meeting is to extract the domain knowledge from the experts, identify features that are in scope and out of scope for the system, and document the features into a highly structured and logical model.

The primary output of the elicitation activity is a feature-level requirements model. During the elicitation meetings, we do not spend time detailing and completing the model itself; rather, we make sure that we are capturing the most important features and structuring the model such that the details can be completed later. As these models become more and more complex, the overall structure becomes increasingly more important. Much like a complex design, it is not uncommon to have to refactor and rethink the structure of the model itself to promote a logical progression during the elicitation activities. Spending time and thought on the high-level structure of the requirements themselves will save time in the long run as a poorly structured model becomes unwieldy and difficult to use.

3.2.1.1 Participants

Table 3.1 shows the participants involved in eliciting the requirements along with their responsibilities.

Tip: Have team leads from remote teams participate in the requirements elicitation.

Typically, it takes significant time to get a remote team up to speed. The time it takes to transfer domain knowledge contributes significantly to this. By having representatives of the remote teams participate in the requirements elicitation activities, the knowledge can be transitioned much more readily. It can help drastically in developing a project context and language that is shared by all and avoid confusion down the line.

3.2.2 Modeling

This section describes the recommended structure of the requirements model that addresses the issues identified in the opening sections of the chapter. We model the requirements in UML (Booch et al., 2005; Fowler, 2004). While some might argue for or against UML (with legitimate reasons

Table 3.1 Participants in the Requirements Elicitation Activity

Title	Responsibility
Requirements Engineer	To elicit and capture the requirements in a model.
Facilitator	To facilitate the requirements elicitation meetings ensuring that the pace and direction of the meeting remains productive. The facilitator also captures questions, issues, architectural requirements, and other concerns on flipcharts as they arise.
Domain Experts	They represent the user's perspective describing the features and the details about how the system will be used.
Product Managers	They identify scope. They are usually only involved when identifying the high-level features.
Architects	Someone who represents the architecture team should also participate in the requirements engineering activities. The other possibility is to have one or more of the requirements engineering team members be part of the architecture team as well.

on both sides), we have found this to be an effective approach given the level of tool support, the ability to incorporate textual descriptions, and the mix of structure and flexibility. We basically model the requirements as a set of hierarchically decomposed use cases with "system" at the root and the detailed requirements at the leaf nodes (Berenbach, 2003, 2004a). The first-level decomposition will be the highest-level features that will be decomposed into sub-features (abstract use cases). These will eventually be decomposed into use cases that are testable (concrete use cases). We have found this approach to offer several benefits (Berenbach, 2004b):

- The UML model is much easier to navigate and understand than free text.
- This model acts as a common blueprint for communication among the stakeholders.
- It can be automatically verified for consistency and completeness, and analyzed for quality.
- It can be used for semi-automatic generation of system requirements, and test and project plans.

The modeling effort begins with a system context diagram that shows the system with all of its external actors. The system is shown as an abstract use case and acts as a single point of entry into the requirements

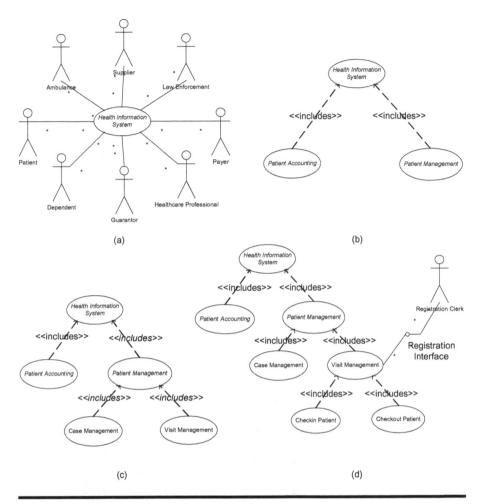

Figure 3.2 Requirements for an HIS (a) system context (b) high-level features (c) sub-features and (d) concrete use cases.

model. The abstract use case is progressively refined to yield concrete use cases. Figure 3.2 shows this for a Health Information System (HIS) developed for an Integrated Health Network (IHN).

The diagram has been intentionally simplified due to limitations of page space. In reality, there will be hundreds of features and thousands of concrete use cases. Therefore, there will be many levels of hierarchical decomposition.

The concrete use cases are services that the HIS must provide and, therefore, represent the detailed requirements for the system. These requirements can be extracted automatically from the model as shown in Figure 3.3 and serve as an input to the project plan.

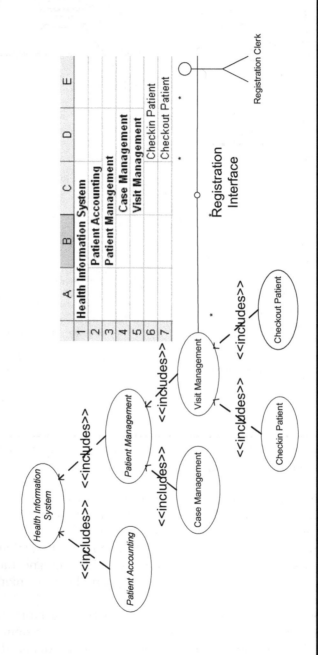

Figure 3.3 Extracting system requirements from the model.

At the end of the modeling activity (although many would say this activity is never really complete), a requirements model exists. We use the model to maintain traceability to the design and also the project plan. We discuss this further in the planning process chapter (Chapter 7); but as you do your estimation and project planning, you must be able to produce a list of modules needed to satisfy a given set of features. This is accomplished by tracing a feature to its detailed requirements and the associated modules that will realize those requirements. In addition, you will bundle features into releases and allocate their development to monthly sprints. With this approach to requirements modeling and traceability, Alberto and Subu could have alleviated their problems to a significant extent.

Tip: Model the requirements using a "breadth first" method.

Often the devil is in the details. If you attempt to model the requirements in a "depth first" way, you often can spend much time discussing the details before the model is stable. Additionally, it can take quite some time before a high-level model can be provided as input to the architects. It is important that there are frequent exchanges between the architecture and the requirements teams. Giving the architecture teams an early view into the high-level features with successive refinements helps facilitate this exchange.

3.2.2.1 Participants

Modeling typically starts during the elicitation meetings (Table 3.2). At this time, the features are modeled and decomposed into sub-features. The major focus is on getting the structure of the requirements themselves correct and identifying the actors involved. At a later time, the requirements are detailed by further decomposing the sub-features into concrete use cases and adding state, activity, and interaction diagrams. During all of these activities, a requirements engineer will do the modeling. There is often a domain expert involved as well (although there may be times when the requirements engineer will go off and draft their understanding, only to review it with the domain expert later on). The list of involved people is a maximal list and will change depending on the particular type of activity being conducted, the level of domain knowledge the requirements engineer has acquired, and the makeup of the project team.

Table 3.2 Participants in the Requirements Modeling Activity

Title	Responsibility
Requirements Engineer	To elicit and capture the requirements in a model.
Domain Experts	They represent the user's perspective describing the features and the details about how the system will be used.
Product Managers	The product managers identify scope. They are usually only involved when identifying the high-level features.
Architects	Someone who represents the architecture team should also participate in the requirements engineering activities. The other possibility is to have one or more of the requirements engineering team members be part of the architecture team as well.

3.2.3 *Requirements Review*

The requirements model can sometimes become unwieldy, difficult to understand, and have conflicting requirements. For these reasons, we periodically review, analyze, and refactor the requirements in support of having a commonly understood and useable model. Tool support becomes critical for managing change in the requirements. As you refactor the model and regenerate your requirements, you do not want to invalidate your project plan, break traceability to the design, or otherwise disturb the process.

Because of the way that we create the requirements model, we are able to do some analysis (syntactic) automatically (Berenbach, 2004b). We can check for model completeness, we can look for violation of various rules (e.g., cyclic dependencies), etc. Other semantic analysis must be done manually by people who know the requirements and the domain. We hold periodic review meetings to accomplish the latter kind of analysis. Those meetings should have both people who were involved with the requirements analysis activities as well as stakeholders who were not directly involved. There are three goals for these review meetings: (1) to ensure that the requirements were correctly understood and translated into the model, (2) to verify that the requirements model itself is readable and makes sense to those who need to understand it, and (3) to further disseminate the requirements themselves. We have found that the best way to get to understand and know the requirements is to participate in some way in the requirements activities themselves. While it is not practical for everyone to participate in the requirements engineering activities, it is

Table 3.3 Participants in the Requirements Review Activity

Title	Responsibility
Requirements Engineers	To elicit and capture the requirements in a model.
Domain Experts	They represent the user's perspective describing the features and the details about how the system will be used.
Product Managers	The PMs identify scope. They are usually only involved when identifying the high-level features.
Architects	Someone who represents the architecture team should also participate in the requirements engineering activities. This is so the architect can become more familiar with the requirements as well as identify requirements that may have a significant impact on the architecture.
System designers	People who are doing the detailed design should be intimately aware of the requirements. These review sessions are a good way to help facilitate that awareness.
Supplier Managers	Supplier managers are the first line of defense for the development teams. For them to be effective, they need to be on the same page as the rest of the project with respect to both the requirements and the architecture and detailed design. Again, having them participate in the review meetings is a good way to facilitate this.

useful to have domain experts, designers, architects, and supplier managers participate in these reviews.

3.2.3.1 Participants

Table 3.3 shows the team members and stakeholders who participate in reviewing the requirements. It has been our experience that four to ten requirements can be reviewed per hour during requirements review meetings.

3.3 Tooling

Consideration of how difficult it would be to maintain consistency between the requirements model, the design, and the project plan while you are refactoring a large complex model should convince you that a sophisticated tool infrastructure is needed. In the ever-changing world of tools, we would have a difficult time describing specific infrastructures (it is also outside the focus of this book). However, you should ensure that there is some automatic way to:

■ Generate readable (and understandable) documentation from the requirements model
■ Have bi-directional traceability between a requirements database and the model
■ Have traceability between the requirements model and the project plan (usually via the design)

In addition, we *highly* recommend prototyping your proposed infrastructure if you do not have one in place. We have never experienced a tool integration effort that performed as advertised.

3.4 Phasing

As discussed elsewhere in this book, there are interactions between the subprocesses that occur iteratively and can be quite complex. The definition of the phases of the software life cycle will impose particular constraints on the outputs of your activities, depending on where you are in the life cycle. As we have and will discuss later in the book, during the inception phase, we are primarily concerned with developing a high-level concept of operations, coming up with rough high-level effort and schedule estimates, and sketching the intended approaches to the issues related to the project.

Later, during the elaboration phase, the detailed design will begin, prototypes of the system will be constructed, requirements will be elaborated, and detailed planning will be conducted. Finally, during the construction phase, the requirements may continue to be elaborated; changes will occur and must be integrated; construction, integration, and testing of the system will take place; and the planning and monitoring of progress needs to continue.

During all of these phases, all the activities described above will take place. They will occur with various levels of detail, however. During the inception phase, the primary need for planning, estimation, and design are the major features that the system will support. This means that the requirements must be elicited down to the feature level, the system scoped at that level, and in some way the features must be prioritized. To support the mapping of these features to the architecture, some elaboration is typically done.

As the planning becomes more detailed during the elaboration phase, sprints are identified, tasks are mapped to sprints, and the requirements activities become more detailed. The high-level mapping of features to modules must get down to the level of interfaces (at least for the first few sprints), which means the requirements must become detailed enough to allow this to happen. Data flows should be identified as much as possible. Customizations and specific kinds of variation should be identified as well. These activities must be coordinated with the project planning and design activities to ensure that the details are available when needed. That is, these activities continue through the elaboration and into the construction phases so the requirements engineers have to understand what requirements need more detailed elaboration first. This will come from both the project plan and the architects. It may be the case that the architects need some more details to make important design decisions. It will also be the case that the project plan will spell out the release order for the features. Requirements engineers should use these to help them plan and prioritize their activities.

3.5 Summary and Conclusions

This chapter described the functional requirements engineering process and how it deals with issues related to GSD. In particular, change management, QA, and the impact of requirements engineering on design, planning, and testing activities were issues that achieve greater significance in a distributed development environment. A requirements engineering process that can manage these effectively is most desirable. In our approach this is achieved through UML models of the requirements with clear traceability to design, project plans, and tests. Our approach also makes it easier to handle change in requirements. Typically, the change comes from feedback through frequent interactions with the customer and stakeholders during the various software development iterations. While in a collocated setting accommodating changes might be easier, in a GSD context orchestrating the change is more difficult because of its potential impact on the different distributed teams. Maintaining traceability from high-level features to concrete requirements, their associated design and tests, and the project plans helps enable managing requirements changes and their impact on distributed teams.

3.6 Discussion Questions

1. What aspects of the project other than requirements engineering are affected by changing requirements?
2. How do the requirements engineering activities described in this chapter address the issues imposed by evolving requirements commensurate with the needs of a GSD project?

3. What might the barriers be for imposing such a process in a given organization?

References

Berenbach, B., "The automated extraction of requirements from UML models," *Proceedings of the 11th Annual IEEE International Requirements Engineering Conference (RE'03)*, Monterey Bay, CA, September 8–12, 2003, pp. 287–288.

Berenbach, B., "Towards a Unified Model for Requirements Engineering," *Fourth International Workshop on Adoption-Centric Software Engineering (ACSE 2004)*, Edinburgh, Scotland, U.K., May 23–28, 2004a, pp. 26–29.

Berenbach, B., "The evaluation of large, complex UML analysis and design models," *Proceedings of the 26th International Conference on Software Engineering (ICSE 2004)*, Edinburgh, Scotland, U.K., May 23–28, 2004b, pp. 232–241.

Booch, G., Rumbaugh, J., and Jacaobson, I., *The Unified Modeling Language User Guide, second edition*, Addison-Wesley, Boston, MA, 2005.

Fowler, M., *UML Distilled, third edition*, Addison-Wesley, Boston, MA, 2004.

Chapter 4

Requirements for the Architecture

Paulo was having trouble sleeping. He had just returned from a last-minute trip around the world to visit various development sites trying to get his project back on track. Development was going poorly. They were far behind schedule and the code to date was unstable. It did not make sense to Paulo; the system they were building was very similar to other systems the organization had built in the past. The components for the system were loosely coupled and fairly well defined. This project should have been a no-brainer. He was convinced that the problem was with the remote development teams; they just did not seem to get it.

In many projects, distributed or not, it is crucial to adequately recognize the requirements as they relate to the architecture early enough that they are reflected in the fundamental design decisions. If they are not, the system may not be able to achieve critical requirements as they relate to performance, scalability, reliability, etc. Problems in these areas are usually not discovered until later in the life cycle, at which point they are difficult to change even for collocated projects. For GSD efforts, these kinds of issues easily lead to the demise of the project. Dealing with these cross-cutting concerns often involves considerable coordination with the teams responsible for many aspects of the system, something that is quite difficult to achieve in GSD projects. In support of the critical success factor "Maximize Stability," we have learned the hard way that it is very important to make explicit these concerns in such a way that they can be accounted for in the architecture.

This chapter discusses our approach for identifying and communicating architecturally significant requirements in general, as well as the specific concerns as they relate to GSD projects. It then discusses the activities involved in soliciting and communicating the architecturally significant requirements.

After reading the previous chapter, it may seem curious that we have another chapter on requirements engineering. We have found that there are really two classes of requirements that are used by different stakeholders for different purposes. The requirements from Chapter 3 are used for designing the functionality of the system. It does not, however, address the gross structure of the system. Object-oriented design techniques aside, many different structures of the system could deliver the desired functionality. In practice, it is often the case that the architecture is being developed more or less in parallel with the requirements. What are the architects using to guide their decisions? How do they know what the critical technical choices are and how to evaluate the options? We take the approach of developing a related set of architectural drivers (or architecturally significant requirements) specifically to motivate the design of the gross structure of the system.

4.1   Background

A software architecture (or the gross structure of the software system) should support *something,* but what is that something? Is it the functional requirements of the system? Well ... yes, but if many different architectures equally support the functionality, then the best architecture is the cheapest to implement ... right? Not necessarily; it really depends on the context. In some cases, achieving a market window may be more important than quality, functionality, or maintainability. In other cases, the architecture could be used to support a product line and initial construction could be two to three times the cost of building a single system. That is, the architecture should support the business goals of the organization. This section explains in more detail how the business goals map to the architecture, what information an architect needs to motivate the design, and how GSD enters into the equation.

4.1.1   How Does an Architecture Relate to the Business Goals?

For all who have been involved with the design of a system, what factors in practice influence your design decisions? How often do you think about how a particular technical decision affects the ability of the organization to achieve its goals? In many projects, you probably do not discuss such issues often. In practice, many design discussions — such as "Should we use an event-based or message-based communication?" or "Should we build our system with .NET or J2EE?" — take place without a clear set of criteria for making a decision. These debates are often more influenced by personal preference, opinion, and other factors that are difficult to quantify than by business criteria. It is the case, however, that these choices may have an impact on an organization's bottom line. We know of at least one case in our own company when particular software architecture choices resulted in the loss of market share and eventual selling-off of a large business unit.

As an example:

> Company A makes all its products through the sale of its hardware devices. The company produces a software application that manages networks of its hardware systems, but currently this is a loss leader (i.e., an application that loses money but enables the sale of its hardware). The executives of the organization recognize, however, that the hardware business is becoming commoditized. They expect the margins on the hardware sales to diminish over the next ten years. To ensure the long-term viability of their business, they have decided to build a new software management system that will turn a profit. The way they envision making this software business profitable is by doing two things:
>
> 1. Reduce the internal development costs.
> 2. Expand the market.
>
> Company A plans on reducing the internal development costs by replacing several existing applications with the new application. The company wants to expand the market by entering new and emerging geographic markets and by opening a new sales channel in the form of Value-Added Resellers (VARs). VARs sell the software under their own brand to support hardware systems of many different manufacturers.

Looking at this example, we can see several areas where the goals of an organization have (or should have) a substantial influence on the architecture of the system without necessarily impacting the functionality. Considerations should be made to support different hardware lines. Different markets may have regulatory considerations, cultural influences (e.g., customers from some regions are willing to pay for highly trained technicians to install and maintain the product, while in other regions they are not), and language considerations (e.g., reading top to bottom, translating alarm messages, etc.).

As more details are discovered, many more influences become identifiable. To what extent can a particular solution support all these goals? What are the trade-offs and risks involved? Is the business comfortable with these risks and trade-offs, or should they refine their goals (e.g., reduce the intended markets, or change the timeline)? All of these are business decisions but require input from the technical folks. Too often there is a disconnect between what the organization wants and what the implementers can deliver. Without some means to bridge the gaps that exist, risk quickly escalates. This is particularly true in GSD projects. Because everything is more complex in a GSD project, it is much more important to have a handle on where a potential mismatch exists between the businesses expectations and the feasibility of the technical solution.

4.1.2 What Influences an Architecture?

As described in Bass et al. (2003), the factors that influence the architecture tend to be the quality attributes; for example, performance, security, modifiability, and reliability. From the example business goals described above, we can see modifiability concerns (e.g., allowing the VARs to "brand" the system), localization, and adaptability concerns (e.g., being able to adapt the system to a new hardware line). There could easily be other concerns, such as performance, reliability, and availability, that are not obvious from the above description. In GSD projects there are some additional factors to consider beyond the typical quality attributes. We discuss these further in an upcoming section.

You often see these requirements defined as "non-functional" requirements. We have found that this can result in a debate that is somehow beside the point. It is often the case that a requirement that is relevant for the architect has both a functional and non-functional component. Rather than focusing on whether requirement X is functional or non-functional in nature, we focus on whether this requirement has an impact on the gross structure of the architecture. One yardstick that you could use to determine this is to ask if you would be able to efficiently accomplish this requirement regardless of whether or not the early architectural decisions took this into account. If the answer is no, then this is a requirement that should be considered by the architect early in the design process.

4.1.3 What Information Does an Architect Need?

It is not sufficient to say (as in the previous section) that a system must be modifiable, adaptable, and allow for localization. Any system is modifiable with respect to something, and a system can be modified with respect to any aspect given enough time and money. The question is: modifiable with respect to what, when, and with how much effort? What specific aspects of the system must be modified? Do they need to be modified at runtime, compile time, commissioning time, or development time? Can they take one hour, two staff weeks, or ten staff years to complete? The same questions go with all the other concerns. They must be specific enough that they can be "testable" with respect to the architecture; for example, an independent reviewer could determine whether the architecture can achieve this requirement. Bass et al. (2003) describe in detail how this can be done. Some additional examples could include:

- If the "adapter controller" fails to respond during normal load, the system will detect that failure and continue to communicate with the field system within two seconds.
- The developers will be able to replace the stand-alone client with a Web-based client in two person-months.
- The system will be developed to C level quality, providing the Connected Device Configuration (CDC) suite of functionality within 12 calendar months and using no more then 360 person-months.
- A systems engineer will be able to import a previously unsupported western language into the system at runtime without degrading the performance of the system below the normal load latency requirements.

4.1.4   What is the Influence of GSD on the Architecture?

So this is a book on developing software using geographically distributed teams. Why then have we spent half of this chapter discussing the requirements for software architecture and only minimally discussed GSD? There are a couple of reasons why we feel these topics are relevant for GSD projects: First, people often do not make explicit the drivers for software architecture. While this is OK in a situation where the system being built is not that much different than the last one and most people involved are experienced in the domain, it can often lead to "gotchas" late in the project. These unwelcome discoveries have been the undoing of many distributed projects. They often require unplanned substantial rework that reaches many aspects of the system. Because of the distributed nature of the project, the teams cannot coordinate sufficiently to rectify the situation in a timely manner.

Second, even if these are concerns that people intuitively know how to deal with, they must be able to make the context of that intuition explicit for the remote teams. The members of the remote teams likely do not share the same experience and intuition and need more help in understanding the motivation and rationale for particular decisions.

It is often said that for GSD you need an architecture that has "well-defined, loosely coupled components." While this is certainly the case, this knowledge is not sufficient to ensure that the architects design a system that can be implemented by the distributed development organizations. It is not uncommon for architects to make technology choices based on the skills of the people involved in the work. Similar considerations must be taken into account for GSD. This is often complicated by the fact that some of the development teams may come from outside the organization and thus are not familiar with the domain. It is also common that particular domain knowledge is isolated within a given division or location. Work units should be considered from the beginning when designing the system. If possible, target teams should be identified for these work units so that suitability between the team and the work to be performed can be determined. In addition, the work units will have different levels and types of coupling with the rest of the system. In general, tighter or more complex coupling implies more coordination between the constituent teams. If you are planning to allocate that work to teams that are not in a position to provide coordination and communication commensurate with the required coupling, then you have a mismatch.

These considerations will often lead to a decomposition that is different from what the architects would otherwise have designed. Along with this, trade-offs are bound to be made with the other requirements on the architecture. These trade-offs must be considered in light of the business goals. Changes in the architecture are not the only option. If there are conflicts that do not offer appealing choices, it is also possible to adjust the organizational structure in ways that will help ensure a match between the technical choices and the development organization's capabilities (further discussed in Chapter 6 on risk).

We believe Paulo's problems result from not paying adequate attention to these factors. Had the architecture been created with due consideration for organization structure and coordination among the constituent teams, he might not be suffering from sleepless nights.

4.2 Architecturally Significant Requirements

4.2.1 Elicitation

We often use a technique for eliciting architecturally significant requirements (ASRs) based on the SEI's Quality Attribute Workshop (QAW) approach (Bachmann et al., 2002; Barbacci et al., 2000). The goal of this activity is to establish a prioritized set of the most important architectural drivers, in the form of quality attribute scenarios, which are mapped to the business goals. We conduct this activity in the form of a structured workshop potentially followed by periodic reviews to evolve the requirements as necessary.

To ensure that the organizational factors also exert the appropriate influence on the architecture, we have developed an approach for bringing this information into the architecturally significant requirements (Hofmeister et al., 2000; Paulish, 2002). This approach aims at understanding the characteristics of the organization, identifying the areas where there is a consideration relevant to the architects, and communicating that concern in a way that allows the architects to act on that concern. This approach is also described in Chapter 6.

Before this activity can take place, the goals for the system must be available. Often, these goals are very general. It is assumed that everyone knows why the organization is building the system. If a concrete plan does not exist for what markets are intended, what the needs of those markets are, the market differentiators, and any special considerations, then it is too early to hold this workshop. If no one can clearly articulate these items, it usually is an indication that there was insufficient business planning for the project. In addition, sponsorship for this process must be secured. Because of the diverse nature of the stakeholders required, a higher-level management person is usually needed to ensure participation.

4.2.1.1 ASR Workshop

We have developed the ASR workshop based on the Software Engineering Institute's QAW (Bachmann et al., 2002; Barbacci et al., 2000). While many of the steps are the same as the QAW, we have tailored the approach in a few areas to better suit our purposes. The basic steps of the ASR workshop are described below.

Step 0: Preparation. This step is performed prior to the workshop. The goal is to ensure that the prerequisite conditions for success have been met. Because of past (sometimes painful) experience, we have formalized this step to allow for a cancellation or postponement of the workshop if the prerequisite conditions have not been met. For this workshop to be a success, three (seemingly obvious) conditions must be met:

■ *Appropriate stakeholder involvement has been secured.* This is often the most difficult aspect of the method. An ideal set of stakeholders could be quite large and include perspectives such as sales, maintenance, quality, service/commissioning, marketing, etc. It is usually essential to have a high-level management sponsor who understands and buys into the goals of the workshop in order to secure the appropriate attendance. It is important that you have in attendance at a minimum:

- Someone who can represent the overall goals of the business with respect to this project or product (the reason for the project)
- Customer or market representatives who can identify the key markets and describe their context and needs (what is required to successfully sell the product or consider the project a success)
- Architects

■ *Business context is known.* This seems like an unnecessary statement; however, after having participated in more than one project where it was not clear why the product was being built, we have explicitly included this. We initially gave very high-level guidance for what we were looking for in the business context presentation; but after having gotten all manner of presentations, we have developed a more detailed template with examples to help guide people as to what information we wanted.

■ *Logistical arrangements are made.* Because it is difficult to secure the time of the attendees, there is nothing more frustrating than wasting their time searching for whiteboard markers, projectors, etc. To avoid this situation, we have created a checklist to ensure that all appropriate arrangements have been made.

Step 1: Present ASR workshop method. The goal of this step is to ensure that all attendees understand the approach and what to expect during the workshop. The stakeholders will have been provided with read-ahead material so that they can start to familiarize themselves with the method, but we have found that stakeholders seldom read or understand the method from the material. We therefore start the meeting with a presentation describing the approach and allow for questions and clarifications. We allocate 1.5 hours for this step.

Step 2: Present business context. By the end of this step we want to have a short, bulleted list of the derived business goals for the project. To do this, we have the business stakeholder present:

- The business context (background on the goals for the projects)
- Key markets (if relevant) describing:
  - Who the intended customers are
  - How important they are (e.g., primary source of profit, not profitable but needed to maintain reputation, etc.)
  - Aspects of the system that would cause these customers to buy this product

- What these customers need to buy or use this product (e.g., customers will not tolerate more than two dropped calls per 100, Value-Added Resellers need to be able to add their own "brand" or look-and-feel to the product, system must comply with local fire regulations in order to be sold in this market)
- If this is a project rather than a product, then similar information is needed about the customers and their expectations
- Other considerations (e.g., platform whose goal is to reduce time to market for product lines x, y, and z by 25 percent)

It is rare that the information will all be available with the desired precision and desired detail. To ensure that there is sufficient detail to allow for a useful workshop, we ask the responsible person to provide us with a draft of the presentation prior to the workshop.

Step 3: Identification of key drivers. The goal of this step is to begin to translate the business requirements into concrete architectural requirements. These are fairly general in nature and provide a context for the next step of generating scenarios. As an example, consider one of the points mentioned above:

> Part of the strategy that we will use to expand the market is to have our system sold by Value-Added Resellers (VARs). VARs want the ability to add their own look-and-feel or the ability to "brand" the software. In addition, they might sell associated hardware devices that are manufactured by another vendor.

From looking at this we can see that the system should be able to have a different "look-and-feel" added to allow the VARs to brand the system. In addition, the system would require the ability to adapt to the various protocols used by the other embedded devices that would be managed by this system. These points are not yet concrete enough to be used as requirements for the architecture, but they are general statements about what the architecture must be able to achieve to support the business goals stated above. During this phase of the workshop, we would enumerate these "key drivers" and use them to drive scenario elicitation.

Step 4: Brainstorming scenarios. The goal of this step is to make the key drivers concrete. We do this by having the stakeholders propose *quality attribute scenarios* (Herbsleb and Grinter, 1999) that represent the specific concerns. The Software Engineering Institute (SEI) has done a nice job of defining precisely what a quality attribute scenario is, as well as cataloging a set of general scenarios to use as a guide. We will not repeat that information here other than to say that it is important that the scenarios be concrete with associated measures identified. For the drivers above, the measure could be in the form of level of effort to add a new user interface, or level of effort to develop a protocol adapter. This is often quite difficult for people to do. They are not used to thinking of the customer's needs in these terms. It is, however, impossible to understand what the architecture needs to achieve without some quantification. What we often do when stakeholders are unable to quantify their needs is to have them make an educated guess, record the fact that this measure is not for sure, and move on. In practice, these measures should be revisited many times during the design process, and it is helpful to know which ones are guesses and which ones are quite firm. At this stage we make no effort to filter, combine, prioritize, or reject scenarios. This is a brainstorming session and we treat it as such. The most relevant scenarios will be identified in subsequent steps. This is not going to be an exhaustive effort. There will be many variants on these scenarios that will not be captured here, but you need to get a representative collection. We often require that each stakeholder propose at least one scenario.

Step 5: Consolidating scenarios. Once we have the raw scenarios we begin to refine them. We do this by consolidating the scenarios. We select scenarios that could be combined, group them together, and then work to identify a scenario that covers the essence of the group. The key to this process is to ensure that the person who proposed the scenario has the final say as to whether the resulting scenario conveys what he or she meant when proposing it. If he or she does not agree, then we either modify the scenario until he or she does agree or keep the scenario out of the group.

Step 6: Prioritizing the scenario. There are several ways to prioritize the scenarios: you can take an inclusive approach and use a protocol where the entire set of stakeholders applies some number of votes to the scenarios that they feel are most important; you can have only the people who represent the business in one form or another determine the importance; or you can use another method for prioritizing. The important thing is that you rank them along two dimensions and that you have a very clear and structured protocol for ranking them (otherwise endless debates will result). You must rank the scenarios both in terms of importance with respect to the business goals (this should be an easy mapping as they are created in the context of one or more key drivers) and difficulty to achieve from an architectural or development perspective. This leads to concerns that are both important to the business and difficult to achieve. There are usually a very few drivers (about three) that end up really shaping the architecture (these drivers may have many scenarios that represent them).

Step 7: Wrap-up and outbrief. The last activity is to summarize the findings of the workshop in an organized and consolidated way, and to let the stakeholders know what will be done with the results and how they will continue to be involved in the process. It is important to remember that these results are not considered final. The workshop essentially ensures that everyone has the same understanding of the goals and direction for the project, a well-defined structure has been established for the architectural requirements, and that a communication channel and common language has been identified between the architects and the stakeholders. At this point, the process for continuing to refine and validate these requirements should be presented (we usually have a defined review meeting with the stakeholders at regularly scheduled intervals).

Tip: Identify no more than five key architectural drivers.

In practice, it is common to have many requirements (even architecturally significant requirements), but usually there are only a very few issues that really drive the architecture. Typically, there are only two or three of these "drivers". While there may be many requirements that make up the drivers, they are variations of the same concern. Much more than that and the architecture becomes too complex. If you find you have many concerns, try to group them into closely related themes. If you still have too many, be sure to clearly prioritize them in such a way that it is clear for which ones the architecture needs to be optimized.

4.2.1.2 Participants

The defined roles for an ASR workshop include:

■ *Workshop leader.* This person is responsible for leading and facilitating the workshop, and must have:
  ■ A thorough knowledge of the goals and method steps
  ■ Knowledge of software architecture
  ■ Excellent facilitation and interpersonal skills (usually there are a diverse set of stakeholders in attendance who have often not interacted in this way before and there is the potential for contention; tact and skill are required to keep the workshop on track and productive)

■ *Workshop scribe*. This person is responsible for capturing the "official" outputs of the meeting. It is often wise to have other workshop team members capturing important points, as well as a backup. This is not just a passive administrative role; it is important that this person is able to:

  ■ Understand the method and the goals so that they can appropriately capture and clarify points to obtain the desired information in the needed form

  ■ Be confident enough to set the pace of the meeting to ensure that important points are captured and approved of by the stakeholders

■ *Workshop team*. These people help in questioning and focusing the meeting. They should be familiar with the ASR method and have architectural knowledge. This is the best role for someone who is new to this approach.

■ *Stakeholders*. These people provide the content for the output.

Table 4.1 describes the stakeholders that should participate in the workshop.

The outputs of this activity are a set of prioritized architectural drivers that are mapped to the business goals. It is usually the case that there are relatively few "real" drivers for the architecture. If you have more than five to seven high-level drivers, then you have too many to manage. At this stage, these requirements can be refined, increasing the number significantly, but they should be able to be easily grouped under a relatively few major concerns.

In addition to (and maybe more important than) the artifact mentioned above, you should at this point have a set of stakeholders who have a common understanding of what the organization is trying to achieve by building this system. Often it is the case that this workshop is the first time these stakeholders will have had such a meeting (in some cases it may be the first time they have ever met), and it is seldom the case that they arrive with a unified concept of what this project is all about. This context and common understanding should be captured and synthesized into the mantra for the project. We elaborate further on this in Chapter 7.

4.2.2 Follow-on Activities

The workshop itself is really the kick-off for the ASR activities, and not the end. We usually follow up these activities with more detailed analyses (usually in areas identified during the workshop) that may include doing more market analysis, further refining the scenarios, identifying special cases and related scenarios, documenting, and more widely distributing

Table 4.1   Stakeholder Participants in the ASR Workshop

Title	Responsibility
Requirements Engineer	The requirements engineers should be knowledgeable about the required features of the system. There is often a direct relationship between the features and the architectural concerns.
Product Managers	The product managers represent the features that the product should have to be successful in the market.
Project Sponsor	The project sponsor funds the development of the product.
Architects	Architects define, describe, and communicate the architecture of the solution; make technical decisions; and perform architectural prototyping. They are responsible for successful completion of a subset of components, and develop specifications and acceptance tests for product components.
Project Manager	Project managers plan the entire life cycle of a product, managing the requirements and the architecture teams per the project plan and commissioning component development teams worldwide.
Customer proxies	Customer proxies represent the needs of the eventual users of the product.

the ASRs. It is important to keep in mind that this is a very iterative approach and is weaved into the rest of the life-cycle activities. While we strongly recommend holding the initial workshop early in the life cycle, we usually have shorter follow-up workshops (structured slightly differently) at regularly scheduled intervals to ensure that everyone stays on the same page throughout the project. The frequency of these meetings generally decreases over time as the architecture and the requirements stabilize.

4.2.3   Documentation

Because the number of these architecturally significant requirements is very small (even for large complex systems) relative to the functional requirements, documentation and management is not as much of an issue. We mandate that these requirements are identified in the architecture overview documentation, along with explanations for how they are addressed and what alternatives were considered. It is helpful when viewing an architecture description document to quickly gain an understanding of the most important issues addressed. It should also be the case that in subsections of the architecture description document, these requirements resurface (sometimes in more detail) when appropriate. Documenting the architecture is described in more detail in Chapter 5.

4.3 Summary and Conclusions

In this chapter we have discussed our approach for deriving the architecturally significant requirements from the business goals. We have also discussed how distributing the development work impacts the design process. Unfortunately, there is still much art in these processes. While we have made some strides in codifying a structured approach for doing this, there remains heavy reliance on experience (unfortunately on experience that is not widespread) in order to execute properly. We have found that the process we have defined and follow helps focus attention in the appropriate areas at the appropriate times so as to avoid some of the pitfalls that have doomed many past projects and result in a quality product — and high quality is the key to high speed.

4.4 Discussion Questions

1. Discuss the importance of architecturally significant requirements to GSD projects.
2. What are some techniques for eliciting architecturally significant requirements other than the one described in this chapter?

References

Bachmann, F., Bass, L., and Klein, M., *Illuminating the Fundamental Contributors to Software Architecture Quality,* CMU/SEI-2002-TR-025, August 2002.

Barbacci, M., Ellison, R., Weinstock, C., and Wood, W., *Quality Attribute Workshop Participants Handbook,* CMU/SEI-2000-SR-001, July 2000.

Bass, L., Clements, P., and Kazman, R., *Software Architecture in Practice, second edition,* Pearson Education Inc., April 2003.

Herbsleb, J. and Grinter, R., "Splitting the organization and integrating the code: Conway's law revisited," *Proceedings of the 21st International Conference on Software Engineering (ICSE 99),* Los Angeles, CA.

Hofmeister, C., Nord, R., and Soni, D., *Applied Software Architecture,* Addison-Wesley, Boston, MA, 2000.

Paulish, D., *Architecture-Centric Software Project Management,* Addison-Wesley, Boston, MA, 2002.

Chapter 5

Architecture

Company ABC was developing the next generation of their embedded system with resource constraints and significant real-time requirements. The architecture was an evolution of ABC's previous (very successful) system. The system was going to be deployed in an environment with an available 64 Megs of RAM (much more than the previous system). The system also had strict real-time requirements for start-up. This time, however, they found they kept blowing their memory limit on run-up. The structure of the development organization had changed over the years and they were now implementing different modules of the system at five sites throughout Europe. This caused many back-and-forth interactions with the different development teams, requiring them to coordinate all the interactions among their components during run-up. The end result was that development took more than twice as long as anticipated, exceeded the original budget by 80 percent, and was still not able to meet the latency requirements or memory constraints for run-up.

In collocated projects, the architecture is often the central artifact that ties together many aspects of the project. It is no different in GSD. Architecting for GSD has special concerns, however. Looking at the critical success factors, it becomes apparent that the architecture is central to many of them. Clearly, the architecture is required to understand the interdependent nature of the tasks. The extent to which you can minimize ambiguity and maximize stability is also dependent on how you conduct and document your architectural activities. It is also the case, however, that the "optimal" design for the requirements is not optimal with respect to the organization that is to develop it. There are problems with remote teams developing a shared understanding vis-à-vis the architecture, there are coordination needs imposed by the architecture that may be difficult to achieve, and it becomes difficult to effectively evolve the architecture as more knowledge is gained. In addition, the ability to conduct the planning and estimation processes effectively relies on having certain inputs from the architecture activities. This chapter focuses on how we support the critical success factors and account for the organization during architecture design activities.

5.1 Background

The SEI defines software architecture as being "…the structure or structures of the system, which comprises software elements, the externally visible properties of those elements, and the relationships among them" (Bass et al., 2003). Another way to think about architecture is as a set of decisions that are made early in the design life cycle that constrain future decisions. In the case of GSD, these future decisions are largely made by remote distributed development teams. In this chapter we discuss how you decide what decisions are important to make, how you can understand the impact of those decisions, and how you communicate them to the rest of the team.

5.1.1 Accounting for Quality Attribute Requirements

Chapter 4 discussed identifying the "architectural drivers" for the system, but did not sufficiently explain what these are. We discussed the process for identifying and ranking the architecturally relevant requirements with respect to the business context, and said that you should have no more than five architectural drivers, but did not go into detail. At the end of the ASR workshop, you might have 20 to 50 requirements. These will be ranked in importance with respect to the business goals, some of which will be very important and others less so. Once you have this ranking, you should have the architects rank the same requirements with respect to their difficulty to achieve. The requirements that end up being very important for the business and very difficult to achieve are the ones that end up being the real "architectural drivers." That is, they end up exerting the most influence over the shape of the architecture. This does not mean that you can ignore the other requirements — only that the other requirements are not going to have as strong an influence on the architecture.

We do not mean to describe the architectural design process in great detail here, but will give general guidance with more detail for aspects that are critical for GSD. There is fairly extensive knowledge on architectural mechanisms for many of the common quality attributes; the important thing is to analyze your options to achieve the ASRs (and thus the business goals). It is a good idea to record the rationale for important decisions so others can benefit from the thought involved (and do not unknowingly violate these decisions). How you go about selecting the order of the drivers and the options is up to you, but you will need to consider them all and you will need to revisit previous decisions often as most of these decisions cannot be made in isolation (we discuss trade-offs in a moment).

5.1.2 Accounting for the Organizational Structure

With some understanding of the intended structure of the developing organization, the architects have a better chance of designing a system that is implementable. The architects should know how many development teams there will be, who (in general) will populate these teams, as well as some characteristics about these people, such as what kind of domain knowledge they have, what their technical background is, where they are located, what organizational units they are from, have they worked together in the past, and their availability. From this information the architects will have some idea how many work units they should have, what kind of effort should be involved for each work unit, what kinds of "skills" to encapsulate, etc.

If we look at the example cited at the beginning of this chapter, for example, we can see that an analysis of the mapping between the dependencies and the organization would have involved significant coordination. Other alternatives could have been chosen, such as more precise memory budgets and scheduling algorithms or partitioning of the system with respect to time and space (while this would have required adjusting the partitioning size, it would have made issues obvious as they arose and made clear the impact of those issues on meeting the overall requirement). Another alternative could have been to change the organization structure; for example, appoint a group that is concerned with the scheduling and resource consumption of the system and have that group manage the coordination in a structured way. The point is that unless these concerns are identified early, the risks cannot be effectively managed (see Chapter 6 for more details).

5.1.3 Making Architectural Trade-offs

As alluded to in Section 5.1.1, trade-offs are an inherent part of the design process. You cannot optimize the architecture with respect to all associated requirements (e.g., optimizing on performance can often hurt modifiability) so compromises must be made. These compromises are fundamentally business decisions. It is typically not the case that architects are ideally positioned to make these decisions (although they often do make these decisions implicitly). Without being informed of an issue by the architects, and without knowing the impact of the issue on the business, the people responsible for planning a project are not in a position to provide input or make optimal decisions. This is the benefit of developing the ASRs in the way we recommend in Chapter 4. It gives a means for the architects and business people to communicate and make technical decisions that impact the bottom line of the business. It is, therefore, important to give the appropriate stakeholders an opportunity to understand the issues and options and provide input. We recommend having regularly held structured meetings to accomplish this.

5.2 Designing the System

Figure 5.1 gives an overview of the architecture design workflow. As mentioned previously, we do not intend to go into detail describing how to architect a system. Rather, we focus on the aspects of the design process

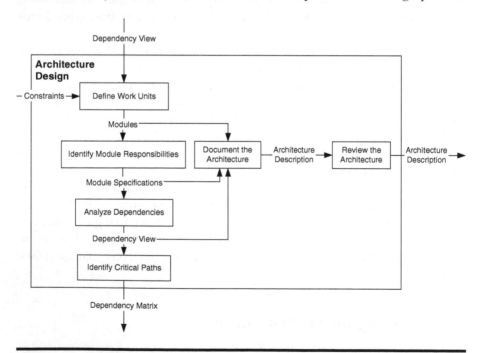

Figure 5.1 Architecture design workflow.

that are specifically relevant for GSD or provide inputs for other processes such as the planning process. In reading the sections below, keep in mind that this is not a sequential list. While we have described these activities independently for clarity's sake, in practice they are interdependent and occur in a very iterative manner.

5.2.1 Define Work Units

At some point the system as a whole should be broken down into functional units that can be allocated to teams to develop. We are not going to go into too much detail about how this is done (in many cases, it is more an "art" than it is an engineering activity), but we will hit on the high points that either relate to GSD or have an impact on other activities described elsewhere in this book.

In design books it often becomes confusing exactly what the authors mean when they use particular terms. In some cases it appears as if the authors themselves are not sure what they mean (in fact, we found that with five authors for this book, we used terms inconsistently quite often). This is particularly true in discussions of software architecture. We will make an attempt to describe what we mean when we use often-overloaded terms. In this section when we talk about decomposing the system into functional units, we are talking about static units (we use "module" to connote a static code unit). In many cases, there will, however, be a reasonable mapping between runtime components and static modules or packages (perhaps the reason why they are so often confused), but it will not be a perfect mapping. There will be more static units than runtime units as things such as utility classes and object models may not exist as runtime entities.

The drivers for how to define the functional decomposition of a system come from many places, for example, previous experience, architecturally significant requirements, available resources, patterns, and organization information. Ideally you will take into account the relevant architecturally significant requirements. Typically, modifiability, extensibility, and variability requirements have a bearing on the decomposition. Availability can also have an impact. If it is the case that you are developing a product line and have identified commonalities and variabilities, you will want to be sure to encapsulate the variable portions of your system to allow for the easy creation of the desired product instantiations. Additionally, if you have different availability needs for various features of the system, you may want to isolate these features (the same goes for real-time performance). These kinds of architecturally significant requirements will (or should) drive the decomposition of your system. In addition, however, you want to be sure to break up your system into implementable units. Chapter 8 (on estimation) gives some guidelines on how to determine the optimal size of the modules, but essentially the decomposition of the system needs to facilitate distributed development.

When we identify implementable units, we want to take into account the teams that are to develop the system. The architects should keep the team composition in their head and ensure that there is a suitable team for the units being identified (this can be done more formally in the review process). If there is no team that is suitable, the architects should attempt to find alternative approaches. If these approaches are less than ideal with respect to the other ASRs, then a trade-off may need to be made. This trade-off can come in the form of a relaxed ASR, restructuring some aspect of the organization (we discuss the restructuring alternatives in Chapter 6 on risk), or an increase of budget or schedule.

As a result of this activity, there is at least an identification of the modules that make up the system, some sort of size estimate, and a description of the responsibility for each module. If there are critical decisions that were made, it is good to document those decisions, what you are attempting to accomplish (usually a reference to one or more requirements), the alternatives considered, and the rationale for selecting the chosen alternative.

As the project progresses, this work will evolve with more complete and stable identifications of the functional decomposition, activity diagrams identifying how the features are realized by these modules, interface specifications, and dependency relationships. We discuss documentation of these and other views of the system in an upcoming section.

5.2.1.1 Participants

Table 5.1 lists the participants who define the work units and their main responsibilities.

5.2.2 Identify Module Responsibilities

At some point the architects will need to determine how the parts of the system work together to realize the features of the system as defined by the requirements (see Chapter 3). There is a tight coupling between this activity and the identification of the work units (described in the previous section). Before conducting this activity, there needs to be both a requirements model and an initial identification of the system modules. This activity is (as with most other things) iterative and thus the requirements model and static module view of the system will likely be refined in parallel with this activity. Obviously, the specific requirements being worked with should be reasonably stable before conducting this activity.

Table 5.1 Participants in the Define Work Units Activity

Title	Responsibility
Architect	The architect owns the architecture and is ultimately responsible for the functional decomposition.
Project Manager	The project manager provides input into the optimal size of modules based on planning activities. The project manager also needs to collect size estimates per module. The project manager also gives input concerning the team characteristics. This is useful to ensure that there are teams that have adequate skills for developing the modules that the architects are identifying.
Requirements Engineer	The requirements engineer helps clarify the requirements inputs and participates in design reviews or other activities to ensure that requirements are adequately addressed.

The static module view, however, will usually evolve as a result of this activity. By looking at the responsibilities in more detail, questions about where particular responsibilities will reside and adjustments to the static view are inevitable.

Chapter 3 discussed how we refine the features identified by the marketing group into concrete requirements. Once we have the detailed concrete requirements, we can identify the system-level requirements (think of these as the external interfaces to the system). We then need to assign responsibilities to various modules in the system such that, in aggregate, they achieve the desired result. In support of our desire to maintain traceability, we do this in UML as well (we create a design portion of the same model that has the requirements). We use interaction diagrams (typically sequence diagrams) to document the tracings through the system. In the process, we identify interfaces and methods that need to be realized for the cooperating modules in the system. These methods will eventually find their way into the schedule (described in Chapter 7 on planning). Figure 5.2 shows an example sequence diagram.

The output of this activity is a set of sequence diagrams describing how the requirements are realized by the system. The design model itself will evolve as part of this process. There will be many methods that have been identified, along with associated Abstract Data Types that need to be agreed upon. The static view will evolve; as well, rules for where to assign module responsibilities will emerge. If these rules are important (i.e., impact one or more of the ASRs), then they should be made explicit and documented.

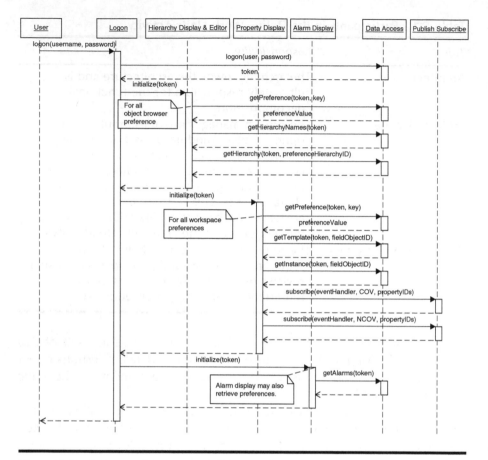

Figure 5.2 An example sequence diagram.

5.2.2.1   Participants

This activity is performed by the architecture team. There is usually some involvement or review by members of the requirements team to ensure that the requirements are being achieved as expected.

5.2.3   Analyze Dependencies

As discussed previously in this and other chapters, it is very difficult to facilitate coordination among teams that are geographically distributed. Largely, the decisions you make during the design of the system dictate the amount of coordination that you will have during the project. It is clear that things such as implicit and explicit calls between modules imply dependencies, but you can have other kinds of less-obvious dependencies as well.

In this context we define a dependency as *an aspect of a module that relies on or provides something to another module or aspect of the system.* That something could be a syntactic dependency such as a reliance on a particular method signature or a particular data construct, a semantic behavior, a timing behavior, or a resource behavior. At some level, virtually every module depends on every other module (e.g., if they all share CPU resources, they have dependencies). The trick is to identify the dependencies that are likely to require coordination among teams. This is necessary to determine the feasibility of your organization developing the solution that is being designed (discussed in Chapter 6 on risk). A useful and practical way to do this is to look at explicit call, implicit call relationships (e.g., publish subscribe), and "uses" relationships (e.g., one module "uses" classes from another module) and develop a dependency matrix (see Figure 5.3). Then as a second step, look at critical runtime requirements from the list of architecturally significant requirements (e.g., performance or availability requirements) and identify the portions of the system involved in realizing these requirements. Looking at the system in this way is something that is typically not done, but it provides insight that can often lead an organization to avoid costly naive assumptions that they may otherwise make.

		1	3	14	4	5	6	15	9	11	16	12	7	10	13	8	2	Number of modules this depends on
Publish Subscribe	1	▪																0
Command Processing	3		▪															0
Configuration	14			▪														0
Value Cache	4	1			▪													1
Data Access	5				1	▪												1
Condition Evaluation	6					1	▪											1
COV Processing	15		1					▪										1
Adapter Manager	9	1	1	1		1		1	▪									5
Property Display	11	1				1			1	▪								3
Alarm Processing	16	1				1			1		▪							3
Alarm Rule Engine	12	1				1	1		1			▪						4
Hierarchy Editor & Display	7					1						1	▪					2
Alarm Display	10					1							1	▪				2
L&R Rule Engine	13	1				1	1			1					▪			4
Rule Editor	8					1				1	1					▪		3
Logon	2					1					1			1	1		▪	4

Number of dependants 6 2 1 1 10 2 1 3 2 2 1 1 1 1 0 0

Legend

1 in bold = uses dependencies
1 regular = regular dependencies

Figure 5.3   An example dependency matrix.

From this activity we have what we call a dependency view of the system. The majority of this work is usually undertaken during the elaboration phase to support the guidance of the distribution of work to teams. If this is deemed a riskier project from a GSD perspective (see Chapter 6), then more attention is paid to the dependencies in the system as the design evolves. If it is the case that dependencies are emerging in critical areas of the system that imply a high degree of coordination, then this should be identified as early as possible so that appropriate steps can be taken (again, see Chapter 6). In some cases, alternative architectural mechanisms can be chosen.

5.2.3.1 Participants

Table 5.2 lists the participants who perform the dependency analysis, along with their main responsibilities.

5.2.4 Identify Critical Paths

To plan the development of the work units, some staging of the development needs to be identified. The way we do this is to identify the "critical paths" in the software. That is, any module with a "uses" dependency indicates that the "user" in that relationship has some intimate knowledge of the "usee." Because the remote development teams are responsible for the detailed design of the internal aspects of their modules, these "usee" modules must be designed (and ideally developed) before the design of the "user" modules. By looking in the system in this way, "critical paths" can be identified.

This activity is done in preparation for the planning, so it is usually started later in the elaboration phase. The responsibilities should be stable (at least for the portion being planned), and the high-level planning should be done. It should be clear what features are assigned to particular releases, and what the dependencies are between those features. This activity results in a type of dependency matrix. This matrix gives the development dependencies among modules in the system.

Table 5.2 Participants in the Dependency Analysis Activity

Title	Responsibility
Architect	The architect is responsible for identifying the dependencies.
Requirements Engineer	The requirements engineer must be available for clarifying requirements.

5.2.4.1 Participants

This activity is conducted by members of the architecture team.

Tip: Keep the architecture team size as small as possible.
Although a number of roles and responsibilities are defined, limit the size of the architecture team. Smaller teams work more quickly and help limit the investment applied to the high-level design phase. Assigning too many architects to the project team can create a "too many cooks in the kitchen" situation that can lead to "analysis paralysis". The roles of project manager and architect are most critical for the project team to make efficient progress during the elaboration phase. Often, the people assigned to these key roles also serve as process mentors, because they very likely are more experienced and have previously done similar projects.

5.2.5 Document the Architecture

Some of the activities above are going to result in particular views of the system being produced. Below we cite additional views of the system and discuss their relevance from a GSD perspective. We do not discuss general issues and goals of documenting a software architecture other than to say to *write the documentation from the reader's perspective*. All too often, architecture documentation is written without much thought given to the reader. We often see a very large architecture document that is given to anyone wanting to know something about the architecture. An architecture document is typically not meant to be read from cover to cover as are novels from your favorite authors. Readers usually have a specific need they are trying to address, and the authors should consider these needs before writing the documents and offer some guidance on how to find the appropriate information. For more information on documenting a software architecture, see Clements et al. (2002).

5.2.5.1 Execution Views

The execution views of the system depict the runtime entities and the mechanisms employed by these entities in interacting with each other. They depict components in the system such as processes, objects and data stores, and connectors that represent mechanisms of interaction between these components. These components and connectors are the elements represented in this view type.

The execution view is useful for the following roles:

1. The domain, architectural, discipline, and technology specialists can argue and reason about architectural properties and quality attribute requirements to which the system must adhere.
2. External stakeholders such as customers and project evaluators can understand the system's principal executing components (including the major shared data sources) and their interactions — therefore serving as a means for verification and validation of system properties.
3. Maintainers of the project can get an overview of the system as a starting point for future extensions or modifications.

Because of this, the execution view is used to determine important runtime dependencies between the elements depicted. A tracing between the static work allocation view and the execution view will provide additional insights into runtime dependencies that exist between the work units of various teams.

5.2.5.2 Implementation Views

The implementation views of the system depict partitions of the system that are unique and are non-overlapping sets of hierarchically decomposable implementation units (modules). Examples of implementation units would be namespaces in the .NET world and packages in the Java world. There are multiple goals in coming up with such a view of the system, including:

- Showing how the source code is decomposed
- Showing the different relationships between these implementation units
- Considering the implementation units that will realize the functionalities as decomposed in the execution views and therefore attain the quality attribute requirements
- Ensuring that the development planning phase has all the requisite inputs to create a feasible plan.

This view type is useful for the following roles:

- The project manager, who must define work assignments that are reasonably decoupled from each other so that they are delegated across multiple remote development teams separated from each other

- The domain and architectural specialists, who must be able to reason about the architectural properties most dependent on such a view of the system (e.g., modifiability)
- The project manager, the domain, architectural, and discipline specialists, who use these views to ascertain the size and complexity of work assignments so that they are able to determine the appropriate level of decomposition to be assigned to a certain team
- The communications specialist, who will know how best to structure collaboration artifacts like the project wiki (see Chapter 12)
- The configuration manager, who is in charge of maintaining current and past versions of the units in consistent and functional packageable assemblies, being able to produce a running version of the system
- Testers, who use the modules as their unit of work to create test cases and perform the tests

5.2.5.3 Traceability between the Various Views

Distributed teams use the multiple views of the architecture to develop modules; and to facilitate this, it is of vital importance that they have a shared mental model of the architecture. In addition to creating the multiple views of the architecture, it is important that the architecture team ensure that the navigability between the views is both usable and correct at all points of time. This means maintaining traceability from the execution views to the module views and to multiple detailed design artifacts that are created much later in the elaboration stage. This is important for the following reasons:

- It allows the project manager, architectural specialist, and the domain specialist to sit down and appropriately understand the dependencies not only between elements of a view but also across views, and this becomes an important tool at the time of allocating execution or implementation units across multiple remote development sites with the aim of minimizing dependencies across sites.
- The remote teams can look at the view that is the basis of the development plan and trace their allocation of software units through multiple views to get a better understanding of their work assignments — a critical step in developing a complete and accurate understanding of the work to be done in each iteration.

5.2.6 Review the Architecture

We recommend conducting at least one formal review before the end of the elaboration phase. We use a method based on the SEI's Architecture

Tradeoff Analysis Method (ATAM) (Clements et al., 2001). While we will not repeat the steps of the ATAM here, it is important that you conduct the review in a similar manner as the ASR workshop. That is, you want to review the architecture against the business goals and the ability of the organization to develop the architecture. To do this, you again need widespread stakeholder participation. This process is aided greatly by a diligent execution of the ASR workshop. The stakeholders know what to expect, the goals have been publicly established, the ASRs have largely been identified, and the goals of such a meeting are commonly understood. The outputs of such a review are a set of risks, non-risks, trade-offs, and sensitivity points. For more information on this process, see Clements et al. (2001).

5.3 Summary and Conclusions

This chapter addressed architecture-related concerns for GSD. It is important to optimize the architecture so that it is easily distributable among geographically distributed teams. Project managers must create work units that take into account the capabilities of individual teams, their abilities to work with each other, and the level of coordination required among them. Identifying modules, their responsibilities, and dependencies among them will assist the project managers in creating these work units. The dependency analysis also helps in identifying critical paths and, therefore, scheduling of the development of the modules. Because architecture is critical to the success of a project, especially one that is globally distributed, it must be reviewed with all the stakeholders. It must also be documented such that the teams involved understand and share the same architectural vision. As emphasized in Chapter 4, high-quality architecture can go a long way toward producing a high-quality product. The techniques illustrated in this chapter help bring focus to technical excellence in the early stages of the software development life cycle.

5.4 Discussion Questions

1. What is the significance of architecture and organization structure in GSD?
2. What is the process by which a project manager can create work units and a feasible schedule for distributed development of a software product?
3. Describe some of the views used in documenting an architecture in addition to those introduced in this chapter. What is the significance of these, if any, to GSD projects?

References

Bass, L., Clements, P., and Kazman, R., *Software Architecture in Practice, Second Edition*, Addison-Wesley, Boston, MA, April 2003.

Clements, P., Bachmann, F., Bass, L., Garlan, D., Ivers, J., Little, R., Nord, R., and Stafford, J., *Documenting Software Architectures: Views and Beyond*, Addison-Wesley, Boston, MA, September 2002.

Clements, P., Kazman, R., and Klein, M., *Evaluating Software Architectures: Methods and Case Studies*, Addison-Wesley, Boston, MA, 2001.

Chapter 6

Risk Analysis

When Joe was working on the BAS project, he sat in a training session on risk management. The instructor suggested that the project management team focus on the few risks that were very likely to occur and could have a large negative impact on the project. As Joe thought of all the potential risks associated with doing global development on such a large scale and his organization's lack of experience with outsourcing, he realized that there would be more than a few risks to worry about.

Looking at the complexity of the BAS project it was clear that there were many potential problems. In fact, the problems were large enough such that they could jeopardize the success of the project. Is there a point in time when these issues should be addressed? If so, could strategies be put in place to reduce the likelihood that these risks would be realized? This chapter discusses risk management as it pertains to global software development (GSD). In many respects, risk management in GSD projects is similar to risk management in collocated software development projects. There are, however, special considerations. Here we highlight the ways in which risk management differs in a GSD context and assume that the reader has a general knowledge of risk management.

Risk management is the primary responsibility of the product (or program) manager. He may be assisted by QA or process experts, but any team member has the responsibility to identify potential risks and actions to mitigate risks. A Risk Management Plan is developed during the elaboration phase, but the plan is implemented and monitored as soon as the first risk is documented.

6.1 Background

This section provides a general background about risk management and discusses sources of risk that are of particular concern in GSD projects. In some sense this information is threaded throughout this book. Each section discusses specific issues that can arise (i.e., risks) related to the activities under discussion. We also discuss ways to identify and address these issues (mitigations).

Why then do we have a separate chapter dedicated to risk management? Have we not covered these topics sufficiently throughout the book? Risk management is a critical project management activity in its own right, with the business goals being the fundamental motivators for decisions. In many ways, a manager does nothing more than manage risk. That being the case, it makes sense to have a structured approach to monitor how well the risks are being managed and where additional attention should focus. GSD, in particular, has some specific concerns that may not be obvious until their impact has been realized. We have seen many projects fail because they did not pay adequate attention early enough to certain factors common in GSD projects. We cite those factors in this section.

6.1.1 What is a Risk?

As with most technical jargon, there are many definitions of risk. Essentially, a risk is the *possibility* of suffering some *loss* (Dorofee et al., 1996). The important thing to realize is that there is some uncertainty that the loss will be suffered. If the loss has already been realized or it is certain that it will be realized, then you are not dealing with a risk — you are dealing with a problem. Looking at the opening discussion of the BAS project: we are not describing risks, we are describing realized problems. At an earlier stage in the project before these problems were certain to occur (when they were still a *possibility*), they were risks.

In development projects, the loss that might be suffered comes in the form of schedule slippages, increased cost, diminished quality of the end product, or even complete failure of the project. In addition to all the traditional issues that can be experienced in collocated projects, GSD projects have particular issues related to coordination, problem resolution, evolving requirements, knowledge sharing, and risk identification. Traditional risk identification and monitoring approaches are often less effective in a GSD context and need to be augmented. We discuss this further below.

6.1.2   The Risk Life Cycle

In traditional projects, one can define the phases and associated activities as a risk life cycle. The Software Engineering Institute (SEI) has identified a risk life cycle (Dorofee et al., 1996) that includes the following steps:

- *Identify*: search for and locate risks before they become problems.
- *Analyze*: transform risk data into decision-making information; evaluate impact, probability, and timeframe, classify risks, and prioritize risks.
- *Plan*: translate risk information into decisions and mitigating actions (both present and future) and implement those actions.
- *Track*: monitor risk indicators and mitigation actions.
- *Control*: correct for deviations from the risk mitigation plans.
- *Communicate*: provide information and feedback internal and external to the project on the risk activities, current risks, and emerging risks.

The key to understanding the above life cycle is that it is continuous. That is, you do not just identify risk at the beginning of a project; you need mechanisms to continuously identify, analyze, plan, track, control, and communicate risks. As the project evolves, the approaches used may change. For example, you may have a more structured diagnostic process that is performed early in the project life cycle to identify major risk areas or themes associated with the project and then have different lighter-weight mechanisms for identifying new risks that emerge as the project evolves. Later in this chapter we describe some structured approaches that we use for risk identification and monitoring.

6.1.3   Risks in a GSD Context

As discussed, GSD projects have some specific concerns. These concerns are often at the heart of the issues experienced. Below we highlight some of the major issues.

6.1.3.1   Coordination

At the heart of the many issues experienced in GSD you will find difficulties related to communication and coordination. It is not often recognized how vital a role informal communication (e.g., around the lunch table or in the hallway) plays in a software development effort. Agile practices have recognized and capitalized on this by institutionalizing practices that encourage ad hoc communication (e.g., pair programming, on-site customer presence, open work areas, etc.). In GSD, you have teams separated by geographic distances that make this kind of communication very difficult and costly. Many of the subtle cues that help people understand each other and provide feedback are not available. The end result is that it is difficult for a project to gain a common understanding across teams about particular tasks. It is also difficult to gauge the extent to which a common understanding has been attained. In the BAS project, there were many assumptions made about what information remote teams needed in order to be productive (e.g., "We'll just give them these module specifications and they should be fine."), and there was no formal mechanism for evaluating the effectiveness of the mechanisms that were being used (mostly design documents).

Research has shown (and our experience is consistent with these results) that tasks executed across sites takes longer (in the study mentioned it was 2.5 times longer) than tasks executed within a single site (Herbsleb and Grinter, 1999; Herbsleb and Mockus, 2003; Herbsleb et al., 2001). What seems to account for this difference is that there is an increase in the coordination required in distributed projects; additionally, there is an increase in the number of participants needed to accomplish a task in a GSD setting (Herbsleb and Grinter, 1999; Herbsleb and Mockus, 2003; Herbsleb et al., 2001). This is an under-recognized fact in GSD projects. The potential for coordination difficulties is often ignored or minimized, and the potential impact on the project is not explored in sufficient depth.

If we look more closely at the role that communication plays in software development and why it is difficult in GSD projects, we can begin to get some insight into why these difficulties are experienced and what kinds of things can be done to mitigate these risks. As said, informal unplanned communication is an important part of software development (Perry et al., 1994). Discussions around the water cooler, at the lunchroom table, or at company functions end up playing a significant role in a software project. These conversations help establish personal relationships, help communicate the skill set and background, and help communicate the activities and tasks of individuals on a project. During the course of these interactions, it can be the case that conflicting assumptions, incorrect interpretations, or dependencies are discovered. It also helps to establish a social network that can be used during the course of the day to resolve questions or problems that you might experience. Knowing whom to go to is not always easy on a large project, but having a well-established social network reduces the time you spend trying to find the correct person. Once you find the person, getting access to him or her and being able to communicate effectively and efficiently is easier if you have an established relationship (Herbsleb and Mockus, 2003).

With the advent of particular technologies such as instant messaging and various chat programs, distributed informal communication is easier now than it was previously. That being said, informal unplanned communication is still very difficult and does not usually happen across sites. Because of this, it takes much longer to find the appropriate person (or people) and coordinate with to take care of a cross-site work item. Consider, as an example, a common situation that occurs during integration time:

> We advocate monthly engineering releases, which includes build and integration testing. It is not uncommon to discover issues during this process, and entering a bug in the bug tracking system along with an assignment of a responsible person or team. The "buildmeister" makes that assignment based on an assumption (or guess) on where the issue lies. That assigned person then needs to do some tracing to discover the source of the problem. Much of the code that is traced may not belong to the person to whom the bug was assigned, often requiring the need to coordinate with other people from other sites. First, there needs to be some knowledge about who the appropriate person is to contact; then the person needs to establish contact and arrange for some appropriate coordination to answer the question. It is likely that the second person has tasks of his or her own to worry about and will not place the same priority as the responsible person (this tends to be more likely if they are strangers), thereby adding to the amount of time it takes to get an adequate interaction.

Looking at this common situation it becomes clear how coordination can take much longer across sites.

Coordination becomes more critical in projects that have ambiguous requirements, design elements, or are otherwise unstable (Galbraith, 1977; Kraut and Streeter, 1995), but it can also be an issue in the most stable of projects. We discuss later various strategies for accounting, monitoring, and mitigating the risks associated with cross-site coordination and communication.

6.1.3.2 Architectural Alignment

As addressed in the chapters related to software architecture, issues can arise due to a misalignment between the system under development and the organization developing that system. A very naive approach to distributing work illustrates this point.

> A project was initiated to develop a large complex platform. This platform was an embedded solution that had resource constraints and hard real-time requirements. In addition, it had complex variability needs as it was to support a wide range of products. During the design, the architects did an elegant job of designing a component-based solution to address the complex set of requirements that the system had. When it came to allocating work, however, they did so without regard to geographic boundaries between individuals. They assigned units of the system according to the organizational unit responsible for that functionality. It just happened to be the case that these units (and thus the teams assigned to these units) were distributed across five locations in several European countries. These locations corresponded to different company acquisitions that were made in recent years and thus these people had not necessarily worked together in the past. A platform was eventually delivered, but it took 120 percent longer than anticipated, exceeded budget by 80 percent, and had quality problems (that were the direct cause of extensive loss of revenue).

While many projects recognize that geographic boundaries should mirror system boundaries in some fashion, it goes a bit deeper. It is always the case that allocated work units of the system need to interact in some manner (to realize the requirements of the system as a whole). This interaction implies coordination of some sort between the teams developing the work units. The question is: can these teams be reasonably expected to coordinate sufficiently to realize these interactions as expected in the desired timeframe? While this question cannot be answered concretely, explicit investigation will yield areas of gross mismatch.

6.1.3.3 Uncertainty and Change

Ambiguity and uncertainty exist to varying degrees in every project. Requirements, design aspects, management practices, and organizational processes can all be areas where uncertainty, ambiguity, and fluctuation might exist. Instability in these areas can be disruptive in any software development process — but in GSD projects the impact is much more pronounced. This subsection briefly addresses these areas of ambiguity and the impact that they can have on GSD projects.

We have yet to work on a project that is scheduled at a relaxing pace with all issues and tasks accounted for in the schedule and all tasks allotted an abundance of time to complete (although we can all hope and dream). It is usually the case that schedules are compressed and time allowances do not adequately account for all of the tasks and issues experienced. It is not uncommon that the project proceeds with a scheduled task (such as engaging a remote team) without having all the prerequisite activities fully completed. That is just a fact of life in today's software projects.

Uncertainty is also a fact of life in software projects. It is important to identify and account for uncertainty in all software projects, but this is particularly true in GSD projects. Because of the ways in which teams interact and the dynamics that can quickly develop in GSD projects, uncertainty (in the form of ambiguous aspects of the system, incorrectly interpreted specifications, or poorly specified items) can quickly spin out of control and bring down a project. Our experience from the GSP project shows that uncertainty can lead to nonproductive teams that become demoralized. This happened when teams had to either do substantial rework through no fault of their own or had to make assumptions to make progress. This was also the case when teams had to sit idle. The point is that areas of uncertainty need to be explicitly recognized and accounted for in GSD projects.

6.2 Managing Risk in GSD Projects

This section begins a more specific discussion of how to identify and mitigate risks in a GSD project. It describes the activities that we have codified in more detail.

6.2.1 Risk Identification

In traditional projects there are several ways to identify risks. There are diagnostic methods such as the Software Risk Evaluation (SRE) (Williams et al., 1999) or the ATAM (Kazman et al., 2000), and you can have risks reported by team members, through periodic management meetings, or by voluntary submission. All of these approaches are equally valid in GSD as well, but they may not highlight specific risks associated with coordination. The degree of risk to the schedule, budget, and quality of the product that derives from distributing some of the development highly depends on the system that you are developing, the context in which it will be developed, and the characteristics of the teams that are going to do the development. The first step in understanding the risk inherent in a project is to get some insight into the organization and look at the distribution options for the system.

We use a diagnostic method for developing what we call a *risk profile* for GSD projects. The profile describes the *capabilities* of the organization that will develop the system, the *coordination needs* implied by the system to be built, and an assessment of the degree of mismatch. This mismatch highlights areas of high risk. This assessment is the input for the planning process. The planning process involves identifying mitigation strategies appropriate for the level of risk exposure with which the organization is comfortable.

6.2.1.1 Determining the Coordination Capability

There are three main components of this diagnostic method: (1) the dependency analysis of the system (described in Chapter 4), (2) identification of the organizational characteristics, and (3) the analysis of the relative "fit" between the two. The goal of identifying the organizational characteristics is to understand the coordination capability of the teams involved in the project. This involves understanding things such as:

- The general background and skills of the individuals that make up (or are likely to make up) the teams
- The domain knowledge of the teams as it relates to the product under development
- The history of interaction across teams (e.g., have they ever worked together before?)
- The organizational separation (e.g., do they have the same reporting chains?) among teams
- Shared culture and language

Each of these items (and many others) either contributes to or hinders the ability of teams to work together. It should be common sense to determine to what category any given characteristic belongs. For example, if members of coordinating teams know each other personally, this may make coordination easier. If, however, they have never met, it will make coordination more difficult. Once these factors have been aggregated, a general picture will emerge. This is not an exact science; rather, it is designed to provide insight into where potential issues might lie and helps to focus the monitoring activities.

6.2.1.2 Participants

This activity can be conducted by virtually anyone who understands the possible project risks. They can interview people, as needed, to gather the risk information and then report the results to the management team for the project.

6.2.1.3   Inputs

To perform this activity, some consideration must be given as to where the development sites might be and who (generally speaking) will populate the teams. It could be the case that this analysis might help inform a selection between sites; but without at least candidates proposed, this activity cannot be conducted. In addition, it is helpful to have some general knowledge about the system to be produced. Any special knowledge (e.g., image processing) should be identified. If general areas of concern are known, it is helpful as well (e.g., safety critical, real-time performance, or 24/7 operations).

6.2.1.4   Outputs

The output of this activity is a profile of the coordination capabilities of the developing organizations. This can be more or less formal as needed and will be combined with the dependency analysis of the system to determine relative fit or mismatch, as the case may be.

6.2.2   Mitigating Risks

During the elaboration phase, it is wise to have as input some concept of the risk profile for your organization. This will allow you to plan the project, distribution of work, and associated practices with the risks in mind. There are areas to consider when mitigating risks. The first is to look at ways to improve your organization's capabilities; the second is to plan the coordination aspects of your project; and the third is to preplan how you are going to adjust your project in the event that the initial coordination plan is not sufficient (the project is not executing as smoothly as desired). We discuss each of these in turn.

6.2.2.1   Increasing Organizational Capabilities

Recall that as part of the diagnostic approach mentioned above, we look at the capabilities inherent in the organization. If a mismatch of consequence is identified, you can look at mitigations in the solution space (potentially change the design of the system) or consider changing some characteristic of the organization. For each item that was considered where your organization (or some teams) did not receive a favorable rating, consider ways in which you could change the aspects of the organization to improve the rating. For example, if it is the case that the teams involved with the development have never before worked together and know nothing about the members of the other teams, then you might consider a personnel exchange, collocating the teams for a period of time, common training, periodic collocated meetings, team building exercises, or some other mechanism to increase the awareness and stimulate a dialogue between members of other teams. As an example, the kick-off meetings used during the GSD project were used for this purpose. Other options could include:

- Unifying tool infrastructure (e.g., have an IDE or framework that constrains development)
- Tighter coupling of management practices
- More frequent builds
- More frequent status meetings
- Cross-team reviews

6.2.2.2 Contingency Planning

Because things usually do not proceed as expected, it is wise to plan for such an eventuality. In GSD projects, this means planning for how and when you are going to adjust the execution of the project. The first thing you want to do is identify and prioritize the dimensions that you can reasonably vary within your organization. These dimensions of variability may include the frequency of builds, frequency and type of status meetings, and maybe even the location of the teams. You should also have some idea of under what conditions you will vary the coordination. This allows for a more structured approach for executing a project. With a bit of forethought, this approach can help ensure that you minimize the negative impact of distributing the project on the quality and schedule of the deliveries.

6.2.3 Monitoring Risks

Monitoring progress and risks within GSD projects is quite difficult. It is difficult to adequately understand what is happening within the teams that are geographically distributed. By the time the deliverables are late or quality issues are discovered, it is likely that the schedule has suffered substantially. It takes much more effort and time to refocus or recover from such situations. It is typically the case that developers have a much better idea of what the current status of a project is at any given time than the managers do. The trick is to make the project much more transparent and allow an open reporting of risks from the people who are in a position to identify them. There are several approaches for doing so. One is to have frequent status meetings in which each member of the team reports status and issues that they are currently facing, such as in daily start-up meetings. This works well but must be adapted as the project grows. It is difficult to effectively get an impression in this way of the overall state of the project for larger projects involving multiple development sites.

We have also created mechanisms for individuals to report issues that they are experiencing, but we have found that it is difficult to get people to proactively do so. One mechanism that we have started using that is proving quite useful is a regular survey (usually biweekly). This survey generally takes less than ten minutes per person and asks questions about how an individual perceives the project is progressing, who they have been interacting with (and how), what they have been spending their time doing, etc. This allows project management to view a summary of the data visually and (after some practice) quickly identify issues. Some issues are instantly obvious, such as a downward trend in the morale of the team members, overloaded individuals (clear when there are a few key people central to many aspects of the project), no interactions between teams where you would expect there to be interactions, etc. Other indicators are less obvious but can be similar flags nonetheless. We have found that by monitoring certain indicators, we have been able to discover issues earlier. These indicators are things such as a spike in unplanned communication (e.g., when it is not associated with a release date) and an unplanned spike in travel. By having monthly management meetings that pay attention to these indicators, as well as scheduled milestones and deliverables, we have been able to discover, investigate, and head off some issues before they became major problems.

6.4 Summary

GSD-related problems, such as communication and coordination, increase the risks to schedule, budget, and quality as compared to collocated projects. It is not uncommon for tasks in GSD projects to take more than twice as long as in a collocated project. If potential risks are identified and mitigation actions are tracked as the development progresses, the project has a better chance of succeeding. The risks and their proposed mitigations are described in the Risk Management Plan.

6.5 Discussion Questions

1. Describe risks specific to a GSD project, and their identification and mitigation strategies.
2. Describe how you might develop a risk profile.

References

Dorofee, A., Walker, J., Albert, C., Higuera, R., Murphy, R., and Williams, R., *Continuous Risk Management Guidebook,* Carnegie Mellon University Software Engineering Institute, 1996.

Galbraith, J., *Organizational Design,* Addison-Wesley, Boston, MA, 1977.

Herbsleb, J.D. and Grinter, R.E., "Splitting the Organization and Integrating the Code: Conway's Law Revisited," *Proceedings International Conference on Software Engineering,* pp. 85–95, 1999.

Herbsleb, J.D., Mockus, A., Finholt, T.A., and Grinter, R.E., "An Empirical Study of Global Software Development: Distance and Speed," *Proceedings International Conference on Software Engineering,* pp. 81–90, 2001.

Herbsleb, J.D. and Mockus, A., "An empirical study of speed and communication in global distributed software development," *IEEE Transactions on Software Engineering,* 29(6), 1–14, June 2003.

Kazman, R., Klein, M., and Clements, P., "ATAM: Method for Architecture Evaluation," Technical Report CMU/SEI-2000-TR-004, Carnegie Mellon University, 2000.

Kraut, R.E. and Streeter, L.A., "Coordination in software development," *Communications of the ACM,* 38(3), 69–81, 1995.

Perry, D.E., Staudenmayer, N.A., and Votta, L.G., "People, organizations, and process improvement," *IEEE Software,* 11(4), 36–45, 1994.

Williams, R., Pandelios, G., and Behrens, S., "SRE Method Description (version 2.0) & SRE Team Members Notebook (Version 2.0)," Technical Report CMU/SEI-99-TR-029, Carnegie Mellon University, 1999.

Chapter 7

Project Planning Process

Joe's anxiety level increased when he checked the requirements database and noticed that with recent stakeholder requests, the number of requirements now approached 7000. He wondered, "How can we implement all these features and still meet time-to-market goals?" Part of the answer to Joe's question is to group the features into "releases" or "versions" that can be iteratively developed and then released to the market when they are ready. Using the design model and critical path analysis, Joe and his colleagues could then define a project plan by which these iterations could be realized.

We have reached the project planning section of this book. This chapter describes the project planning workflow and Chapter 8 provides details for cost estimation. We describe how a multi-year project plan is created. We use an iterative time-boxed approach to achieve synchronous development among the various geographically distributed development sites. Because late deliveries of software modules happen even in the best of all software projects, we discuss strategies for handling them in synchronized, global development.

7.1 Project Planning: An Overview

Figure 7.1 gives a simplified overview of the activities involved in project planning. While the diagram shows the activities as largely sequential, these activities are not only iterative; they are also split across phases of the project. How these activities are phased largely depends on the details

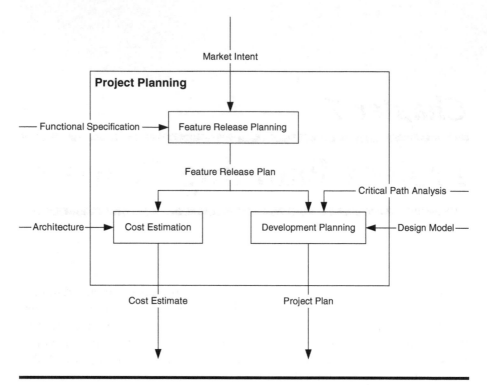

Figure 7.1 Project planning workflow.

of your specific process for the development life cycle; however, we give some guidance on this in Chapter 8.

The feature release planning process starts with the identification of "bundles" of features that comprise saleable solutions. We call this a feature release plan; depending on the needs and complexity of your system, this may or may not need to be a separate artifact. These bundles can then be prioritized. In our organization, it is usually the product manager who leads this activity.

Based on the planned releases identified in the feature release plan and the functional decomposition done during the architectural definition (shown as the design model in Figure 7.1), the modules needed to realize these features can be identified. As the design evolves, specific tasks for development teams can be identified. Using the feature release plan and critical path analysis (described in Chapter 5), we can begin assigning these tasks to sprints. These activities are quite complex and are highly coupled with other activities such as requirements engineering and architecture definition. It is not possible to have well-defined stable information before the planning process begins, so it is typically the case that an initial high-level projects plan and cost estimate are developed, and then further refined iteratively. Upcoming sections and chapters provide more details about these processes and provide concrete examples.

7.2 Feature Release Planning

Feature release planning involves "bundling" features into planned external releases of the system. This is an activity typically under the product manager's responsibility. These position titles are often overloaded and may differ from one company to the next, but the point is that this is a person who is typically responsible for and has insight into identifying the features that will allow a product to be sold in the marketplace. This will be somewhat of an iterative activity as the optimal set of initial features will depend on the timeline or effort involved with the development, the current customer base, and the state of existing legacy products. A migration plan for sunsetting legacy products can be developed in conjunction with the feature release plan. Sometimes, one can segment the market, whereby the old and new products can be sold simultaneously until the new product grows its feature set. At some point in time, old products must be sunsetted, when they will no longer be maintained by your organization.

The goal of this activity is to identify the minimum set of features that can be sold in the marketplace. This minimum set of features is identified as the first release, and the remaining features are bundled into subsequent releases.

An example feature release plan, reproduced from Paulish (2002), is illustrated in Figure 7.2. In this figure, Schedule Maker is the name of an example set of features to be developed. The features listed are all allocated to various releases; and as the feature release plan evolves, those releases are broken down into internal engineering releases. These engineering releases correspond to Scrum sprints (Schwaber, 2001, 2004). The integration and test plan will be based on the feature release plan.

	ER1	ER2	ER3	R1	R2+
Schedule Maker					
Search Consumer Tree for Scheduled Events	√			√	
Create a new Schedule	√	√	√	√	
Handle Report	√			√	
Handle Acquisition		√		√	
Optimize Acquisitions					√
Handle set Parameter Scheduled Events		√		√	
Display and manual Update of Schedules			√	√	

Figure 7.2   Example excerpt from a feature release plan.
Source: **Pearson Education, Inc.**

As seen from Figure 7.1, both the market intent and the functional specification are inputs for this activity. To begin the process and come up with a first draft of the feature release plan, the requirements engineering activities should have made reasonable progress and a first version of the functional specification must be available. That is, the major features for this product must have been identified (see Chapter 3). Another prerequisite for this activity is some kind of market intent that describes what the business goals are for developing this product (why the company is building this product). This establishes what the company hopes to achieve with the release of the product and can have a substantial impact on the prioritization of features. As the project and migration plans are refined, the feature release plan can be revisited to see if the originally identified set of features still makes sense.

7.2.1 Participants

While the primary responsibility for developing a feature release plan lies with the product manager, there are several people typically involved with this effort. Table 7.1 provides a typical list of participants and highlights their primary responsibility with respect to this activity.

Table 7.1   Participants in Feature Release Planning Activity

Title	Responsibility
Product Manager	Product managers have ownership for this activity. They are responsible for providing or arranging an understanding of the marketplace, an understanding of the legacy products, and an understanding of the competition. They also should be able to represent the needs of the end user.
Architect	The architect is involved in this process to begin to provide input as to the time required to implement a given set of features.
Requirements Engineer	The requirements engineer provides input into the requirements that make up a given feature. This can be useful for scoping the set of features and beginning to talk about effort.
Project Manager	It is useful to have project managers involved enough in this process that they can begin to lay out a draft schedule for planning purposes.

Tip: Force product management to define the minimal feature set.

Product management will likely have a difficult time defining the minimal set of features that could be sold and thinking in terms of iterations where additional features are released to the market over time. This is because it is easier to sell a product with a rich feature set that is available in the market. Development will likely need to force product management to put priorities on features and delay some features to later releases. Often, there is a demand such as, "I need all the features ASAP." Convince product management of the value of having some features early and then additional features later. One way to do this is to calculate the sales revenue lost for each week that the product is not available in the market.

7.3 Development Planning

Figure 7.3 gives an overview of the activities involved in development planning. Your features should not only be specified as to the sequence of development, but will also need to be allocated to software modules per the architecture design model. You must also specify the sequence of module development (see critical path analysis in Chapter 5). Thus, features will become available and integrated as they are developed within individual modules owned by the distributed teams. When enough modules and their implemented features are available, a product version will be defined and made available for customer use. If the requirements model is developed as described in Chapter 3, the detailed requirements can be automatically identified for each feature. Likewise, the modules and associated methods needed to realize each requirement can be automatically derived from the integrated requirements and design model. It is not so easy, however, to determine the sequencing of module development. The various dependencies across modules must be determined, along with the availability of appropriate resources.

In addition to the tasks identified above, there will likely be other activities that must be built into the plan. For example, if there are aspects of the architecture that are currently unclear, or risky with respect to the ASRs, it may be wise to develop a proof-of-concept prototype early on. These kinds of tasks should be enumerated and added to the schedule as well.

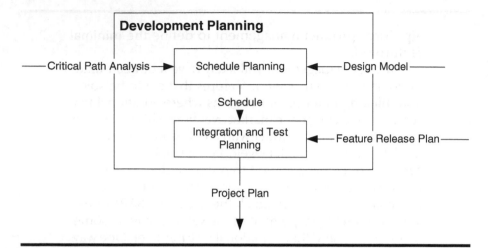

Figure 7.3 Development planning workflow.

The dates for each sprint (referred to as engineering releases) in the schedule are fixed in time. Thus, each development team must release an operational version of its module to the central integration and test teams on the date specified. Each team has a little bit of flexibility with respect to the features that are delivered. The release must be stable enough to be integrated and tested. But, if some features are missing, they are planned for development during the next sprint. What is most important is that the release date is fixed. No team can slip the release date. In some cases, a development team might not participate in the engineering release (e.g., during a local holiday time); however, in this case, the release would be skipped and the team would release on the next fixed date for the next sprint. The current sprint is planned in detail. Future releases are less well-defined with high-level project plans. Tasks that are not accomplished in the current sprint are replanned for the next sprint.

> **Tip:** Pick release milestone dates that are easy to remember.
>
> Pick release dates that are easy for everyone on the development team to remember — for example, the last Friday of the month. With monthly sprints being done each month, every component development team can get into the routine of doing an engineering release on that day every month. Be careful of local holidays when planning multi-site development projects in different

countries. You might adjust the normal release date for the month of a major holiday (e.g., November or December). Also, keep track of when key team members are on vacation. Some teams might skip a release if they are all planning to be on vacation (e.g., during some summertime months in some European countries). Be aware that seasons may be reversed. For example, when working with sites in North and South America.

Adjustments to the schedule are inevitable as estimates are inaccurate, unanticipated problems arise, or teams under-perform. The difficulty comes in when trying to minimize the impact of these replanning activities across the teams. As many tasks are interdependent, delays by one team may cause idle time for other teams. When teams are idle or are given busy work, they can quickly become disenfranchised. It is a good idea to have some contingency plans in place so that you have an understanding up front of how you can move tasks around in the event of schedule deviations. An adequate critical path analysis of the system helps ease this process.

Tip: Identify contingency tasks.

When performing the critical path analysis, it is likely that largely independent tasks will be identified. These tasks should be explicitly flagged as tasks that can be moved up in the schedule in the case that a team over-performs or teams are in danger of becoming idle.

7.3.1 Participants

The architecture team is responsible for identifying the modules and associated methods required to realize the features in the feature release plan and for identifying the phasing of the development of these modules. There is usually some back-and-forth, however, between the architects and the project or product managers. As the schedule evolves, the feature release plan can be revisited and potentially revised. As the estimated release date is identified, trade-offs between release date and functionality may be required to meet a desired market window.

7.4 Cost Estimation

During the inception phase, an initial estimate is done in conjunction with the architecture definition. We recommend that the system is broken up into components of no more than 100 KLOCs (thousands [kilo] of lines of code) requiring no more than 120 staff months of effort to develop. We realize that this is a guess at best (although the more experienced the architects in the target domain, the better the estimates will be), but it is usually good enough for this phase. This allows for a first cut at planning and cost estimation. The real purpose of this exercise it to get a go/no-go decision from the sponsors of the project, but it is also useful as a draft for later in the life cycle. We describe the estimation process in more detail in Chapter 8.

7.5 Phasing of the Planning Effort

While the various phases differ from company to company, there are typically four phases (see Chapter 2) in one form or another. Project planning takes place primarily in the following three phases:

1. *The Inception Phase*: takes a look at the system to be built and determines whether or not it makes business sense. To determine this, the requirements and architecture are first explored, a high level plan is put together, and a rough cost and effort estimate is calculated.
2. *The Elaboration Phase*: primarily involves preparing for the construction of the system by detailing the requirements, elaborating the architecture, validating the architecture through construction of a vertical slice (Hofmeister, C. et al., 2000), and refining the plan.
3. *The Construction Phase*: involves the primary construction of the system, with the development teams in full swing, the periodic delivery, integration, and testing of functionality, and the monitoring and controlling of progress.

From a planning perspective, the needs are different, depending on the phase of the project and the information available. This section gives more detailed explanations for how we phase the planning activities.

7.5.1 Planning during the Inception Phase

The primary goal of the *inception phase* it to determine if the project makes business sense for the organization. To do this, there must be some estimate of the relative cost and benefit of building the system. As

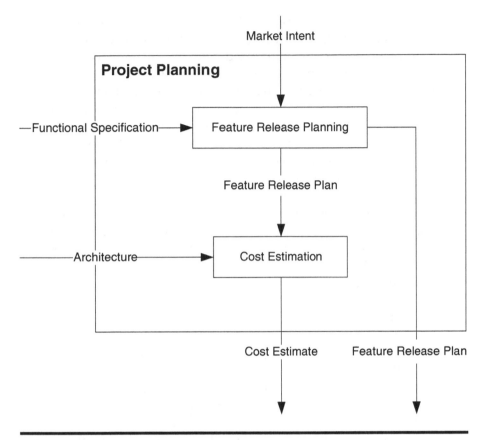

Figure 7.4   Planning workflow during the inception phase.

discussed in Chapter 6, during this phase the first draft of the feature release plan and the cost estimate is determined. Figure 7.4 gives an overview of the project planning activities during the inception phase.

It is important to at least consider what the alternatives are with respect to:

- Time to market
- Feature richness
- Quality
- Migration plan for current customer base
- Associated infrastructure that is needed (e.g., associated tools needed to effectively sell and commission a system such as data conversion tools, engineering tools, graphics tools, etc.)

A strategy can be identified for how the business goals are to be achieved. This strategy should also give guidance for how trade-offs could be made as difficulties are encountered. For example:

Assume we have a company that produces products for the consumer market. This market has a short life cycle where new technologies are introduced into the market every six months. The majority of the sales and the highest margins go to the company that first introduces a new technology to the marketplace. This company is developing a radically new and different product that (the company feels) will change the direction of the marketplace. In this case, it is vital that they are the first ones to the marketplace. While the company would never admit that it is OK with turning out products with quality problems, when push comes to shove, the company recognizes that it is better for business to release a product early to the marketplace — even if it is short some of the planned features and has some stability problems. They could then gain market share and have a later release, fixing the issues without any adverse effect.

Having this background will allow the product manager to use this guidance when creating the feature release plan as well as reflect this philosophy in the development plan that will be put together later. We have too often seen the situation where managers (or individuals) at the local level make assumptions about what is important (e.g., we cannot reduce scope, we need to deliver everything!), making decisions that conflict with the real business goals of the organization.

At this stage, product managers can identify what they think an ideal set of initial features are, what they believe the absolute minimum set of initial features might be, and what they might vary to effect these minimal sets (e.g., if we change the initial market from X to Y, then we can drop features a, b, and c; or, if we add feature z to our legacy product, then we can extend the life of that product, reduce our initial set of features in the new product, and offer them simultaneously until the second feature set is released at which point the legacy products can be sunsetted). It is not important to create a large formal document, particularly if you have an adequate requirements database. It is, however, important to capture rationale for your decisions (as well as alternatives) as this background information can be useful later on and is usually lost.

Independent of creating the feature release plan, the architects will be working on identifying the driving architectural concepts and doing a first-level functional decomposition on the system. Based on this functional decomposition, a first-cut effort estimate can be done (as described in Chapter 8). You should keep the business goals in mind so that the cost and effort estimate can reflect the time-to-market goals appropriately.

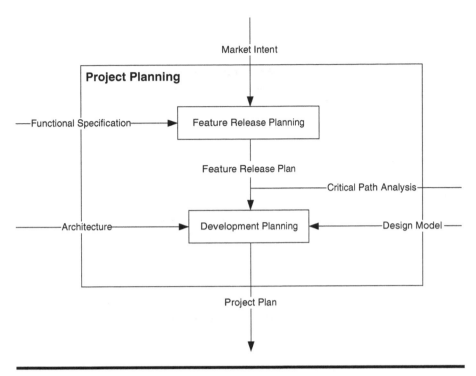

Figure 7.5   Planning workflow during the elaboration phase.

7.5.2   *Planning during the Elaboration Phase*

Throughout the elaboration phase, the requirements and architecture become progressively more stable. This allows for the tasks to become more granular, the estimates to become more accurate, the releases to be broken down into engineering releases, and the schedule to become more refined. It is usually the case that planning is done continuously throughout the execution of the project. During the elaboration phase, the first few sprints will be planned in detail, and subsequent sprints planned in progressively less detail. As the project proceeds, the plans can be adjusted and future sprints planned with more confidence. Figure 7.5 gives an overview of the project planning activities during the elaboration phase.

7.5.3   *Planning during the Construction Phase*

Planning will continue throughout the construction phase. At the end of each sprint, there is a post mortem that will look at issues that were experienced during the previous sprint, and also look at progress made. The issues may either result in task adjustments or process adjustments.

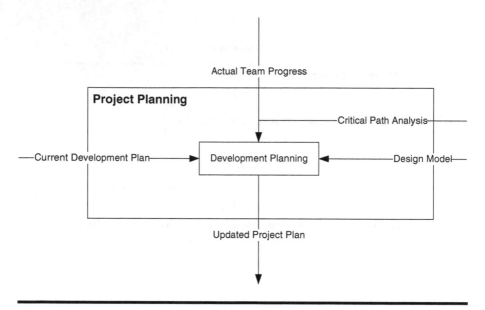

Figure 7.6   Planning workflow during the construction phase.

There is then a detailed planning session for the upcoming sprint. In addition, the planning team is refining the plan for upcoming sprints during the execution of the sprint itself. The major adjustments are done during this time. At the pre-sprint planning meetings, usually only minor adjustments are allowed. Figure 7.6 summarizes the project planning activities during the construction phase.

7.6   Summary and Conclusions

This chapter provided some guidelines for release planning. Because we use an iterative approach, the software development is broken down into small monthly sprints in which the product features are developed over time. In addition to development, the release of features to the market grouped into versions is also planned. A key task is the definition of the minimally featured product for the first release to a customer site. Also, planning must be done concerning how older products will coexist with the new product, and when and how older products will be sunsetted.

7.7   Discussion Questions

1. What should be the maximum size or effort for an individual component?

2. What should be the calendar time between engineering releases?
3. What is the significance of critical path analysis to development planning?
4. How is project planning different from one phase of a project to the other?

References

Hofmeister, C., Nord, R., and Soni, D., *Applied Software Architecture*, Addison-Wesley, Boston, MA, 2000.

Paulish, D., *Architecture-Centric Software Project Management*, Addison-Wesley, Boston, MA, 2002.

Schwaber, K., *Agile Project Management with Scrum*, Microsoft Press, Redmond, WA, 2004.

Schwaber, K. and Beedle, M., *Agile Software Development with Scrum, 1st edition*, Prentice Hall PTR, Upper Saddle River, NJ, 2001.

Chapter 8

Project Estimation

On one warm summer afternoon, Bill's boss, with soda can in hand, showed up at his office and told him that he needed his project cost budget estimate for the next fiscal year by Monday. He also added, "Because you will be in the construction phase by then, I'll also need your development staff headcount, your office space requirements, and any software development tool license costs." While he was speaking, his mobile phone rang, and he waved his soda can at Bill and quickly disappeared down the hallway.

As his boss walked down the hallway, Bill began wondering how he would determine the project cost budget for the construction phase. He had estimated projects before, but using his staff at his location. For this global development project he would need to estimate the resources required at remote development sites in addition to his local staff. He would also need to allocate and distribute the work between his site and the remote sites. He did not personally know the staff at the remote sites, and he had no idea how well they would perform. During the inception and elaboration phases, Bill had a relatively small team of requirements engineers and software architects working for him. For the construction phase, he would be responsible for a much larger team of distributed developers. Based on time-to-market needs, Bill suspected much of the development would be done in parallel and thus a large development team would be required. These new developers would need to be acquired and they would need a place to work, training, and tools. As Bill thought about all these needs, it seemed like the temperature rose a little more in his warm office.

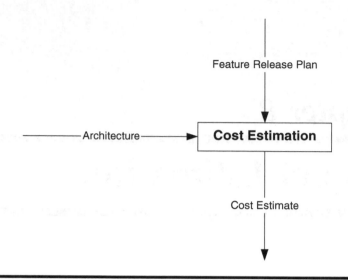

Figure 8.1   Cost estimation workflow.

This chapter describes an estimation approach for the development of software modules in a distributed development project, a way to validate the original estimate through bottom-up estimates, and the process for estimating effort for the monthly sprints. It also discusses the execution and refinement of the estimates during the various project phases. See Figure 8.1 for a summary of the activities involved in project estimation.

8.1   Top-Down Estimation Approach

The functional decomposition of the architecture (Chapter 5) identifies the functional units of the architecture that will be implemented by the distributed development teams. An estimate of the development cost for the construction phase can thus be developed by estimating the effort for modules that must be developed over the various iterations, and adding in the resources required for central team functions (e.g., architecture, requirements engineering, testing, and project management). It should be recognized that such an estimate is done during the inception and elaboration phases. The accuracy of such an estimate in the inception phase is usually ±80 percent and improves to within 20 percent in the elaboration phase. A primary input to the estimation process is the size estimate for each work allocation unit as determined by the architecture team.

Table 8.1 Participants in Project Estimation

Title	Responsibility
Product Manager	The product manager is responsible for the estimation activity.
Architect	The architect provides size estimates for the modules.
Requirements Engineer	The requirements engineer verifies that the identified features are satisfied (only at a high level).

8.1.1 Who is Involved in This Activity?

The product manager is responsible for the estimating activity, but other team members also have a role. The architects provide input for the size estimate and the requirements engineers may be involved to verify the details of the features are taken into account. Table 8.1 summarizes the primary participants and their roles.

8.1.2 What are the Inputs and Outputs?

The prerequisites for developing estimates (during the inception phase, these estimates are largely SWAGs or guesstimates) include having an identification of the modules to be developed and some size estimates for these modules. The more historical data that is available, and the more confident the architects are in the size estimate, the more accurate the effort and cost estimate will be. If the historic data is not calibrated for distributed projects, then additional effort must be factored in based on the additional cost of collaborating across development sites. The extent of the impact that distribution will have on the projects depends on the characteristics of the project and organization. Input from the risk analysis activities can help to inform this estimate. In our experience, we have found that distribution generally imposes an effort factor of 1.2 to 2.5 times that of collocated projects.

The outputs of this activity will be:

- An effort estimate, both in terms of staff effort and calendar time
- The number of development teams as well as the size of the development teams

■ The effort and size of central team activities (e.g., architecture elaboration, requirements engineering, integration and test, and project management).

The formality of these outputs depends on the needs of your organization. This estimate can be refined as the inputs stabilize.

8.1.3 Global Development Assertion

We have observed that software engineers working on small development teams are generally more productive than engineers working on large teams. This is a consequence of the increased communication required among team members in larger teams, which results in cognitive synchronization problems (i.e., mismatches in shared understanding) that are described further in Chapter 13. Our global development assertion is summarized below:

■ If work allocation units are small and fit within an architecture framework and their requirements are modeled, their development can be distributed around the world.
■ Centralized control will be necessary to support the architecture, high-level business requirements model, system integration and validation, project planning, user interface high-level design, quality assurance, and development of critical shared modules.
■ If each module development team size is kept small (e.g., ten people or less), agile processes can be applied to increase productivity and decrease development times.

Operationally, what this assertion means is that we put a constraint on the architects to design a structure where work allocation units are relatively small; that is, they can be developed within about a ten staff-year investment (i.e., ten people for twelve months). Thus, our resulting organization structure is a collection of small distributed development teams coordinated by a central team. The distributed teams are small enough where good daily communications are enabled among the team members. Furthermore, if possible, the architecture is structured such that the need for communications between teams is minimized (e.g., loosely coupled architectures). Work is allocated to the distributed teams so that inter-team communications occur within a development site or only with the central site, and communications among module development teams at different sites are minimized.

The negative effect of increased software development team size can be observed by doing some "what-if" analysis using a cost estimation tool. As the estimated code size for a software project increases, the time and number of staff to develop the software increase. If one increases the proposed schedule using such cost estimation tools, the effort and resulting development cost decreases along with the peak team size. However, there is business pressure to get products to the market quickly. Also, requirements and technologies are more likely to change during longer-duration projects. Thus, development team sizes are often larger than ideal (from a productivity perspective), and large teams with their increased communications needs are less productive. Our rules of thumb state that no team should be larger than ten staff members, and no single development site should have more than 100 engineers (or ten teams of ten). The maximum team size is a somewhat arbitrary number, but basically it strives to be able to put the entire module development team in one conference room for say a Scrum stand-up meeting. Ideally, the entire module development team should be able to work within approximately ten meters of each other.

We can illustrate these concepts using cost estimation tools. Consider the output from the Estimate Pro tool for a project of 50 KLOCs as illustrated in Figure 8.2.

To reduce the development schedule from, say, 12 months to 10 months requires approximately two times more development investment. These curves are very nonlinear, which we interpret as the significant negative

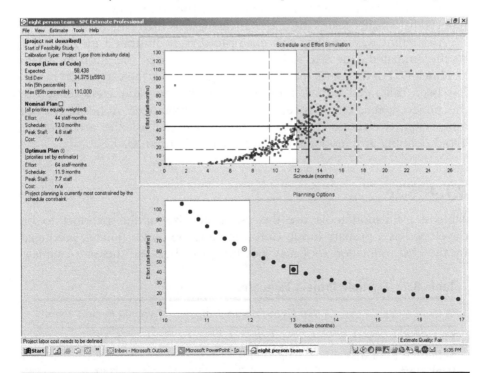

Figure 8.2 Effort versus schedule trade-off.

effects of communications for larger teams. For an example of the impact of module and development team size, one can ask the following question:

> For developing a software system estimated to consist of 100K function points with 800 software developers available, would it be better to organize as 100 eight-person teams or two 400-person teams?

If we enter 1K function points into our cost estimation model for one of the 100 eight-person teams and 50K function points for one of the two 400-person teams, we get the estimates summarized in Table 8.2 below.

Comparing these two organizational structures says that, for this example, the 100 smaller teams can develop the product in less than half the time and effort than the two larger teams. What is most remarkable is the schedule: approximately five years of development time for the larger teams as compared with approximately one year for the smaller teams. Of course, this example does not take into account that the 100 work allocation units developed by the smaller teams must be integrated more than the two developed by the larger teams. From this discussion we would like to emphasize the trend rather than the actual numbers. We recognize one could argue with the validity of the numbers above. The trend, however, accurately reflects that smaller teams are more advantageous than larger teams.

A different way to view this example data is illustrated in Table 8.3. As the estimated code size to be developed increases, the effort increases nonlinearly. For this particular example organization, the estimation model has been calibrated to past project data, including parameters related to the project team's experience, skills, and environment. Adhering to our ten-person, twelve-month rules of thumb, we can ask the architects to avoid defining any modules that are greater than 60 KLOCs.

8.1.4 Size

All cost estimation tools use the estimated size of the product to be developed as a primary input. Unfortunately, the cost estimates produced by the cost estimation tool may not be good, because the size estimate

Table 8.2 Example Project Estimates

	100 Eight-Person Teams	Two 400-Person Teams
Effort (staff-months)	64	7118
Schedule (months)	11.9	59.1
Peak staff	7.7	340

Table 8.3   Code Size versus Effort

KLOCs	Effort (SM)	Schedule (months)	Peak Staff
10	3	5.5	0.9
20	9	7.1	2.0
30	24	8.6	3.8
40	46	10.1	6.3
50	56	10.6	7.5
60	85	11.8	10.3
70	117	12.0	14.6

inputs may not be good. It is very difficult for an architect to estimate the size of a software module prior to developing it. Different approaches and units for size estimation have been debated in the software metrics literature (Moeller and Paulish, 1993; Paulish, 2002). We will not engage in this debate here, but do suggest that the architects select an approach that is most comfortable for them. For the case study projects described in the later chapters of this book, most of the module estimates were given in lines of code and they were estimated by counting the lines of code developed for earlier projects that had similar modules to the new product being estimated. Thus, experience is important when estimating the sizes of new modules to be developed.

8.1.5   Effort

Cost estimation tools provide staff profile outputs where effort is smaller at the beginning of the project, peaks toward the end of development, and then drops off again as the product goes into a maintenance phase. The effort is calculated under the curve of the staffing profile. We are suggesting a highly iterative, synchronized approach where modules are developed in parallel to achieve the best time-to-market. The architecture is designed to minimize the dependencies among modules and keep the module size small. The consequence for development is that module development teams can be kept small and the need for module teams across multiple locations to communicate is minimized.

As a consequence of the iterative, synchronized nature of our approach and the use of sprints to achieve monthly development progress, we do not recommend that module teams are built up over time within an iteration. Rather, we recommend that the entire module team is available at the beginning of the iteration and remains together at a constant size throughout the iteration. Additional teams can be added or the team sizes can be adjusted for the next iteration. This flat staffing approach can increase overall effort, but it is oriented toward reducing time-to-market such that team start-up time, communications, and efficiency are improved within the module development team. We also seek to keep the module teams staffing stable, so that domain experience can be built up over time. This helps support our goal that remote module teams over time become more like "competence centers" that are able to maintain and enhance modules for the central team, rather than merely "extended workbenches."

Effort estimates will vary significantly, depending on who is doing the estimate. This is due to a wide variation in software engineering staff productivity and experience. If someone has performed a similar task in the past, they will likely be able to perform the new task more easily than someone who has never performed such work. Ideally, the effort estimates should be done by the individual(s) who will be actually performing the work. But, with offshoring approaches, it is not likely that the project planning staff will know *a priori* the experience level of the remote team members who will develop the module. Thus, there is a need for estimation modeling, but the reality of development will be different, depending on who will work on the development. Involving the remote teams in the estimation process is discussed below.

8.1.6 Schedule

In today's business environment, time-to-market is a pressure with which every project manager must deal. Software system development projects often need time for technical concepts to evolve and mature. Ideally, a software engineer wants to be able to think about his technical approach before implementing it, and also have plenty of time for testing and rework until a quality product is realized. This conflicts with the business need to realize products quickly; thus, many software engineers feel pressured to achieve high quality within tight schedule constraints. The worst-case scenario is when a project is working with an unrealistic schedule and everyone recognizes it and the schedule starts slipping. This is why we put an emphasis on meeting all milestone dates and dividing the project into iterations with monthly fixed sprint dates where demonstrable progress is made every month. With shorter times between milestones, the project can be better focused and, if necessary, replanning can occur more frequently.

8.1.7 Top-Down Estimation Steps

To help solve Bill's problem with how to estimate the development budget for the construction phase, we describe an estimation approach in eight steps:

1. *Calibrate a cost estimation tool.* Select a cost estimation tool (see Section 8.3) and calibrate it for your organization. This is done by looking at past development projects and adjusting the parameters or cost driver attributes (Boehm, 1981; Boehm et al., 2000) of the model such that the estimates coming from the tool are close to the actual prior development costs. Develop a table similar to Table 8.3, using the calibrated cost estimation tool.

2. *Estimate module sizes.* Get size estimates from the architecture team for each software module identified within the architecture. We use the term "software module" loosely here to mean a work allocation unit that a remote development team will implement as a piece of operational code that will fit within the architecture framework described by the architecture team. Impose constraints on the architecture team so that there are no more than about 150 modules within the design and no individual module is estimated to be more than about 100 KLOCs (or 60 KLOCs for the organization calibrated in Table 8.3). With these constraints, this approach should only be applied to software systems estimated to be 15 MLOCs or less. You can constrain your architects to define modules less than 100 KLOCs, depending on your development environment. The primary constraint is to define modules that would be allocated to the remote teams that could be developed with ten people in less than a one-year iteration. When your architects estimate a module that is greater than the size constraint, you ask them to go back and refactor the module into smaller ones.

3. *Allocate modules to development iterations.* You will need to work closely with the architecture team and the "buildmeister" to understand the sequence in which the modules should be developed. Bigger modules will take longer to develop. We have described approaches for iteration planning in Section 7.2. If your architects have met the size constraints you have given them, no individual module iteration time will be more than one year in duration.

4. *Estimate the code size for each iteration.* Add the sizes for all the modules allocated to each iteration. Calculate the average size of a module for each iteration. Note that when you generate your development plan, you will use the actual size estimates for each module. Using the average size per iteration at this point is a little easier for determining quickly the estimated development cost for the construction phase.

5. *Estimate development time, effort, and peak staff for each iteration.* Using the average size of a module for each iteration, calculate the development time, effort, and peak staff size using the calibrated

cost estimation tool or from the table you developed in Step 1 (see example Table 8.3).

6. *Estimate the iteration development time and average team staff size.* Set the iteration development time to the nearest whole number of months and the average team size to the nearest whole number of peak staff for each iteration.

7. *Estimate the development schedule time.* Calculate the development schedule time by adding the development times for each iteration and then adding in some validation testing time at the end based on what you have experienced on prior projects (e.g., two to six months). This validation testing time at the end can be considered a stabilization sprint.

8. *Estimate the development cost.* Calculate the development effort in staff-months by multiplying the average team size by the iteration duration by the number of modules plus the effort of the central requirements, architecture, project management, and testing teams for the project duration. The development cost estimate is calculated by multiplying the total number of staff-years by the average staff-year cost for your organization. This would be the cost if your organization were to develop the product at your site. If you are planning to offshore the module developments, you would use the average staff-year cost for each supplier organization to calculate the development cost, which should be less than the cost at your site.

As you prepare the development plan, you will likely consider different development scenarios and compare the relative development costs, depending on the number of iterations, selected suppliers, size of the central team, etc. You will develop a high-level staffing profile and development schedule that you can review with your management prior to committing to a development plan. An example staffing profile is given in Figure 8.3.

As a short example of how you would estimate the cost for the construction phase using the eight steps above, let us assume that you have 20 modules that need to be developed and you split the development work over two offshore sites. Also assume that you divide the development project into two iterations, each consisting of ten modules to be developed with five teams each allocated to sites A and B. The total estimated code size to be developed for the first and second iterations is 300 KLOCs and 500 KLOCs, respectively. Thus, the average module size is 30 KLOCs for iteration 1 and 50 KLOCs for iteration 2. Using Table 8.3, you could plan your first iteration for nine months with an average team size of four engineers. Iteration 2 would be planned for eleven months and an average team size of eight engineers. Thus, for the ten teams, iteration 1 would

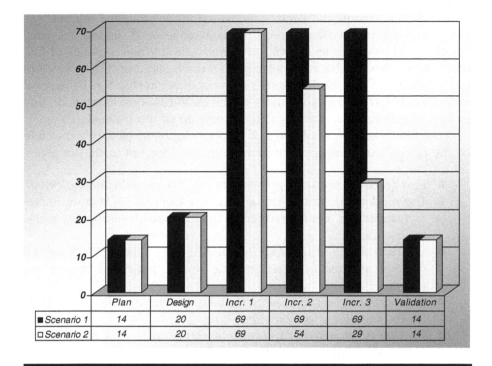

	Plan	Design	Incr. 1	Incr. 2	Incr. 3	Validation
■ Scenario 1	14	20	69	69	69	14
□ Scenario 2	14	20	69	54	29	14

Figure 8.3   Example staffing profile.

require 360 staff-months (30 staff-years) and iteration 2 would require 880 staff-months (73.3 staff-years). You estimate that during the construction phase, you will need two architects, two requirements engineers, three testers, two supplier managers, and yourself working at your central site, which is a total of 200 staff-months (16.7 staff-years). If the staff-year cost at your site is $150K, at site A it is $100K and at site B it is $80K, then your cost estimate for the construction phase is about $2.5M for your site, $5.2M for site A, and $4.1M for site B, for a total estimated cost of about $12M. When you work on the development plan, you will need to look at scheduling and staffing the individual modules within the two iterations, but for now you can tell your boss that he should request a budget of about $12M for development work over the 20 months from the start of the construction phase. In fact, you probably should ask for about $22M, because an early estimate such as this one could very well be 80 percent off the mark.

8.2   Bottom-Up Estimate

As candidate development teams are identified, it is wise to have them give independent estimates for developing the modules. The central team, in an effort to identify the iteration times for the incremental release, will have done a top-down estimation for an average-sized module for each iteration. Development teams will be staffed with a whole number of full-time staff members who are available from the beginning of the development iteration to its end. This is useful as a validation step for the original estimates, to have the development teams establish some credibility, and to have the development teams take ownership of the estimate.

To initiate the commissioning of the development of a new module by the central team, the application module development teams are given:

- *Part of the integrated requirements and design model to implement.* The model is described using UML (see Chapter 3). Feature implementations are communicated to the remote development teams via use cases.
- *Software architecture description.* The architecture is described using an architecture description document or a design model (see Chapter 5).
- *Acceptance tests.* The acceptance tests that the module must satisfy for the increment are provided.
- *Iterative development plan and integration dates.* A skeleton schedule is provided that specifies the duration for the module development iteration and the fixed dates for iterations to be released to the central integration and test team.
- *Module interface specification.* This specifies how the module to be developed will interface with the architecture framework.
- *Vertical slice prototype implementation.* This is a thin prototype implementation of minimal executing functionality across all layers of the architecture to be used as an implementation example for the module development teams.
- *UI Style Guide.* This specifies the user interface appearance design to be used.

Upon delivery of the commissioning documentation package to the remote site, the development team at the site will be given one week to respond with a bottom-up effort estimate to develop the identified modules per the specified iterative development schedule. Experience from past projects suggests a rule of thumb that four hours per person are required for a bottom-up module effort estimate. If each member of a module development team does an estimate and the team size is limited to ten staff members, then forty hours could be applied to the bottom-up estimate per module during the one-week response time.

It is suggested that the central team accept without question module development estimates that are within a range of about twice the top-down estimate provided by the estimation tool (see Table 8.3). Estimates should be questioned that are significantly less than or more than twice the top-down estimate. The estimates for potential high-risk modules should also be reviewed and possibly adjusted. It is also suggested that each module development team is staffed with a fixed team size for the full duration of the increment. Of course, some key staff can be applied across all the module teams (e.g., architect, subject matter expert, quality assurance specialist, project manager) at a specific development site.

Tip: Do not promise your management large development cost savings through offshoring.

Although the hourly labor rates may be less for off-shore sites as compared to your central site, the lack of domain expertise and the additional communications required may offset any cost savings. For example, if the remote site labor rates are one third those of your local rates, but the remote team needs to rework their implementation two additional times to get the product functionality correct, then there is no development cost savings. We have observed that remote teams may require six to twelve months before they will match the central site's productivity when working with a new domain or technology.

Although the staff-year rates can be substantially lower for offshore sites as compared to your central site rates, some of the development cost savings will be offset by the communications cost overhead associated with working over multiple sites. Supplier managers at the central site will need to work with the remote teams, travel budgets will be increased, and rework will need to be done due to miscommunications. Consider also that you will be outsourcing large amounts of the code development, but coding efforts may represent only 20 percent of the overall product development cost. Furthermore, the maintenance costs associated with a successful product may equal or exceed the development costs. The costs associated with launching a new product to the market, for example to train the sales force, may also equal or exceed the development cost. Thus, although the hourly labor rates for certain countries may attract your management's interest, make certain that they are factored into the overall product development, launch, and maintenance costs.

8.3 Estimation Tools

Software cost estimation tools have been used since business managers requested estimates of the cost to develop new software products. A seminal book on the subject of software cost estimation is Boehm's *Software Engineering Economics,* published in 1981. This book describes the COnstructive COst MOdel (or COCOMO) model. *Software Cost Estimation with Cocomo II* was published in 2000. In addition to COCOMO, commonly used software cost estimation tools are based on SLIM, PRICE-S, and function point analysis (FPA) (Albrecht and Gaffney, 1983; Jones, 1991; Paulish, 2002; Putnam, 1992).

The price of a software cost estimation tool can range from nothing (where one can find a simple calculation tool based on COCOMO on a public Web site), to thousands of dollars (where the tool is bundled into a software metrics consulting engagement where past and future projects would be analyzed based on the environment and productivity data of existing organizations). Many tools come loaded with historical data from products developed for specific industry segments. If your organization does not have good historical data from earlier product developments, you can match your product with similar products and calibrate the tool based on industry data. Many software project managers today carry a cost estimation tool on their laptops so that they can do "what-if" analyses while traveling.

The graphs, charts, and tables produced by cost estimation tools seem to impress nontechnical management. But these pretty charts can often contain very inaccurate estimates when the size inputs are inaccurate or the tool is not calibrated correctly. Nevertheless, these tools are good at helping development managers to remember all the parts that go into a cost estimate and provide an overall schedule framework (e.g., "There is no way this product will be developed in three months; or if it is, it will be the first time in the history of our company."). Furthermore, the project manager can use the estimation tool and top-down schedule to educate management and set appropriate expectations so that schedules, team size, and risks are realistically considered before full-scale development begins with the offshore development sites.

8.4 Summary and Conclusions

The project planning and estimating approach described in this chapter is based on the assertion that large software products can be developed globally if requirements are modeled and the architecture design divides the functionality into small modules that can be incrementally implemented.

This is based on the observation that smaller software development projects are easier to manage and smaller development teams are more productive. Furthermore, many of today's agile software development processes are optimized to work best with development team sizes of ten staff or less. Thus, our global project planning approach uses a central team to manage a collection of small development teams, each contributing to the development of a software module that fits within the software architecture.

The approach to dividing a complex system into a number of smaller modules can be observed within other engineering disciplines. For example, the Boeing 777 aircraft design was divided into 240 subsystems. Approximately 10,000 staff in total were assigned to the development, but much smaller teams worked on the development of each subsystem (Smith and Reinertsen, 1997). Dividing a big job into a collection of smaller tasks is necessary for designing, planning, structuring, organizing, and estimating any engineering project.

8.5 Discussion Questions

1. How should one estimate any development cost savings associated with offshore sites?
2. What is the relationship between module development team size, agility, and productivity?
3. What is the learning time for a remote team to become productive working in a new domain?
4. How much of the overall product development, product launch, and maintenance costs will be spent on coding related tasks for your product?

References

Albrecht, A. and Gaffney, J., "Software function, source lines of code, and development effort prediction: a software science validation," *IEEE Transactions of Software Engineering*, 9(6), 639–648, 1983.

Boehm, B., *Software Engineering Economics, 1st edition*, Prentice Hall PTR, Upper Saddle River, NJ, 1981.

Boehm, B., Horowitz, E., Madachy, R., Reifer, D., Clark, B., Steece, B., Brown, A., Chulani, S., and Abts, C., *Software Cost Estimation with Cocomo II, 1st edition*, Prentice Hall PTR, Upper Saddle River, NJ, 2000.

Jones, C., *Applied Software Measurement: Assuring Productivity and Quality*, McGraw-Hill, New York, 1991.

Moeller, K. and Paulish, D., *Software Metrics: A Practitioner's Guide to Improved Product Development*, IEEE Computer Society Press, Los Alamitos, CA, 1993.

Paulish, D., *Architecture-Centric Software Project Management*, Addison-Wesley, Boston, MA, 2002.

Putnam, L., *Measures For Excellence: Reliable Software, On Time, Within Budget*, Prentice Hall, New York, 1992.

Smith, P. and Reinertsen, D., *Developing Products in Half the Time: New Rules, New Tools*, John Wiley & Sons, New York, 1997.

Section III

ORGANIZATION STRUCTURE

Chapter 9

Software Development Teams

On Paul's most recent project, he led a small team of software developers and testers who worked well together. A few of the team members were new hires coming directly from the university. By the time they made their first customer release, many of the team members had become friends as well as colleagues. Although they sometimes had to work extra hours to meet their delivery schedule, some of the team members would get together after work to attend a baseball game in the summer or a hockey game in the winter. Paul enjoyed working with this team, and he liked to read some of the jokes they e-mailed to each other as well as the code they produced.

For Paul's new project, he was expected to manage a group of development teams, some of which were located far away from his workplace, specifically in India, Slovakia, and Brazil. He did not hire or even meet these remote engineers. He only knew the hourly rates that his company would be paying them, and that his management was keen on enforcing a hiring freeze at his local workplace and offshoring large parts of their product development work. Paul was apprehensive about how he would be building, managing, and monitoring these remote development teams. He also suspected that he would not be attending any baseball or hockey games with these new, remote team members.

This chapter outlines the organizational structure for geographically distributed global software development teams, designating relevant roles and their responsibilities, and how communication, coordination, and control are handled among such teams. It also provides mechanisms for tracking the progress of projects undertaken by these teams.

9.1 Structure of a GSD Project

As previously mentioned, coordination and control become more difficult due to distance as software development teams are geographically distributed. We attempt to minimize excessive communication by optimizing the amount of collaboration between teams. Collaboration can be optimized by breaking the software system architecture into loosely coupled subsystems and modules. Each team can then work relatively independently of the others on a given subsystem or module. The modules are defined based on the features that must be implemented for the product and the structure of the software system as described by its architecture.

In our approach, a small architecture team is part of the central organization, with members assigned full-time from both onshore and offshore sites. The team operates as a project, with a product manager responsible for the entire product life cycle. Requirements engineers located at the central site capture and analyze the features requested by stakeholders.

Chapter 8 listed the artifacts that the central team delivers to the remote development teams to enable them to plan and estimate the effort for the modules they will be developing. These artifacts are created during the early phases of the project when the central team is small and collocated at one site. We strongly recommend that these central team tasks are staffed with some members of the future remote development teams who have temporarily relocated to work at the central site. Ideally, the time spent at the central site (e.g., six months) is used to "train" the future remote team member on the application domain, architecture, tools, and processes that will be used during the development. These team members will hopefully become leaders of the remote development teams upon returning to their home sites. They will begin working with supplier managers, who are employees of the central site that help manage the relationship and projects with the remote sites or the suppliers of the modules to be developed. Thus, generally the process break point between a collocated central team and the remote development teams is at the point in time when detailed design is initiated. The central team will remain together while the development progresses, but some team members will return to their home sites.

With this rotation of staff between the central site and supplier site, some of Paul's apprehension with regard to working with unknown

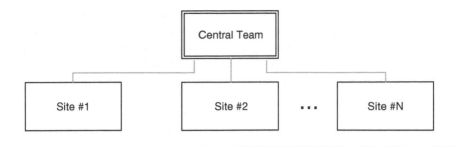

Figure 9.1   Example global development organization.

resources is minimized. Paul may not know everyone at a remote development site, but he should have about six months' experience with some of the key people at the remote site who had worked with him at the central site. We believe this type of personal contact is necessary to support communications with the remote sites during development. Knowing supplier colleagues personally in advance seems to be particularly important when something goes wrong on the project. Remote problem resolution is particularly difficult when staff at both the central and remote sites have never before met each other or worked together.

As described in Chapter 2, the collocated central team makes up the project team during the inception and elaboration phases. As the construction phase begins, remote development teams are added to the project, and the overall team size increases as a collection of loosely coupled teams. The overall project organization takes on the form illustrated in Figure 9.1, where staff sitting at multiple sites are now working on the project.

The central team functions that are first organized during the inception and elaboration phases are continued through the construction phase. The central team controls the remote teams. Conceptual design and requirements engineering are done by the central team, modules are designed and developed by the remote teams, and then the product is integrated and tested iteratively as code is delivered from the remote teams to the central team. Thus, the central team is the control and communications center that enables global development. The functions performed by the central team include:

- *Requirements engineering.* Analyze requirements requested by stakeholders. Allocate features to releases and modules. Develop requirements model. Provide domain expertise to development teams.
- *Software architecture design.* Design and describe the conceptual architecture. Initiate the high-level design (possibly with the support

of remote teams). Review and monitor design as it is implemented. The software architecture design team can also develop prototypes to investigate architectural trade-offs and determine technical feasibility. These prototyping resources could be at the central site or remote. The software architecture team will also determine the technologies, tools, and processes to use for the development.

■ *Project planning.* Make estimates. Develop schedules, budgets, and processes. Select remote development sites and allocate work. Determine sprint goals.

■ *User interface design.* Develop user interface style guide. Perform usability analysis and testing. Prototype user interface workflows.

■ *System integration and validation.* Develop build plan. Develop module acceptance tests. Develop system tests and conduct testing as the product is incrementally developed.

■ *Quality assurance.* Determine quality processes and checks. Assist with project risk analysis. Review supplier site processes and artifacts. Assist in defining review processes. Assist in developing development processes.

As described in Chapter 8, a documentation package is transferred from the central team to each remote module development team. This documentation package is used to help communicate to the remote teams the work that will be done in accordance with the development plan. The work to be done is scoped to be implemented by a relatively small module development team (a maximum of ten engineers). The roles of the development team members are described below but, in general, their skills will be multifunctional, including domain, design, development, and testing expertise. Furthermore, the remote development teams will be linked to the central team, primarily through their supplier manager but also to the central team functions listed above such as software architecture design and system integration and validation. In fact, for each module there will be a focus group formed, such that the remote teams work with multifunctional experts from the central team. For example, if development team A in India is working on the user interface framework module, their focus group may include Bill, who wrote the functional specification for that module; George from the architecture team; Aaron from the user interface design team; Dan the supplier manager; etc.

Based on the above, the overall project organization will consist of remote development teams that will fit within the organizational structure of their local company that report to a central team made up of technical experts as described above. The remote teams supply code and other artifacts to the central team, who then use them to build a product. However, we recommend that such a supplier relationship is established for the long term. Thus, over time, with an exchange of technical artifacts and staff, the remote team may become a competence center of the central organization. Over time, the remote organization will develop more applications for the central organization and become increasingly more involved in early phase activities. Furthermore, for such a relationship to be successful over time, we recommend the exchange of staff as short- or long-term delegates between the central and remote sites. For any organization, but especially for ones crossing national and geographic boundaries, its success will depend on the trust among peers and their reporting relationships. Such trust across, up, and down the organization can only be built up over time and based upon personal interactions. For the current state of software engineering practice, we doubt that an outsourcing approach where specifications are sent to a remote site and the central team waits for the code to be delivered back to them will be successful (Herbsleb et al., 2005).

Figure 9.2 gives an example organization showing the relationship between the central and remote teams. The product manager has the overall responsibility for the life cycle of product development. The chief architect is both the head of the architecture team and has overall responsibility for technical decisions affecting the project. The members of the remote module development teams report to a local R&D resource manager at their site. The remote teams report to the project manager at the central location, primarily through their assigned supplier manager. The focus group for each module connects the various functional specialists between the central and remote sites.

Figure 9.2 gives an example of the relationship between the central team and one remote site. Similar modules or applications should be collocated whenever possible. Modules are clustered into applications or subsystems and assigned to the development teams within a single site not to exceed 100 engineers at the site. The organization structure is such that the remote sites normally communicate with the central site. However, occasionally, communications among multiple remote sites may be necessary, such as when two modules require an interface that must be worked on by both teams. It may also be valuable for sites to share best practices information as experience is obtained. This could be helpful to bring on new teams or for teams to learn about processes used by other teams. However, this should be initiated carefully over time, because the various sites may initially be viewed as competitors of each other until competence centers build up unique expertise and trust.

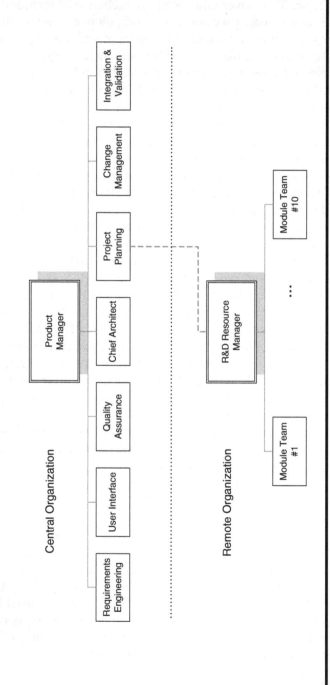

Figure 9.2 Relationship between central and remote teams.

Tip: Resist any suggestions to turn the central team into a "virtual" team during the inception and elaboration phases.

We have observed that activities such as requirements analysis and architecture design require close, frequent interaction among the team members. Thus, we feel strongly that such activities must be collocated. Because it is also desirable to bring potential remote team members into these teams during these early phases of the project, logistics issues will surface. When remote team members are relocated to your site, the costs will increase due to travel and living expenses. Staff relocating without their family members may become homesick or require unexpected return trips. Ideally, remote staff will be able to work at the central site with their family members present. If not, scheduled trips can be planned such that the central team works together for a few weeks, and then everyone returns home for a couple weeks. However, we have had mainly bad experiences trying to manage central team functions that are not resident at a single site.

9.1.1 Roles and Responsibilities

Table 9.1 summarizes the roles and responsibilities of the central team, and Table 9.2 summarizes the roles and responsibilities of a remote team.

Perhaps the two most critical roles on any development project are the product manager (or project manager for larger projects) and the chief architect. The roles and relationships between the chief architect and the product manager are discussed in Hofmeister et al. (2000) and Paulish (2002), respectively. Essentially, the chief architect worries about the various technical parts of the project and the product manager worries about the project management parts (e.g., schedules, budget, organization, staffing, status). For global development projects, the product manager and chief architect must make decisions for a team that is geographically distributed and not under their direct control. Thus, in addition to the usual required management and technical skills, they must be able to work with staff from differing company and country cultures. Their communication skills will be stretched as they attempt to lead staff whom

Table 9.1 Roles and Responsibilities of the Central Team

Role	Responsibility
Product Manager	Owns the product determining the market needs; does release planning deciding the feature set that must be part of a release.
Project Manager	Plans the entire life cycle of a product, managing the requirements and the architecture teams per the project plan and commissioning component development teams worldwide.
Supplier Manager	Plans the entire life cycle of a component and manages a remote component development team.
Subject Matter Expert (SME)	Provides expertise on the business that the project is to support. Reviews requirements artifacts and screen mock-ups.
Requirements Engineer	Captures customer requests. Establishes policy for vetting customer requests into requirements. Develops the analysis model and glossary. Translates the analysis model into requirements documents.
Architect	Defines, describes, and communicates the architecture of the solution. Makes technical decisions. Performs architectural prototyping. Responsible for successful completion of a subset of components. Develops specifications and acceptance tests for product components.
Process/QA Expert/ Buildmeister	Provides process support and training on the various activities. Supports the automated build/test, configuration management, and defect tracking systems used by the architecture project team. Manages failures to build and test. Responsible for support of development, inspection, and QA tools. Responsible for assuring traceability of project artifacts.
UI Designer	Develops UI specifications, screen mock-ups, UI prototypes, and UI tests for delivered components.

they may have never met and who may have performance incentives different than their own. We recommend that staff assigned to these roles have intercultural experience or are given intercultural sensitivity training early in the project. Furthermore, they will need to be flexible and adaptable as project progress and status change due to events beyond their control; for example, political conditions in the countries where their development teams are located.

Table 9.2   Roles and Responsibilities of the Module Development Team

Role	Responsibility
R&D Manager	Plans the entire life cycle of a module and manages the module project team(s).
Architect	Acts as a proxy customer resolving issues related to the domain or the architecture. Makes technical decisions related to module architecture and design.
Designer	Designs modules using appropriate design patterns.
Developer	Implements modules and continually refactors to maintain their quality.
QA Expert	Tests the module as a unit as it is developed.

The overall project communications and coordination are controlled by the central team. Technical activities are controlled by the leaders of the functional technical teams. Project activities are controlled by the product manager, project manager, and supplier managers. The project is planned as development iterations made up of monthly sprints. The goals of each sprint are planned centrally, using the build or integration and test plan. We recommend that project plans are communicated at a high level. Detailed planning should be done by each module team for each sprint. Delivery dates are fixed, but there will be some feature migration between sprints. Integration is mainly the responsibility of the buildmeister, who is a member of the central team and understands the architecture.

Tip: Get everyone involved.

It is often difficult to gauge the level of participation and understanding of all team members on a remote team. Usually, a single person will act as the "voice" for the team and thus limit insight into that remote team by the central team. One way to overcome this is to assign roles to all team members (in addition to being developers) and require these team members to report some status, answer questions related to their role. This can help to engage all team members and allow an opportunity to discover issues earlier.

9.2 Size

In previous discussions, we have suggested that teams be no larger than ten people and sites have no more than ten teams. This is just a rule of thumb. While we know of some examples where sites have contained upwards of 300 people and still been successful, these projects all started small. Adopting a geographically distributed approach toward developing software is a fundamental paradigm shift and an organization needs time to adapt. Jumping into a large distributed project without having past experience is a recipe for disaster. Initially, we recommend starting with no more than two or three sites totaling less than a hundred developers. At steady state we have not seen any successful projects with more than seven or eight sites.

If you have a project that is larger than the suggested limits mentioned above, we recommend alternate approaches to minimize the maximum team size. One option is to increase the overall development schedule and introduce additional iterations. Another option is to further partition the system into distinct subsystems such that the projects could be considered largely independent. The adoption of a true product line approach has helped many projects achieve such a separation.

Tip: Make sure each team can fit in one room.

We have given a rule of thumb that no module development team should be larger than ten engineers. If teams are using Scrum daily stand-up meetings, they will need a place to meet. Thus, your project will need conference rooms or work areas for team meetings, and the maximum team size will be constrained by the sizes of these meeting areas. If you are seeing team meetings where the team members cannot comfortably communicate with each other within one room, consider reorganizing.

9.3 Summary and Conclusions

The organization for your global development project will be different from a project that you would do completely at your facility. Although you will use many of the management practices that have worked for you previously, you will need to compensate for the large communication paths to distant development teams. Furthermore, you will have less control over the project and be working with staff whom you will not know and may never meet. You will use your supplier managers as key members of your team to help bridge the communications gap to the remote teams. You will also view the relationship with your suppliers as a long-term one, where over time they become extensions to your own organization.

9.4 Discussion Questions

1. How important is it to get to personally know some key remote team members before initiating the construction phase?
2. How do you set up an effective global project organization that spans company and country boundaries?
3. What are the key project roles for making technical and project management decisions?
4. At which phases of development are collocated teams necessary?

References

Herbsleb, J., Paulish, D., and Bass, M., "Global software development at Siemens: experience from nine projects," *Proceedings of the International Conference on Software Engineering (ICSE 2005)*, 2005, pp. 524–533.

Hofmeister, C., Nord, R., and Soni, D., *Applied Software Architecture*, Addison-Wesley, Boston, MA, 2000.

Paulish, D., *Architecture-Centric Software Project Management*, Addison-Wesley, Boston, MA, 2002.

Chapter 10

Supplier Manager

Ann was born in Wisconsin, attended college at Purdue, and is now working for a large software company outside Chicago. Although she has visited other parts of the United States and Europe on business trips, and has been to Disney World a few times on family vacations, she considers herself very much a "Midwesterner."

Ann's company is keen on reducing product development costs by offshoring some of its work to companies in India and Eastern Europe. As a result of Ann's recent positive performance leading a small development team, her manager is considering offering her a new position as a supplier manager. Ann is not clear what the role of a supplier manager is, but she has been warned by her manager that it will involve much travel to remote development sites, and that she should "get her shots and check the expiration date on her passport."

This chapter describes a key role for managing offshore development sites. The supplier manager is a member of the central team who manages approximately eight to ten software developers at remote development sites. Various organization models have been applied concerning where the supplier manager sits physically and within the global project organization. We discuss the characteristics of an effective supplier manager and some of the challenges of this role.

10.1 Roles and Responsibilities

To describe the roles and responsibilities of a supplier manager, we first give some development definitions that we have adopted and as described in Cockburn (2002):

- *Multi-site development:* carried out at relatively few locations with complete development groups developing subsystems with well-defined subsystem interfaces.
- *Offshore development:* designers in one location send specifications and tests to programmers in another country. Offshore location lacks architects, subject matter experts, designers, and testers.
- *Distributed development:* has been characterized as "sun never sets development," as members of a single team can be spread across many locations such that development occurs around the clock. This requires that daily communications occur among collaborating team members. Open-Source development is a type of distributed development with different philosophical, economic, and team structure models. In Open-Source, anyone can contribute code but a gatekeeper protects the code base. All communication is visible to anyone.

In our GSD approach we send specifications to the remote sites in other countries but we also build up the expertise of the remote team by including them in early phase activities at the central site. The supplier manager helps build this expertise bridge between the central and remote teams.

Within Siemens, we define software outsourcing as developing some or all of a software product outside the local development organization facility or in another Siemens division. Usually, software outsourcing refers to development work done outside the company. However, Siemens has fully-owned and majority-owned subsidiary companies in countries such as India, Brazil, China, and in Eastern Europe where such outsourcing software development work is performed.

Communications and development are done within a corporate intranet, and patent disclosures are jointly written by team members with all intellectual property owned by the parent company. The work is done in accordance with a simple internal contract that specifies goals, deliverables, costs, payment options, escalation policies, and termination procedures. Sometimes, bonus or malus agreements are put in place to reward or punish a remote team based on their performance. But most contracts are set up such that the remote supplier organization's incentive to perform well is to sustain and grow their funding from central business organizations over time. Ideally, a remote team that performs well will be funded for multiple iterations, across multiple fiscal years, and be invited to contribute to the maintenance of the products they develop as well as participate in new product developments. Thus, the supplier manager facilitates technology transfer from the central site to the remote site such that the remote site over time becomes a competence center of the central business. This model works well within Siemens, assuming that the business grows over time. When the business is shrinking, the remote sites are usually the first to be cut off.

We define global software development (GSD) as involving development teams that are geographically distributed. This often involves teams from different organizations and different countries. Thus, one of the skills that supplier managers must develop is the ability to work effectively and communicate with engineers from different cultures in countries other than their own. Obviously, another characteristic of the supplier manager is a willingness and interest in foreign travel.

There are risks associated with GSD as identified below compared to development at a single site that the supplier manager helps manage:

- Lack of control of schedule, cost, quality
- Potential loss of core competencies
- Time and distance
- Cultural, communications, language misunderstandings
- Complexity
- Currency exchange rates
- Political

Working across national boundaries creates a number of political risks that are not experienced during single-site development projects. Some of these political risks can be managed by supplier managers, and some are beyond their control. When unforeseen political events occur, the supplier managers will play a key role in communicating the risks to the central team and formulating alternate plans. Example political risks include:

- Labor:
  - First world versus third
  - White-collar workers versus blue
  - Commoditization versus specialization
  - CIOs, CFOs, and CEOs versus developers
  - Big business versus labor
  - Automation versus craftsmanship
- Government:
  - Weapons of mass destruction

- ■ Immigration
- ■ Education
■ Industrial:
  - ■ Intellectual property
  - ■ Balance of power
  - ■ Vendor/supplier relations

Coordination and control become more difficult due to distance as software development teams are geographically distributed. The supplier manager's role is to reduce these distances by functioning as the communications interface between the central and remote organizations. To some extent, the artifacts that the central team delivers to the remote development teams enable them to plan and estimate the effort for the modules they will be developing. However, the supplier managers, who are employees of the central site, will help manage the relationship and projects with the remote sites.

We believe the personal contact that the supplier managers provide is necessary to support communication with the remote sites during development. Knowing supplier colleagues personally in advance seems particularly important when something goes wrong on the project. Remote problem resolution is difficult when staff at both the central and remote sites have never met each other or previously worked together.

Therefore, we can summarize the responsibility of the role of the supplier manager on a global software development project as:

> Manages the resources (approximately eight to ten engineers) and projects at remote software development sites, manages the relationship between the supplier and the central organizations, and facilitates communications between the central and remote teams.

10.2 Desired Skills

The supplier manager has many of the skills of a software project manager plus a few more. From Paulish (2002) we have reproduced the tasks and skills of a software project manager in Table 10.1.

A supplier manager will need to work with team members from both the central and remote teams. Thus, his or her communication and intercultural skills may need to be more advanced than a project manager for a single-site project. A skill that could be used effectively by a supplier manager, for example, could be the ability to speak a foreign language. The project work might all be done in the English language but the

Table 10.1   Role of the Project Manager

Task	Description	Desired Skills
Create a project vision	The project manager must be able to communicate a vision of successful project completion	Marketing, business climate, technology trends, experience from earlier projects, communications, goal setting, consensus building
Direct, coach, and mentor	The project manager must be directive, function as a mentor to inexperienced team members, or function as a coach to more experienced team members, depending on the situation	Communications, empathy, technical
Make decisions	The project manager must make timely decisions concerning the project so as not to hold up the work progress of team members	Global analysis, communications, trade-off analysis, business climate, political climate
Coordinate	The project manager must coordinate the necessary communications among team members and provide organizational support to avoid wasting the time of team members	Time management, organizational, communications
Work with team members	The project manager must interact with all team members, especially the chief architect	Team building, team member, communications, consensus building, interpersonal, social, intercultural

Source: Pearson Education

supplier manager can use the native language of the remote team for social communications. Furthermore, some understanding of the culture of the country in which their remote team is working will be useful.

A high degree of flexibility and mobility will also be useful for supplier managers. It is likely that supplier managers will need to make frequent, long trips to remote development sites. It is better if they view such travel as interesting rather than a difficult chore. We encourage our supplier managers and other staff working on a global development project to join frequent flier and hotel programs. Sometimes, travel does not progress as planned, and the ability to be flexible can help avoid potential hardships. On the BAS project, it was observed that some of the participants at project meetings in foreign locations seemed to be overly jet-lagged. This may contribute to inefficient meetings, short tempers, impatience, and the like. This is one reason why we recommend that central team functions be collocated. Supplier managers will learn to compensate for these travel-related hardships.

Supplier managers will benefit from having well-developed social skills. In Siemens it is customary for visitors to remote sites to be invited to evening dinners or social events during their visit. We encourage such social engagements, as they help build teamwork. However, such events create personal decisions for visitors concerning how late to stay awake, what to eat, drink, etc. Good social communication skills are helpful to define the constraints of such interactions; for example, "I'll be pleased to have a couple beers with you this evening but I cannot eat spicy food before bedtime."

Supplier managers may require deeper technical skills than a project manager at a single site. Project managers at a single site who need technical information can usually walk over to an expert and ask a question. Supplier managers at remote sites, depending on time zone differences, may experience that their technical experts back at the central site are sleeping when they need technical information. Thus, we desire our supplier managers to have good technical skills and domain expertise. In fact, many of them contribute to developing the early phase artifacts that will be turned over to their remote development team, and they well understand the product requirements and system architecture.

Tip: Note how people introduce themselves at a remote site meeting.

You will learn much about your suppliers when you visit them. If team members are introducing themselves to each other as well as to you, it is not likely that the team has successfully worked together previously. At some sites, staff turnover is high enough that long-term working relationships are never formed among the team members. Because you are investing in your supplier to become your competence center over the long term, do whatever is in your power to form highly productive teams and keep them together working on your project for years.

10.3 Organizational Models

Our rule of thumb for supplier managers is that each one should be responsible for from eight to no more than ten remote developers. Our preference is that supplier managers are part of and reside at the central site, but it is expected that they will make frequent trips to the remote sites. Table 10.2 lists the various supplier manager organization alternatives and their pros and cons.

The overall project communications and coordination for a global development project are controlled by the central team. Technical activities are controlled by the functional team leaders within the central teams. Project activities are controlled by the product manager and supplier managers. The project is planned as development iterations made up of monthly sprints. The goals of each sprint are planned centrally using the build plan.

Detailed planning should be done by each development team for each sprint, with the support of the supplier manager. Delivery dates are fixed but there will be some feature migration between sprints.

Table 10.2 Supplier Manager Alternatives

Employee of	Resident at	Pros	Cons
Central	Central	Strong control	Less contact with remote engineers
Central	Remote	Less project information/ communications	More contact with remote engineers (living expenses)
Remote	Central	More project information/ communications	Additional cost to supplier
Remote	Remote	Strong control of remote team	Less project information/ communications

Based on the above, we believe the best alternative is to have the supplier manager be part of the central organization and sit at the central team site. Frequent trips will be made to the remote sites, especially for the kick-off meeting for a new iteration and to view the results of each sprint. Thus, one should plan for one trip per month by the supplier manager to the remote sites, or about 25 percent of supplier worktime will be at the remote sites. In addition, technical specialists from the central team may also visit for reviews, workshops, and audits with the remote teams. Monthly demonstrations by the remote teams help the supplier manager gauge the progress of the team, and often help build the confidence of the remote team as they see their own progress and the overall project progress.

Suppliers prefer to retain someone from their own staff at the central site even after remote development begins. Clearly, they use this person to bridge the communications gap between the remote and central teams. Although such a role is useful, we do not see this individual replacing the role of the supplier manager as we have defined it. Perhaps this alternative role could be better described as an account manager. The central site may balk at funding such a role when they have an adequate number of their own employees working as supplier managers. Such an alternative may work best when the supplier has other projects with other central site organizations in the same country, and the account manager can be spread across different projects. We have observed that our internal suppliers use an account manager in the United States very effectively to help orient their staff that comes to work at the central site for early phase activities. We have also observed that they often temporarily relocate their staff to the United States with their family members. This helps relieve homesickness and the need for frequent trips home during the early phases of the project.

From case studies done within Siemens, we believe there are also some benefits to moving staff from the central site to the remote development site organizations as long-term delegates. This is possible within Siemens because the suppliers are subsidiary companies. These delegates are trusted employees of the central site company who are often selected to help establish the presence of the company in a foreign country. In general, most exchanges of staff seem to help the working relationships between the central and remote teams. In particular, if the development or relationship is not progressing well, communications between the central and remote teams are often increased, and this can be effectively accomplished by physically exchanging staff. Such staff should be selected for their communication skills, and they serve as "bridges" between the central and remote teams.

Based on our experience, we believe that at the current state of software engineering practice, personal technical interaction is necessary to keep a global development project on track. Thus, although good documentation is clearly important, we do not believe a pure *offshore development* model as defined in Section 10.1 can be successful for complex software development projects.

Tip: Delegate trusted staff to new remote sites.

In this chapter, we have discussed the importance of supplier managers who work for the central team but spend part (e.g., 25 percent) of their time at the remote development sites. Earlier we also discussed the importance of key remote team members working at the central site on early phase tasks. In addition, consider delegating staff from the central site into key positions at the remote site. In some cases, the low costs for remote teams may be the result of hiring very inexperienced staff. With your trusted staff working in the remote organization, they can assist in interviewing, training, and building a shared understanding, and the various activities that will help accelerate bringing the remote team(s) up-to-speed for your project.

10.4 Intercultural Issues

We have observed over many projects that multicultural variables can be a factor that may influence a global development project (Kopper, 1993). These variables can be strengths for the project or impair project progress, depending on how they are managed. In Siemens, cultural factors can originate from multiple countries, and also from different company cultures, as Siemens has acquired many companies over time.

Cultural variables often affect the basic values of development team members including punctuality, the balance between work and personal time, conflict resolution, etc. For example, as the stress level to meet delivery dates for the project increases, remote teams may question each other's commitment to the project and complain that "they are on holiday when we have work that needs to get done."

We have stressed the need for supplier managers to understand intercultural issues and be able to communicate them. However, this need also extends to all project team members. We have observed that successful projects often develop their own project culture that borrows from the country and company cultures. Communications are repeated frequently and delivered using different media to help support different learning styles and languages. Staff from multiple sites visit each other frequently, and they get to know each other outside the work environment.

We have also noticed that successful projects invest in team building and multicultural training. This is required for supplier managers, but is also valuable for the entire team. Often, the outputs of such training can be very practical processes such as defining a common way to conduct meetings throughout the project.

Tip: Encourage best practices sharing.

It is inevitable that comparisons will be made among your teams and suppliers. Make these comparisons a positive motivator rather than a negative one by encouraging "best practices sharing." If you see an innovative process, tool, or technology being used by one team, initiate introductions within another team so they can learn from the experience. Do not ask, "Why can't your team be more like team A?" If you are managing teams from multiple suppliers, they may be business competitors of each other. Your interest should be to use the best practices for your project, and make certain that all your teams are highly motivated and productive.

10.5 Summary and Conclusions

As a supplier manager, you are an important member of your project team to help bridge the communications gap to the remote teams. You will view the relationship with your suppliers as a long-term one, where over time they become extensions of your own organization. Your capabilities will be stretched as you compensate for differences in distance, culture, and language that you have not encountered to the same extent on single-site projects. You will be held responsible for the progress of the remote development teams you oversee and their working relationships with the central team members. In summary, you can view your role of a supplier manager as a "traveling software project manager."

10.6 Discussion Questions

1. What types of skills are desirable for supplier manager, and where do you recruit them?
2. How are remote development team members recruited, interviewed, and assigned?
3. What are some of the cultural factors that might influence the values of staff from various countries working on the project?
4. How do supplier managers communicate with remote team members? How frequently do they visit the remote sites?

References

Cockburn, A., *Agile Software Development*, Addison-Wesley, Boston, MA, 2002.
Kopper, E., "Swiss and Germans: Similarities and Differences in Work-Related Values, Attitudes, and Behavior," *International Journal of Intercultural Relations,* Pergamon Press, New York, 1993, pp. 167–184.
Paulish, D., *Architecture-Centric Software Project Management*, Addison Wesley, Boston, MA, 2002.

Section IV

MONITORING AND CONTROL

Chapter 11

Quality Assurance

Ron was just assigned responsibility for quality assurance for the BAS project. He was told that most of the development work would be done in Bangalore. He was puzzled by how he could assure the quality of code developed by staff he never met, and he had no influence on their development process.

This chapter focuses on strategies for monitoring the quality of a globally distributed software development process and the software product. The process is continuously improved through measurements and audits that determine when and where a process is broken. Analysis of key metrics data, prevention of defects, and continuous testing are strategies for improving the quality of a product.

11.1 Background

The IEEE defines software quality as:

1. The degree to which a system, component, or process meets specified requirements
2. The degree to which a system, component, or process meets customer or user needs or expectations

The corresponding definition for quality assurance (QA) is as follows:

1. A planned and systematic pattern of all actions necessary to provide adequate confidence that an item or product conforms to established technical requirements

2. A set of activities designed to evaluate the process by which the products are developed or manufactured

While we like the IEEE definition for software quality, we feel the definition for quality assurance limits the scope to ensuring that the established technical requirements are met. In our view, QA activities also include measures for ensuring that the established requirements accurately reflect the customer or user's needs. We believe in the idea behind the agile tenets that users and customers are not always able to accurately describe what they need; the old "I can't tell you what I want, but I will know it when I see it" syndrome. We therefore adapt the IEEE definition of QA to be:

> "A planned and systematic pattern of all actions necessary to provide adequate confidence that an item or product conforms to established technical requirements and the customer or user's needs and expectations"

That is, QA involves answering the following questions:

- How do we know that we have accurately established what is wanted and needed?
- How do we know we have built a system that realizes the requirements as expected?
- How do we know that the system built behaves and will behave as expected now and in the future?
- How do we know that the system that has been built will not do unexpected things?

This chapter describes the issues with QA in a global context, how we have addressed these issues, and discusses software maintenance for products built using GSD. We follow the format established in the remainder of this book and not discuss the details of QA that are no different in GSD than in collocated projects or do not have an impact on other activities described in this book.

11.1.1 QA in a Global Context

Why is QA different in a global context? If we have structured rigorous approaches for QA on our current projects, why will they not work for GSD? QA in GSD may be different for the very same reasons that were mentioned over and over again in this book. In collocated projects there are often informal safety nets that make up for deficiencies in the process. That is, it may not be the QA process itself that brings many issues to light; rather, it is the constant close interactions of the team members that surface issues (or perhaps that is in some part the QA process). These safety nets do not exist in GSD. In addition, the impact of issues can be magnified in GSD projects. If you have ever seen semi-trucks on the highway with multiple trailers attached, you know that the impact of small corrections made by the driver is amplified as it is telegraphed through the trailers. Corrections that would not be an issue when driving a car can have disastrous effects on these trucks. The same is true for GSD.

When you ship a specification to a remote team, it is much more difficult to get a sense for whether they sufficiently understand the nature of their tasks. In collocated projects, you can meet face-to-face, establish a working relationship that facilitates communication, pick up subtle cues that may indicate discomfort with or confusion about tasks, etc. In GSD, you typically send a specification into the cyberspace ether, have a teleconference, and expect that the teams will let you know if they have problems or questions. Compared to a distributed project, a collocated project provides increased opportunities to have insight into the execution of the individual tasks. You get to know who the key people are on the team, what their approach is, and how well things are proceeding. This information not only helps for identifying issues, but also helps resolve issues more quickly.

When a problem is discovered in a GSD project, it is more difficult to recover from it than in collocated projects. It is more difficult to know who to hand off the problem to, know who all the parties are that should be involved in solving the problem, adjust schedules and shift tasks to account for unanticipated efforts or tasks, and in general keep the issue from derailing forward progress. Depending on the type of issue (e.g., requirements misunderstanding, syntactic issue, semantic issue, or behavioral issue), it will likely be discovered at different times. The further away you are from the generation of the issue, the more difficult it will be to identify and correct the source of the issue. It is not uncommon to assign the issue to an individual and have it be reassigned several times before the issue is resolved. Each reassignment was accompanied by some investigation of the issue as well as investigation for who else could be involved. This takes time away from other tasks and may ultimately require some negotiation or collaboration across teams that are difficult to conduct efficiently. A reassignment of tasks can have ripple effects throughout the project. If a team is involved in developing something that is on the critical path for planned features, a missed delivery could mean that other teams are sitting idle waiting for another team's delivery.

11.2 Measuring Process Quality

As previously discussed, coordination and control become more difficult due to the geographical distribution of teams. We want to put processes in place that will ensure we deliver a product of high quality. The issue is that GSD projects differ so drastically from one project to another that it is difficult to definitively say that particular practices will be effective for a given project. In looking at past GSD projects across Siemens, we did not find significant correlations between particular practices and the success of the project. What this means is that it is doubly important to define measures that will give you early warning indicators that the process needs adjusting. This section discusses some practices that we have used successfully, what some useful measures could be, and how to evaluate these measures and improve the processes accordingly.

11.2.1 Defining Processes

While it very well may be the case that your organization has a Software Engineering Process Group (SEPG) and has standard processes defined for your software development, there are many details that are either tailorable, not addressed at all, or are not standard across the teams involved in the current GSD project. The requirements engineering process, for example, describes how to model the requirements in a way that facilitates automatic generation of the test cases. Certain aspects of the project, however, must be defined on a project-by-project basis — things such as the infrastructure(s) used for the project, the detailed management practices, the team-level development practices, the build frequency and process, etc. Selection of these details can be viewed as balancing risk with overhead. As discussed in the risk chapter (Chapter 6), selection and tailoring of the particular processes should be done in light of the characteristics of the project at hand (we called this a "risk profile" in Chapter 6). Defining these processes is really just a starting point, however. The selection is an educated guess, the accuracy of which will depend on many factors. It is prudent to go a step beyond and make some contingency plans as well. In what ways could the processes reasonably be adjusted if the project is not going as desired (see Chapter 6 for more details)?

11.2.2 Defining Measures

Once we have our processes defined, we need to know how to monitor them. One issue (that has been cited over and over again) is that visibility into the progress and current state of a GSD project is difficult to achieve.

Often, problems are not apparent until very late in the game, thus causing major corrections to be made (picture the semi-truck here). We need to define measures that will give early warning indicators that things are not proceeding as planned, allowing us to act before major issues are realized. This is not so easily done. We would like to be able to give concrete guidance (beyond the standard Goal/Question/Metric approach), but unfortunately all we can do here is share some heuristics that we have learned over the years.

Some items that can be monitored and may be warning indicators of an issue include:

■ *Increased communication.* When people are having trouble with their work, they usually start to find someone to help. This means they pick up the phone, start e-mailing more frequently, or have face-to-face meetings. How does this help? Well, if you are able to monitor any of these things — such as a sudden spike in unplanned travel by members of the teams, increased traffic on list servers, etc. — it may be worthwhile investigating the reasons for this. Some of these things could be explained by the schedule (e.g., during integration time or before deliveries communication tends to increase), but they may also be indicators of an impending issue.

■ *Unusual reduction in scope delivered during a sprint.* Because of the agile nature of the planning process, it is normal to have the scope for each sprint adjusted somewhat, but this normally stabilizes over time. If a team suddenly delivers much less than what it had expected, it is wise to figure out why. Sometimes, the reasons behind the issue could involve several teams, and it is best to have the central team get involved early in the interactions so as to be aware of and manage these exchanges.

■ *Morale of the developers.* We have observed that there is a high correlation between a developer's perception of progress and the actual schedule (and conversely, a poor correlation between the manager's perception of progress and the actual schedule). If there is a way to track the frustration level of the developers, that is often a good indicator of the current state of affairs. The people dealing with the issue on a daily basis will know that a problem is pending long before the management. It is also the case that teams can easily become disenfranchised if they are left idle or feel they are given busy work. This is also an indication of either poor planning, poor performance by another team, or problems with the requirements or design.

- *Frequent changes in the requirements or design.* While this is expected early in the project as the execution begins, if the requirements or design change frequently it is wise to investigate the cause and impact of these changes.

It should be noted that new remote teams will take some time to reach their best productivity. From our case studies of Siemens global development projects, these new remote teams may need six to twelve months to achieve their best productivity. Thus, goals for early sprints should be modest and become more challenging over time.

11.2.3 Improving Processes

As a central team quality manager, you have responsibility for continuously improving the global development process that is in use. This must be done incrementally and carefully so as not to perturb the development progress. You will work with your remote site process improvement champions to provide support for their local processes and work with your local management to introduce planned improvements.

11.3 Measuring Product Quality

Product quality will be measured by tracking the counts of defects identified during the incremental testing of the previous release (Paulish, 2002). The defect counts will be obtained from a change management tool where you will be able to summarize the priorities, counts, and status of defects as they are reported by the test team. You will have quality criteria related to customer shipments; for example, "No product will be shipped if any known priority level 1 or 2 defects are outstanding."

11.3.1 Defect Types

The term "defect" is much broader than an error; it is any deviation in the product from its "fitness of purpose." As previously discussed, fitness of purpose is defined as a product's ability to meet the expectations of its users. Therefore, defects can manifest themselves as:

- *Coding error.* This is typically a syntactic error.
- *Incorrect feature.* This is a logical design error, also referred to as a semantic error.
- *Missing feature.* This is an absence of a vital requirement.

- *Misunderstood feature.* This is a faulty understanding by a developer or designer of a customer requirement.
- *System behavior.* This manifests itself as a system performing poorly, missing deadlines, and not behaving as expected under certain circumstances (e.g., when a fault is introduced).

11.3.2   Issues with Product Quality in a GSD Context

If we look at the defects above, we can begin to see how there are additional issues maintaining product quality in a GSD setting. It is the case that the compiler catches syntactic issues (e.g., interface mismatch), so this is easily addressed even in GSD, but semantic errors are much more difficult. We must have sufficient correctness and coverage of our test cases to uncover semantic errors in GSD. While this is also true in collocated projects, the likelihood of experiencing such an issue is greater and the implications of having such a defect introduced are much worse in GSD. Differing assumptions across teams such as U.S. Dollars versus Euros (does anyone remember the Mars Rover?) can introduce logic errors as well as problems that are isolated within a single team.

Misunderstood requirements are more likely in a GSD setting. When a project is collocated, it is not uncommon to have face-to-face meetings to augment specifications. These meetings are not only more effective, but they allow an opportunity to gauge the level of understanding of the recipient. As previously discussed, this safety net is not available in GSD. In GSD projects, you rely solely on the QA procedures in place. Hopefully at this point you have a better sense for why and how maintaining product quality can be a much more difficult task in GSD projects.

11.3.3   Strategies for Maintaining Quality in a GSD Context

For global development, one of the recommended better practices is automated code inspection. Remote teams will do code inspections with their local team members and may even use such techniques as pair programming. However, for global development it is good to establish coding standards across all the development teams. If the code is analyzed using a tool to check for violations of the coding standards, it will be easier for any team member to understand product code and some defects may be discovered prior to integration.

We describe an "extended workbench" type of model where components are developed remotely and then brought together at the central site for integration and verification. Thus, different levels of testing are done at the central and remote sites. Some of the recommended better practices for testing include:

- The central team enumerates acceptance test cases derived from the high-level functional requirements.
- The remote teams create automated test classes as part of each iteration for their respective task assignments.
- The central team specifies and executes integration tests at the central site. These are defined when an iteration is under way and are executed at the end of each iteration.

Prototypes for various purposes may also be a good idea. Sometimes it is very helpful to do UI prototyping to help solidify the requirements as well as verify that the remote teams have a common understanding of the requirements. In addition, we recommend first developing a "vertical slice" of the architecture. This is to facilitate earlier testing of the system-level features, to verify the riskier parts of the architecture, and to ensure that the remote teams adequately understand and are able to implement the design. Along these lines, we have also used static analysis to verify compliance with the architecture and various coding guidelines. This is something that can be automated, provided there is sufficient tool support and the design is done in sufficient detail.

While it places a higher burden on the central team, delivering acceptance test cases along with the specifications as part of the work package given for each sprint is quite helpful. We have found that the test-driven development approach helps to ensure that the developers understand and address the important requirements.

As part of the requirements process, we conduct regular reviews of the requirements by the domain experts to validate that we have not missed any vital requirements and that the requirements as captured reflect the user's needs and desires. This is greatly aided by our approach to modeling. The visual representation of the use cases in UML lends itself to understanding even by nontechnical people. It also allows for automatic generation of test cases and increases correctness and coverage of test cases.

11.4 Product Maintenance

Once a product is made generally available, it enters the maintenance phase of its life cycle. At this stage, the focus shifts from product quality to customer satisfaction. Not much can be done about product quality as it has been deployed at customer sites with all of its defects that went undetected. How do we make sure that customers are not dissatisfied as a result of these defects making their way into the product? While maintenance quality is an issue for any software product, fixing defects effectively and efficiently in a product developed by many suppliers at disparate remote sites can be challenging. In this section we look at product maintenance in GSD projects, the need for long-term relationships with suppliers at remote development sites, and strategies for fostering such relationships.

11.4.1 Product Maintenance in a Global Context

Product maintenance quality is judged by the efficiency and effectiveness of the maintenance process. Typical measures instituted to assess this quality include (Kan, 2003):

- *Fix backlog:* a measure for the rate at which fixes for reported defects become available
- *Fix response time:* a measure of the mean time of all defects from the time they were reported to the time they were fixed; defects can be categorized and response time measured by severity level
- *Delinquent fixes:* a measure of those fixes for which the turnaround time exceeds the required response time
- *Fix quality:* a measure of bad fixes, that is, fixes that do not correct the defect or inject further defects

It is clear from looking at these metrics that a maintenance process will be as effective and efficient as the people involved in such a process. The effectiveness and efficiency of the people involved will depend on their intimate knowledge of the product being maintained; there is no substitute for that. It is obvious that the people most intimately involved with the product will be the same people who developed it. We must, therefore, leverage the suppliers from remote sites not only for the development of the product, but also its maintenance. It should be noted that how the suppliers are affiliated to the central organization that owns the product can add another dimension to the maintenance process. How maintenance issues are handled when the central organization and the suppliers are part of the same corporate legal entity will require a different approach than when they are two independent legal entities. We provide more details in the following sections.

11.4.1.1 Need for Long-Term Relationship

Team building is a challenging task in a distributed environment, one that requires considerable effort such as travel for acquainting onshore team members with their offshore counterparts, creating a single virtual development site with shared change and build management systems, and communities of practice where team members can go to have their questions answered. It is therefore beneficial to retain a relationship with offshore teams for a longer duration or else a similar start-up effort must be expended each time a new partner is found.

But as cited in the opening remarks, establishing long-term collaborations with offshore teams is even more critical for the ongoing support and maintenance of the product under development.

Offshore teams, therefore, must be treated as an extended workbench of the central business unit that owns the product it delivers. With this model, the central team plans to build the remote site into a competence center for their business over time. Thus, training of remote staff is an investment in the future of the business. The efficiency of collaboration will improve over time (Lasser and Heiss, 2005). Thus, one may experience the cost benefits of global development only after a few years of collaborative work, or perhaps on the next project, rather than the first project with a new site.

11.4.1.2   Strategies for Fostering Cordial Relations

There are a number of possible approaches for developing a good working relationship with your suppliers working at remote development sites:

- *Trust.* A long-term relationship will not be successful without mutual trust. Trust must be earned and takes time to build. The trust-building time period can be reduced by "doing what you say." It is suggested that response and delivery dates are met. Commitments made by each partner should be upheld, and schedules should be met.
- *Respect as colleagues.* As part of the strategy to build up a remote competence center, staff at the remote supplier sites should be treated as respected potential colleagues. This is different from treating the remote staff as short-term contract laborers. This respect implies investment in building up the technical skills and domain knowledge of the remote staff, with the assumption that the relationship will continue for an extended time.
- *Exchange of staff.* Often, the best way to transfer technology and build trust between organizations is to rotate staff between sites. Our approach to global software development encourages moving remote team members to participate in early phase activities at the central site. We also recommend that some central team staff work as extended-stay delegates at the remote sites.
- *Planning and developing competencies.* Remote sites should be planned to be given an area of responsibility for which they can become a competence center. For example, for the BAS project, the development site in Slovakia was planned to become the

competence center on closed-circuit TV (CCTV) equipment and applications. They start by developing working prototypes and CCTV applications, until they become technology experts for this domain.

■ *Keeping teams together.* Because a long-term relationship is being nurtured, it is important to attempt to try to keep together key members of the product team. As economic conditions improve in low-wage countries, software engineers may have a tendency to "job-hop" to boost their salaries. Suppliers should attempt to keep their teams together over multiple years of development and maintenance. This can be done by providing interesting and long-term work, but also with financial enticements such as a long-term incentive program (LTIP) or periodic bonuses.

■ *Teamwork.* Not only must there be good teamwork within a component development team, for global development there also must be good teamwork between the remote and central teams. Select staff with better communications and social skills. Some staff is talented with "bridging skills," for example, bringing together opposition, understanding different cultures, language skills, etc.

■ *Long-term planning.* Share your long-term plan with your suppliers. Although the business climate changes and thus plans must change, let suppliers know about anticipated head-count requirements, necessary skills, and other pieces of the "big picture."

■ *Negotiating price.* Do not squeeze your suppliers on hourly labor or other rates to save small amounts of money. Chapter 9 recommended that component development estimates within about a factor of two as compared to the top-down estimate be accepted. Your supplier labor rates may already be 20 to 30 percent of your rates. Pressing for an additional 5 to 10 percent discount may harm the relationship more than the value of the savings realized.

Tip: Control your purchasing people during contract negotiations with suppliers.

Many purchasing staff members have incentives to reduce costs by a specified percentage of the contract value. In many cases, they may not be aware of (or care about) the business or project goals associated with the contract. Impress upon your purchasing staff that if the software does not work when it is delivered, it does not matter how little you paid for it.

11.4.1.3 Affiliation of Suppliers to the Central Organization

When suppliers are not part of the same legal entity as the central organization, it is very likely that they are part of different organizational units with a different reporting structure or independent companies. Once they finish a development project, they will move on to the next project. Under such circumstances, it becomes important for the central organization to work out a strategy for prioritizing and allocating customer change requests when they arrive to the appropriate members of the supplier organization. This can be problematic, given that each organizational unit may have conflicting business goals and objectives. One strategy might be to formally award a maintenance contract to the supplier teams and offer further incentives through engagement in future development projects. As discussed in the previous section, the objective is to treat a supplier as an extended workbench and evolve it as a competence center. The central organization must, therefore, make the suppliers part of its business strategy for the future.

In case suppliers are independent legal entities, the central organization has to worry about turnover should the supplier be located in a highly volatile region. We have observed high turnover rates in companies located in Bangalore, India, for example, as it has become a popular location for many multinational companies. Strategies cited in a previous section for long-term incentives may help in these circumstances.

11.5 Summary and Conclusions

Quality assurance practices are critical for the successful outcome of a global development project. The central site quality assurance champion must partner with colleagues at the remote sites to help control and improve the development process. Quality problems are better prevented and must be detected prior to customer shipment.

11.6 Discussion Questions

1. Discuss some of the measures and strategies for maintaining process and product quality in a GSD context.
2. What is the significance of maintaining long-term and cordial relations with suppliers at remote sites?
3. How long should one expect for a remote development team to reach peak performance?
4. How does the central quality expert work with experts at the remote sites?

References

Hofmeister, C., Nord, R., and Soni, D., *Applied Software Architecture*, Addison-Wesley, Boston, MA, 2000.

Kan, S., *Metrics and Models in Software Quality Engineering, second edition,* Addison-Wesley, Boston, MA, 2003, pp. 105–110.

Lasser, S. and Heiss, M., "Collaboration Maturity and the Offshoring Cost Barrier: The Trade-Off between Flexibility in Team Composition and Cross-Site Communication Effort in Geographically Distributed Development Projects," *Proceedings of the IEEE International Professional Communication Conference (IPCC 2005),* Limerick, Ireland, 10–13 July 2005, pp. 1–11.

Moeller, K. and Paulish, D., *Software Metrics: A Practitioner's Guide to Improved Product Development*, IEEE Computer Society Press, Los Alamitos, CA, 1993.

Paulish, D., *Architecture-Centric Software Project Management*, Addison-Wesley, Boston, MA, 2002.

Chapter 12

Infrastructure Support for Global Software Development

The first of six distributed teams had just joined the Global Studio Project (GSP) and Zak was trying to set up infrastructural support that would not only meet the demands placed on the project by the technology and the architecture, but also by the distributed nature of all the teams. The key issues that the central team was contending with were how to enable and facilitate communication within and among the teams and how to ensure that up-to-date project artifacts were made available across the organization. With the software configuration management set up in particular, the build-meister needed to figure out a way to manage and merge the code branches specific to the different sites participating in the development effort.

This chapter takes a look at strategies and tools for infrastructure management in a global software development environment and gives practical guidance on how such efforts can be better managed. In particular, the chapter covers the following aspects:

1. Criteria for selecting the infrastructure for global software development (GSD)
2. Infrastructure required for communication and coordination, knowledge management, and software configuration management
3. Processes used to facilitate the usage of the infrastructure appropriately and effectively

12.1 Criteria for Selecting the Infrastructure

In line with engineering and planning activities, preparing an adequate project infrastructure for distributed development is a significant project success factor. Infrastructure tools must support accessibility, collaboration and concurrency, processes, and awareness and integration. Conventional tools may not address these requirements very well; and if this is detected too late, the deployment of those tools and migration of artifacts will be costly and time consuming, and eventually disruptive to the project (Gersmann, 2005).

12.1.1 Accessibility

The tools must be available at all development sites. This means that the project team members at the sites must be provisioned with licenses. Additionally, the problem of network connectivity should be addressed. Depending on the network topology, there may be conflicts among sites, thus making data exchange and connectivity difficult. If the tools depend on network connectivity, they must support this connectivity in a restricted network environment. If the system under development is a distributed system, this also applies to the network connections required by the system. The infrastructure coordinator must document and address these issues. This means that probably some tools will not qualify for deployment in a distributed setting and, therefore, they cannot be used. Tools supporting distribution and limited network connectivity (for example, Web-based solutions, or tools using HTTP as a communication protocol) may need consideration. Should this not be possible, the infrastructure coordinator must arrange the required modifications to the network configuration or to the infrastructure setup.

12.1.2 Collaboration and Concurrency

Depending on the field of application, the tools must support collaboration and concurrency. Collaboration here does not necessarily refer to real-time collaboration, but also asynchronous collaboration, which is often the case with geographically distributed teams particularly in different time zones. Concurrency refers to the extent to which different parties can collaborate explicitly or implicitly on a single artifact. Implicit concurrency support can come in the form of optimistic access control and merging functionality.

This functionality can be provided by the revision control system in the form of text-based merge utilities or by the applications themselves in the form of format-specific merge utilities. Explicit concurrency control requires locking of artifacts or smaller fractions of an artifact for modification. Those systems usually require an online working mode. To minimize the potential for conflict, the artifact entities that are managed by the tools should be as small as possible and then aggregate into larger entities. The quality of collaboration and concurrency support is important, as it determines the ease of use and thereby the probability of adequate adoption by project team members.

12.1.3 Processes

Two dominant issues relating to the choice of infrastructure are the extent to which tools enforce a particular process or allow flexible definition of a process. Unfortunately, it is difficult to find tools that support both. The more flexibility a tool provides, the less it is possible to enforce specific processes by technical means. Tools that provide high structure and enforceability often are tailored to specific processes and workflows, and thus they provide little flexibility. Depending on the nature of the project, the project manager and infrastructure coordinator will have to make a decision for either one of those tools. In the context of distributed development, flexible tools should probably be preferred over specific tools, as those tools are seldom designed for distributed development. The selection of flexible tools, however, results in higher manual process enforcement activities.

12.1.4 Awareness and Integration

The infrastructure should support awareness of communication and technical artifacts. Awareness could, for example, be supported by making as much information as possible available in a single location and linking different artifacts for navigability. Using traditional documents, it can be difficult to refer to individual entities within the document. For traceability reasons, however, it is preferable to have the ability to support direct addressing of individual entities. To achieve traceability and navigability, different vendors provide integrated tool sets. The problem is that integration is limited to what has been anticipated and provided for by the tool vendors. Thus, appropriate trade-offs should be made; some tools may be more structured and support enforcement, while others may be more flexible and easier to integrate. As investments into infrastructure and tools are usually long term, they should be carried out carefully and under strict consideration of the project's (and organization's) requirements (Gersmann, 2005).

12.2 Communication and Coordination

The lack of an infrastructure supporting the two complementary communication needs in software development projects (Herbsleb and Moitra, 2001) (official communication such as updating project status, and informal spontaneous conversation between team members) disrupts the ability of developers and management to work as a cohesive team. There are at least two dimensions of the problem (Gernmann, 2005). First, there are problems concerning the communication infrastructure and usage policies. Equally important are the communication processes that prove difficult to set up and enforce, are error-prone, and are susceptible to ambiguities and loss of awareness.

GSD projects are challenged by both aspects of this problem. Software development, particularly in the early stages, requires much communication (Perry et al., 1994). Due to distance and time zone issues, it is difficult to sustain ongoing informal conversations among distributed teams, often resulting in misalignment of activities and rework. Distributed teams frequently resort to ad hoc communication mechanisms. There may be redundancies in communication, imposing an overload when the central team has to respond to same or similar queries. Different communication styles and media are used within the same team at different times, therefore losing consistency of messages.

12.2.1 Communication and Collaboration Strategy

The key drivers for the communication and collaboration strategy are an increase of information accessibility to all stakeholders in a disciplined manner and the creation of an environment of participation where all stakeholders contribute to the information exchange.

There have to be effective mechanisms in place for managing both kinds of communication — transient information (information with local impact and a short time span of significance) and persistent information (information that has a significant impact on different teams or that must be documented to be accessible later). E-mail can be a valuable means of communication for transient information, as it is quick and accessible. Due to various reasons, however, it is not well suited for persistent communication. It cannot be easily used to structure information, to guarantee an equal information level for different stakeholders, or to guarantee the availability of information when it is required. Due to the lack of structure and organization, e-mails typically will not be an information source used to retrieve information after days or weeks of receipt. To accomplish a significant reduction in communication overhead in the long term, information must be accessible without the need for explicit communication or inquiries. Absolute transparency of communication and documentation is required, and the central team members assume the role of facilitator instead of being an authority to report to (Gersmann, 2005).

12.2.2 Communication and Collaboration Infrastructure

The communication and collaboration infrastructure should be designed carefully so that it supports the communication strategy and its key goals, which are accessibility, collaboration and concurrency, support for the processes, and awareness and integration. In subsequent sections we describe the infrastructure that has proven quite effective in our experience.

12.2.2.1 Mailing Lists for E-Mails

E-mail communication can be accomplished through the use of mailing lists, which simplify the sending of mails to complete teams and ensure that all team members are addressed. The use of mailing lists also allows the automated filing of mail into specific folders and the archival of mail. All central team members should be copied on each site- or team-specific mailing list (Gersmann, 2005). There should also be a mailing list for the central team, as well as one for facilitating inter-team interaction with the architects and leaders of each team subscribed to it. Considering that e-mail is the most frequently used mode of communication, the mailing lists significantly simplify mail management.

12.2.2.2 Infrastructure for Weekly Meetings

The central team should conduct weekly management meetings with each of the remote sites. To facilitate this, a mix of conference bridges, video-conferencing, voice chat, and desktop sharing technologies can be used. The conference bridges enable telephone conferences with multiple distributed participants — this service allows the teams to use a fixed phone number and conference room code to dial into conferences and provides further features such as noise cancellation. Videoconferences can be used for kick-off meetings with the remote sites and for other extraordinary meetings. Voice chat can be used when rooms with telephones are sometimes not available for the remote sites. Desktop sharing technology can be used to ensure that both parties (the central and remote teams) have the same view of the world (artifacts being referred to during the course of these meetings).

Tip: Have the remote team submit questions in writing prior to meetings.

By requiring remote teams to submit questions in writing, the central team can be sure to provide well-thought-out and consistent answers to the remote teams. It allows the central team the opportunity to interact internally and iron out any confusion or disagreement in advance. It helps to avoid confusion by either having a debate while meeting with the remote team or having to later change or modify an answer. It also ensures that members of the central team who are not participating in the meeting will be aware of the question and understand the answer. We also recommend posting all (appropriate) questions and answers somewhere accessible to all teams.

12.2.2.3   Discussion Forums for Interactive Discussions and Queries

Remote teams can be subscribed to discussion forums on various pertinent topics as a means by which they can solicit information from the central team. This ensures that the queries are categorized and made persistent, allowing all remote teams to access each others' queries, thereby saving considerable overhead to the central team. Figure 12.1 shows a snapshot of a discussion forum for the Global Studio Project, one of the case studies described in more detail in Chapter 14.

Tip: Verify remote teams' understanding of directions.

One way to help ensure that remote teams have adequately understood directions or answers to questions is to have them repeat back the answers that they understood in their own words. This can be done verbally, or in writing, by having them record the question and answer in meeting minutes, or posting the question and answer to a discussion forum. The latter two have the advantages of also being available to the other remote teams.

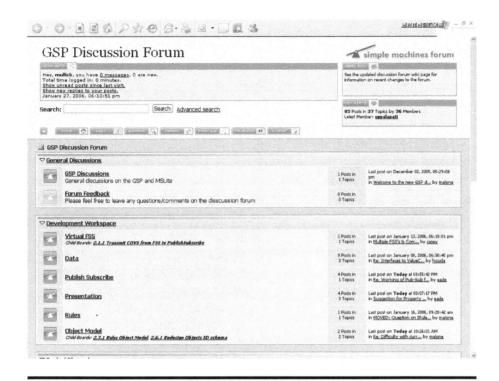

Figure 12.1 Discussion forum for Global Studio Project.

12.2.2.4 Defect Tracking and Change Management

Similar to the discussion forums, common tools must also be provided for defect tracking and change management, with an adequately outlined defect tracking and change management process that is enforced to support effective usage of such tools (Figure 12.2).

What is important to note about almost all the infrastructure setup discussed in this chapter is that open-source tools have been utilized (after considerable research and analysis against previously described criteria) for the Global Studio Project so as to avoid or circumvent the challenge of availability.

12.3 Knowledge Management: Software Design, Models, and Documentation

The lack of effective information-sharing mechanisms, poorly maintained software design and corresponding documentation, and collaboration on

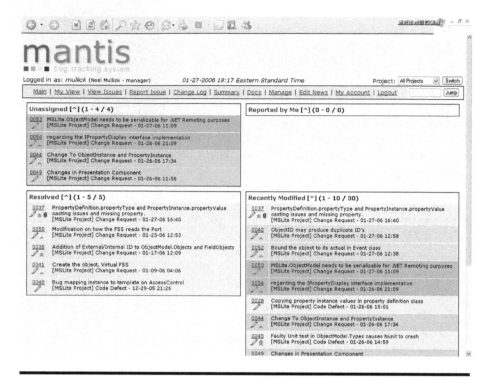

Figure 12.2   A defect tracking tool called Mantis.

artifacts all exacerbate the issue of managing knowledge in a way that harnesses the true potential of GSD. Technical issues such as discrepancies in networks, incompatible data formats, and different version of tools across sites also exacerbate the problem of knowledge management (Hersleb and Moitra, 2001). The asynchronous nature of most communication mechanisms poses a further challenge to effective knowledge management by causing delays, adding ambiguity to messages, and adding redundancies and obsolescence into the communication. This also results in the remote sites having a mental model of the system discrepant from that of the central team and from that of each other as well — therefore making the system implementation deviate from its design.

A very important observation gleaned from our experience is that in the absence of a central infrastructure, most sites will set up their own local infrastructure. Setting up a central infrastructure in isolation does not extenuate the problem of knowledge management. The central team is also required to set up processes and guidelines for usage of the infrastructure and enforce these in order for it to be utilized successfully.

12.3.1 Selecting the Knowledge Management Infrastructure

The knowledge management policies and processes should center on building a shared, collaborative knowledge base. This knowledge base should comprise all project-related information, such as technical documentation artifacts, managerial artifacts, processes, practices, infrastructure, etc. The stakeholders must be aware of the fact that the mere production of documents is not a value in itself, but that it is a means toward providing all members with the information they need.

Thus, the policies should stimulate indirect communication utilizing the knowledge base in favor of direct communication that emphasizes short-term goals and is only valuable in the current context. To increase awareness, the knowledge base should provide intelligent notification mechanisms that update stakeholders on recent modifications. It should be logically structured for ease of navigation and clustering of related information into specific realms.

Of course, the knowledge base will not eliminate the need for direct communication. Nevertheless, the central team, as facilitator, should monitor carefully that direct communication is not employed as a substitute for documentation activities. Direct communication will serve as a mechanism for coordinative activities in the process of building the project knowledge base. If, for example, issues or questions emerge during weekly or unplanned meetings, this must result in an action item that will be resolved by the central team or a remote team, and should thus manifest itself in the knowledge base. The central team must also monitor and enforce the maintenance of information, which the remote teams provide.

The knowledge base should be partitioned into a public or global section and a semipublic or team-specific section. Thus, continuity, consistency, and transparency can be maintained while still allowing teams to collaborate internally utilizing the same mechanisms as for global collaboration. Separate repositories should not be tolerated by management, as they do not reflect the principles of transparency but do prevent other teams from accessing this information, thus reducing awareness. As the project may necessitate the utilization of semi-structured and structured documents, different tools or techniques must be employed. In general, it should be considered worthwhile to keep as much of the stored information centralized using a single tool to improve accessibility. Providing stakeholders with templates for the major artifacts will increase consistency and also provide guidance to the teams, thus facilitating a semi-formal definition of expected work products. Especially in the institutionalization phase, the central team members should place their main focus on enforcing the communication policies and processes. One member from each remote team should assume the role of a documentation manager and be held responsible for the adequate implementation of such policies and processes. Due to the delay that indirect, asynchronous communication imposes, it is not always suitable for immediate resolution of issues. In such cases, e-mail or telephone conversations should be used (Gersmann, 2005).

To summarize, the key aspects of knowledge management to be considered for the infrastructure setup for GSD include:

1. Provide a central, cohesive knowledge base and keep as much information as possible in this repository.
2. Define and enforce indirect, documentation-centric communication processes.
3. Provide structural guidance and templates.
4. Have a documentation manager role within each team responsible for maintaining the structure.

12.3.2 Knowledge Management Infrastructure (Gersmann, 2005)

The centerpiece for the knowledge management infrastructure is the concept of a knowledge base, as discussed above. The requirements on this knowledge base, especially support of availability in restricted network environments and support for collaboration and concurrency, suggest a Web-based collaboration platform. The advantage of such a platform is the disentanglement from complex deployment, the accessibility by means of standard browsers, and the use of a ubiquitous network protocol (HTTP) available in nearly all network environments. Modifications to online resources are immediately visible to all stakeholders, and one common scheme can be used to reference artifacts directly (in the case of the WWW, this would be a URL). The limitations are that the information is only available when the user is connected to the Internet, some workflows are not very convenient when implemented with Web-based tools, and appropriate tools do not exist for all the tasks that must be carried out by the stakeholders. Thus, it may be necessary to combine Web-based tools with conventional client-only tools and client/server tools for different activities.

Simple content management tools — called *Wikis* — have gained popularity recently. These tools provide a system where Web pages can be manipulated immediately in the browser window by employing a custom formatting syntax that is relatively simple to learn and use. These tools are suitable for the creation of semi-structured documents. New documents can be created easily, references to documents within the Wiki can be set using a special syntax, and other artifacts outside the Wiki can be referenced if they are addressable by means of a URL. Images and other objects can be embedded into the pages.

Although formatting and layout options are not as rich as provided for by conventional tools, the capabilities are certainly sufficient to create technical documentation. The documents need not be strictly sequential, but can be broken up into logical parts that can be kept and manipulated on separate Web pages. This is particularly useful for requirements, architecture, and project plans, as these artifacts are typically broken down into smaller parts and traceability can be maintained by linking the different pieces.

Should the project need to utilize more sophisticated tools, one approach might be to employ an export functionality provided by those tools and extract a Web page representation of those artifacts. When a revision control system is employed that allows for Web access to the entities under control, those Web pages can be added to revision control and be referenced from the primary documentation, which is kept in the Wiki. Similarly, it may be possible to reference artifacts in the Wiki from the documentation generated by those tools. If not, complete documents are created using engineering tools but specific artifacts that support the written documentation (such as model diagrams), those artifacts could for example be exported as a graphic image and embedded into the documentation. The disadvantage of this approach is the need to maintain traceability and consistency mostly manually. On the other hand, this need also arises frequently if different dedicated tools are employed that do not integrate with each other.

The utilization of Web applications enables the centralization of the tools that are being employed, while still providing high accessibility to the stakeholders. This property has positive effects on collaboration capabilities exposed by the tools. Because there are no distributed databases, collaboration is simplified, as all modifications are immediately visible to the stakeholders without the need for dedicated synchronization actions.

The Wiki implementation has been successfully used in the GSP case study and it is provided on the accompanying CD. The central team was able to prepare for GSD better using a Wiki for most documentation. The requirements (use cases, models, screen mock-ups), architecture (different views with different levels of detail), design documentation, project plan (teams, roles, organization, tools, infrastructure, etc.), schedule, and collaboration spaces are the major artifacts that were hosted in the Wiki. Discussion pages for each Wiki page allowed for maintaining the rationale for decisions taken, and the notification feature allowed for increased awareness. Early enforcement was employed to direct discussions on the discussions forum. Issue tracking was supported by a specific tool. Templates were provided to the teams for the work products of some major activities. The central team paid special attention to the maintenance of structure and accessibility, and then subsequently to the enforcement of the Wiki as the central knowledge base. The central team kept video recordings of key meetings with on-screen recordings of screen contents that were made available through the Wiki. The video recordings of requirements and architecture review meetings, for example, were provided to the teams to allow for a more natural consumption of requirements and design rationale and context. On-screen recordings were used as a replacement for written installation and deployment manuals. On-screen recordings overlaid with audio could also be utilized for a more natural walk-through of technical artifacts, for example when the UML model was discussed verbally.

Different types of projects certainly expose different needs for communication, documentation, and knowledge management. Depending on the methodology in use, the documents will be more or less formally structured. Big projects are more likely to have formal, highly structured requirements databases, stricter configuration management processes, etc. No definite recommendation for the knowledge management infrastructure can be given here because it largely depends on the project requirements and available options. In general, lightweight tools should be preferred over tools that impose specific processes and structures to be able to provide ease of use and flexibility.

12.4 Software Configuration Management

Software configuration management (SCM) is the discipline of managing how software is modified and built through source code control, revision control, object build tracking, and release construction. It involves identifying the configuration of the software at given points in time, systematically controlling changes to the configuration, and maintaining the integrity and traceability of the configuration throughout the software life cycle (Paulk et al., 1993).

SCM plays a pivotal role in the success of any software development project. We have found from our experience that when pressures increase on a software development project, processes are often abandoned, especially in lower process maturity organizations — and one of the first to go is the process that governs the administration and usage of the SCM infrastructure.

Software configuration over the years has expanded in scope to include configuration management of artifacts other than just software and, therefore, is (or should be) an activity that needs to be managed effectively from the beginning of the software development project until not only the end of the software development project life cycle, but also until the end of the life of the software itself.

12.4.1 Selecting the Software Configuration Management Infrastructure

For software configuration management in GSD projects, it is important that the members of the project team receive information about what the others in the team are doing, how the project is developing, its status, which changes have been done and by whom, etc. When co-developing the same source code in distributed repositories, it is important to have a frequent or flexible (i.e., on-demand) transfer mechanism because developers often need to see each other's changes (Asklund et al., 1999).

It is also important to support the sharing of files and concurrent, simultaneous changes. Solutions using "locking" and exclusive access to files must work efficiently, as it is difficult to resolve situations where group members, located at different sites, must wait for each other. Of course, all this must occur on multiple (and disparate) networks to integrate work across multiple sites.

12.4.2 The Software Configuration Management Infrastructure

In the Global Studio Project (GSP) a software configuration management tool was initially used that did not prove suitable for distributed development over public and medium-bandwidth network connections — and both our experience and publicly documented research supported this hypothesis. Moving into the elaboration stage of the project where multiple distributed teams had started joining the project, the central team realized the importance of the software configuration management infrastructure and decided to port to the Subversion revision control system, allowing access to the repository over standard HTTP and having the advantage of accessibility even in restricted network environments. An open-source plug-in for the integration between Visual Studio (the Integrated Development Environment (IDE) initially selected) and Subversion existed but experimentation showed that it was not usable for production environments. Additional issues concerning the combined usage of Subversion and Visual Studio surfaced, but the central team was able to overcome them.

12.4.2.1 Integration and Build Management

The coordination of distributed software development is an important success factor. The automated nightly builds and continuous integrations become a major component in collaborative software organization and management. In a multi-person, multi-platform environment, they provide fast feedback to developers on new code submissions and facilitate collective work on different or the same parts of the software. Multi-platform nightly builds, based on the recent versions of the software packages, try to compensate for technical failures, test the newly built software, identify possible problems, and make results immediately available to developers spread over different institutions and countries (Undrus, 2003).

There are a wide variety of open-source tools that can be used for build management and integration. NAnt, for example, is a build tool. Unit and integration testing can be performed using the NUnit testing framework. For the .NET platform, CruiseControl.NET integrates NAnt, NUnit, and Subversion, and can be effectively used for continuous integration (Fowler and Foemmel, 2005). It can serve as a framework for automated builds and tests, meaning that every time a developer commits source code to the repository, the tool checks out the latest version and runs the build file and unit tests. The results of this build and the tests are compiled into status and error logs, which can easily be accessed by means of a small Web application that represents the project dashboard. Thus, the current integration and testing status is easily accessible by all developers. An additional feature that can be achieved by the utilization of NAnt is the automated generation of API documentation that is also available on the Web site, so that all developers have easy access to it.

12.4.3 SCM Processes to Facilitate Global Software Development

Just like technology is meant to serve a business need, the CM infrastructure would not meet its objective without it being coupled to a process that is meaningfully defined and diligently executed. Process support for CM implies (1) the "formal" definition of what is it to be performed on what (a process model), and (2) the mechanisms to help or force reality to conform to this model (Estublier, 2000). It has also been observed that better and more flexible process support was the feature most missed in many CM tools, as nearly every CM system relies on its own predefined and somewhat inflexible product life cycle (Estublier, 2000).

With the distribution of software development efforts across geographical boundaries, the need for concurrent development has been imposed on all practice areas associated with such development, including CM. A prerequisite for geographically dispersed development sub-units working concurrently on a single software system is that they are allowed to and can make simultaneous changes to the same artifact or set of artifacts.

By letting developers work in different parallel development branches, they can, despite the concurrent nature of the work, work in an isolated "sandbox" and in that way avoid using each other's temporary changes. However, the isolation results in the possibility that, without being aware of it, they may make changes that are in conflict with each other. These conflicts must be resolved when the branches are subsequently merged into a common development branch.

Concurrent development can be achieved at different levels. At the system level, sub-products or different functions are developed in parallel (concurrent system development); and at a lower, more detailed level, several developers can make simultaneous changes in different versions of the same file (concurrent software development). The lower the level, the greater the possibility for a high degree of concurrent work, but also the greater the risk of conflicting changes. There are two main ways of reducing the risk of conflicts.

First, a good product structure (architecture) makes it possible to make dependencies more obvious and distribute the work to different parts of the product. The more independent the parts are of each other, and the better their interfaces are described, the smaller the risk of conflict. It is then relatively easy to distribute the areas of responsibility, as different parts of the product, to the different developers or project groups.

Second, a high degree of awareness of what other developers or project groups have worked with and are currently working on helps reduce the risk of conflicts. Concurrent development on a low, detailed level requires more awareness than on a higher level. With concurrent work at the system level, knowing if and when an interface is being changed may be enough; whereas two developers working on the same module would probably like to know if and when the other starts working in the same file.

12.4.3.1   Well-Defined Tasks

Well-defined tasks result in increased awareness in the sense that a person knows with what the others should be working. This is an important aspect with collaborations over long distances. It also reduces the risk for misunderstandings (e.g., due to cultural differences). However, it gives no "real" awareness through system support; that is, what actually happened yesterday, or what is happening right now. By defining the tasks for each developer, one does not decrease the reasons for concurrent work at the lower levels.

12.4.3.2   Exclusive Areas of Responsibility

Another common technique is to allocate *exclusive areas of responsibility* (e.g., a set of files or modules). Especially during *new development,* this is often possible by having a suitable product structure, and to split the work between developers such that they become responsible for different parts of a product. Clear tasks and well-defined interfaces result in the work, particularly between locations, being done quite independently. Despite this, awareness is important and some GSD projects are now looking for a greater connection between development at different locations, with a possibility of seeing on a daily basis how work is progressing, rather than during weekly status meetings. Because only one person is allowed to make changes in a file due to the division of responsibility, branches at the file level are rarely used.

During *maintenance,* it is more difficult to make the same division of responsibility. Instead of breaking down associated tasks (e.g., change requests) into too small pieces that should be performed by different people in their respective areas of responsibility, it is better to enable a developer who notices a simple error in another person's module to, at least temporarily (possibly in his own branch), quickly correct the error so he can test his own changes. This is particularly important when developers are situated in different locations (although it may be more difficult to achieve). The person responsible for the module should then be informed that somebody else has made a proposal for a change, to be able to decide whether it should be integrated (merged) into the main branch.

When the division of responsibility is too great, it easily becomes too static and therefore limits the developers in what they can do. Some people also believe that the working mode according to "new development" outlined above is only caused by inadequate support for distributed development and that it is a concession to get simpler CM in the absence of branches. Instead of this, the normal working mode should be that every new functionality is implemented by a responsible person, who then implements the complete change in all affected files. It should also be stated that the maintenance of, and further development of, a successful product are the greatest part of its life cycle (at least 80 percent according to some sources). Therefore, the formulation of tools and processes just for new development rather than for further development or maintenance is a common but, and in this respect, serious mistake.

Tips: Some practical rules for software configuration management (Asklund et al., 1999):

1. Replicate the information at the different development locations so that everyone can work on a local server. Synchronize the replicates regularly and frequently, preferably automatically using tool support.

2. Do not lock files to prevent simultaneous development, particularly if the lock restrains developers at other locations. Instead, make it possible for developers to create a temporary branch themselves. The temporary branch should then be merged with its original branch as quickly as possible and discontinued.

3. Create a good product structure that gives an early, natural division of the work. A good structure decreases the need for branches. Where branches are still being used, a good structure reduces the risk of conflict at the subsequent merge.

4. Do not use too strict a division of work with people being responsible for individual files or modules. This easily leads to static and inflexible change management where several change requests affecting the same files cannot be managed concurrently, particularly if the same change request might affect areas of responsibility in several places.

12.5 Summary and Conclusions

The three pillars of effective infrastructure management for GSD are (1) communication and collaboration; (2) knowledge management; and (3) software configuration management. An effective communication and collaboration infrastructure must aim at increasing information accessibility to all stakeholders in a disciplined manner and the creation of an environment of participation where all stakeholders contribute to the exchange of information. The centerpiece for the knowledge management infrastructure is the concept of a knowledge base. In fact, this knowledge base need not consist of a single tool, but can be created from a set of tools that integrate well (Gersmann, 2005). As far as software configuration management is concerned, Estublier (2000) observed that better and more flexible process support was the feature most missed in the majority of CM tools, as nearly every CM system relies on its own predefined and inflexible product life cycle. And this is what makes SCM for GSD more challenging. Just like technology is meant to serve a business need, the CM infrastructure would not meet its objective without being coupled to a process that is meaningfully defined and diligently executed. A good strategy during any development is to try to limit the dependencies between the developers, especially if they are situated in different locations. This is often mainly done during the structuring (architecture) of the product to be developed. The system is divided into modules or components, which are then developed by different groups separately. However, it turns out that despite good structuring, dependencies between the components remain. This becomes clear when interfaces must be modified or when the components will be integrated. These are examples of situations when one (although one has tried to avoid it) requires an overview and synchronization between the groups working on different components (Asklund et al., 1999).

12.6 Discussion Questions

1. What are the three pillars of infrastructure management for GSD?
2. When should the infrastructure for a GSD project be set up? And how long is it necessary to maintain it?
3. In the context of GSD, is a CM tool supporting a regimented workflow better or a tool that supports the definition and maintenance of a flexible process? Why?

References

Asklund, U., Magnusson, B., and Persson, A., "Experiences: Distributed Software Development and Configuration Management," Lund University, Lund, Sweden, 1999.

Estublier, J., "Software Configuration Management: A Roadmap," *Proceedings of the Conference on The Future of Software Engineering*, Limerick, Ireland, 2000, pp. 279–299.

Fowler, M. and Foemmel, M., "Continuous Integration," Retrieved 09/27/2005, 2005, from http://www.martinfowler.com/articles/continuousIntegration.html.

Gersmann, S., "Development of Strategies for Global Software Development," Technische Universität München (Munich, Germany) and Siemens Corporate Research (Princeton, NJ), Masters Thesis, 2005.

Herbsleb, J. and Moitra, D., "Global Software Development," *IEEE Software*, 18(2): 16–20, 2001.

Paulk, M., Curtis, B., Chrissis, M.B., and Weber, C.V., "Capability Maturity Model for Software, Version 1.1," CMU/SEI-93-TR-024, 1993.

Perry, D.E., Staudenmayer, N.A., and Votta, L.G., "People, organizations, and process improvement," *IEEE Software*, 11(4): 36–45, July/Aug. 1994.

Tellioglu, H. and Wagner, I., "Negotiating Boundaries — Configuration Management in Software Development Teams," Vienna University of Technology, Vienna, Austria, 1995.

Undrus, A., "NICOS System of Nightly Builds for Distributed Development," CHEP2003, San Diego, CA, 2003.

Chapter 13

Communication

MNC Corporation was six months into a globally distributed software development project when it discovered that a highly complex network of project work processes had taken hold among its six different locations around the world. Software engineers at some locations came to know of their counterparts in other locations, which led to the opening up of innumerable communication channels among them. Frequently, these engineers communicated requirements, agreed on interim deliverables, and created and exchanged software products implementing those requirements. There were, however, some locations where the engineers kept to themselves and rarely communicated with their remote counterparts. Their understanding of the work allocated to them was fraught with uncertainty, inconsistency, and ambiguity.

MNC Corporation now had a daunting task of streamlining the communication channels. Too much communication, when left uncontrolled, would create an undue overhead and a complex web of work processes; too little communication could stifle information exchange, knowledge sharing, and team building. What is the right balance? How must MNC approach this problem?

This chapter looks at communication drivers and barriers in globally distributed software development projects. Understanding them can provide insight for developing strategies to effectively manage communication between distributed teams and coordination of their activities. Techniques that can be used to track communication between geographically distributed teams to uncover the dependency structure of a development project are also discussed. Critical task dependencies require intense communication, and these techniques allow managers to identify such dependencies and foster richer communication between the collaborating teams.

13.1   Communication Drivers

Task interdependence and organization bond in our experience and also supported by the literature are the key motivating factors for transfer of information among collaborating teams (Sosa et al., 2002). The higher the degree of interdependence among tasks, the greater the need for communication; this need increases even further if such communication is fraught with uncertainty and ambiguity. Under such circumstances, collaborating teams typically interact to:

- *Reduce ambiguity.* In the face of imprecise information, ambiguities must be removed to more precisely define problems or reach consensus on solutions to problems.
- *Maximize stability.* When information is lacking, critical information (as it becomes available) must be communicated to reduce this deficit.

Organization boundaries create a sense of identity among members belonging to the same group. This bond leads to a higher frequency of communication among them, as opposed to members of different groups.

These drivers achieve greater significance in globally distributed software development projects because interrelated tasks performed by members belonging to different geographically distributed organizations can become challenging to coordinate and control.

Tip: Minimize task dependencies.

Managers must identify interrelated tasks and minimize dependencies among tasks performed by geographically distributed groups that have no organizational bond (e.g., no previous history of working together). Software development, especially in the planning stages, is an activity requiring intense communication. Distance between distributed teams, compounded by their unfamiliarity with each other, will make this communication very difficult.

Tip: Facilitate communication between teams with interdependent tasks.

For critical task dependencies, managers must facilitate intense communication among the teams involved. Distance between teams and unfamiliarity among team members may have to be overcome by collocating these teams.

13.2 Communication Barriers

We have found the following factors as hindrances to information exchange among communicating development groups (Sosa et al., 2002):

■ *Physical distance.* Distance negatively impacts communication. The physical separation is, however, most significant for the first 50 meters, after which there is a drastic drop in communication and it is immaterial whether collaborating groups are located in two different buildings, cities, countries, or continents (Allen, 1984).

■ *Overlapping working time.* The probability of synchronous communication decreases with a decrease in the overlap of the working hours between communicating groups. Face-to-face communication drops rapidly, the telephone is used among groups with some overlap in working time, and e-mail is the preferred media when there is no overlap in working time.

Tip: If possible, avoid remote sites with large time zone differences with the central site.

A difficulty with North American central sites working with Indian and Chinese remote sites is the large number of time zones between the sites. This restricts the possibility of impromptu telephone conversations. Even when teleconferences such as daily stand-up meetings are scheduled, it is likely that at least one of the participants will be physically tired. We knew one supplier manager on the east coast of the United States who would call his India-based team before he retired for the evening. He would then call them again upon waking, as they were working while he was sleeping. When problems are arising on the project, it is probably not conducive to restful sleep. For business and market reasons, it may not be possible to avoid these large time zone difference situations. When faced with this situation, try to allocate work packages to the remote site that will not require telephone communications, or set up an organization structure where they will be a satellite organization to another site (e.g., a European site that will overlap work hours with the east coast of the United States and India).

■ *Cultural and language differences.* There is a tendency among humans to seek out similar others with which to communicate. Therefore, two groups have a higher probability of communicating if there are fewer differences in their culture and language. It is also the case that written asynchronous communication media such as e-mail is the choice of collaborating groups with significant differences in language.

Tip: Facilitate written asynchronous communication.

Managers must facilitate written asynchronous communication among collaborating groups where there are significant differences in language. This helps team members in developing personal contacts. These contacts play a significant role in how people obtain information, learn to do their work, and solve cognitively complex tasks. Research shows that documents are of considerably less value, and software engineers overwhelmingly get their information from other people (Kraut and Streeter, 1995). There is, therefore, no substitute for an interpersonal network.

■ *Organizational motivation and trust.* In GSD projects involving products that are likely to replace legacy systems, organizations supporting the legacy systems are less likely to trust their collaborators as they perceive them as a threat to their job security. These organizations are also less likely to be motivated to be enthusiastic participants in the new undertaking.

■ *Personal relationship.* Communication is less likely to occur between collaborating teams unless the team members get to know each other.

In globally distributed development projects, managing activities of groups separated by several time zones with significant differences in culture and language can, therefore, be challenging to coordinate and control.

Tip: Be aware of seasonal work habits across development sites.

Central sites in North America will often be working in time zones near to those of South American sites. However, the seasons may be reversed. Thus, typical vacation time periods, or time periods of high or low productivity, may be out-of-synch between sites. Plan your schedules accordingly. For most places in the world, it is not likely that there will be high productivity or output during the last week of December.

13.3 Communication and Coordination

Communication has been recognized as key to improving product development performance (Sosa et al., 2002). In particular, coordinated teams have a higher level of performance, especially when tasks are interrelated (Kraut and Streeter, 1995; Malone and Crowston, 1994). Yet, as previously mentioned, in GSD projects coordinating interrelated activities that require intense communication can become challenging. Improved communication and coordination can be achieved through the application of the following three concepts from organizational theory (McChesney and Gallagher, 2004).

1. *Coordination theory.* This theory stipulates coordination as the act of managing dependencies among activities. Primitives of coordination theory can be used to identify coordination dependencies and coordination mechanisms for managing such dependencies. Some examples of such dependencies and mechanisms are:
   a. A shared resource dependency, such as a code module, can be managed through the use of a configuration management tool.

    b. A prerequisite constraint dependency, such as approval of a change request before it can be allocated to an engineer, can be managed through the use of a change management procedure.

    c. An accessibility dependency, such as communication of an approved change request to an engineer, can be managed through an automated or manual task allocation system.

    d. A usability dependency, such as the need for a complete specification for a change request, can be managed through the provision and automated enforcement of a standard template for change requests.

    e. A fit constraint dependency, such as daily builds by multiple teams, can be managed through the use of a standard build procedure and software configuration management.

    f. A task/sub-task dependency, such as the breakdown of project tasks into sub-tasks for management of task complexity or task allocation purposes, can be managed through work breakdown structures and PERT/CPM planning techniques.

2. *Communication genres.* These are communicative actions habitually used by members of a community to achieve some purpose. In the software community, for example, meetings and reviews are typically used at various stages in the software development life cycle to approve or provide feedback for the artifacts under consideration.

3. *Collective mind.* Shared understanding is critical for the success of a project; it reflects how well the collaborating teams understand aspects of the problem they are trying to solve. That is, are they focused in the right direction to achieve their common goal? Collective mind theory articulates that shared understanding is fostered through interactions with collocated team members and becomes difficult to achieve in a geographically distributed environment.

Coordination mechanisms from coordination theory and the communication genres are formal communication mechanisms, whereas collective mind is achieved through informal communication. In our experience and supported by the literature, formal communication mechanisms are desirable for routine tasks and are more effective when projects are certain; in the face of uncertainty and incompleteness, informal communication plays a key role (Kraut and Streeter, 1995).

Most software development, unfortunately, deals with ill-defined problems with information that is uncertain, incomplete, and subject to change. The challenge for distributed development, therefore, is to devise efficient and effective means for informal interpersonal communication. This form of communication is more critical in the early phases of software development when the problem to be worked on is analyzed. It is important for all involved to have a common understanding of this problem so they can work successfully toward creating a solution. Once the project is past the inception and elaboration phases, information tends to become more stable and certain, and the need for intense informal communication diminishes.

Tip: Achieve shared understanding among project teams.

Members of the remote teams can engage with the central team during the inception and elaboration phases when requirements are being analyzed and the architecture is created. At the end of the elaboration phase, some of the remote team members are relocated to their home site where they can act as local experts, creating a shared understanding of the requirements and the architectural vision.

During the construction phase, as remote teams are implementing the system, experts from the central team can periodically travel to the remote sites where they engage the remote team members in using the very system they are building. This technique is sometimes called "eat your own dog food." By exercising the real-world scenarios that demonstrate how the system will be used, the remote teams build a better awareness and knowledge of the problem being solved.

Such exchanges of members between central and remote sites are also valuable for face-to-face interactions that help in building interpersonal networks.

13.4 Communication and Control

While good communication and coordination are important for improving product performance, too much communication can be detrimental. Left uncontrolled, it can lead to numerous communication channels among collaborating teams, creating a complex web of project work processes. It can also create situations of overload and misinformation, thus reducing attention on task relevant information. Communication also comes with a cost such as for international telephone calls or airline tickets.

Minimizing dependencies among distributed tasks and facilitating interaction among teams collaborating on highly interrelated tasks can be one

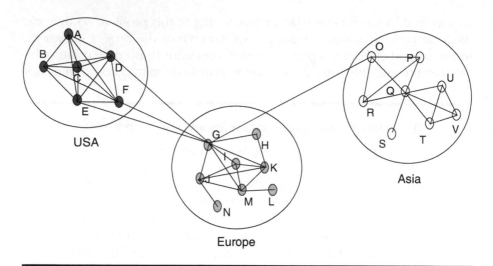

Figure 13.1 Communication patterns between teams at three different locations.

strategy to foster communication in a controlled manner. To achieve this objective, one must be able to track communication among different groups to ensure those groups working on interrelated tasks are interacting adequately. Section 13.4.1 describes a technique for such tracking; it is called "Social Network Analysis" and is beginning to receive some attention in the software engineering community.

13.4.1 Social Network Analysis

Social Network Analysis (SNA) is a survey-based technique that can be used to uncover interactions among groups of individuals (Scott, 1991). A graph called a sociogram is created based on responses to questionnaires focused on how people communicate and the effectiveness of such communication. These graphs can visually depict these interactions, allowing one to see patterns of communication and intervene at critical points, such as those where intense communication is desired. Figure 13.1 provides an example.

The nodes in this graph represent individuals and the edges represent communication paths. Circles have been drawn around clusters to visually highlight areas of intense communication. The sociogram in Figure 13.1 shows many interesting aspects:

- ■ The team in the USA is much more tightly integrated than the teams in Europe and Asia; all members of this team interact with each other.
- ■ The teams in Europe and Asia have members at the periphery who do not interact with most of their team members; on the European team, these members include N and L, and on the Asian team S.

- The Asian team is fragmented; there are really two subgroups — one consisting of O, P, Q, and R, and the other consisting of Q, T, U, and V. Member Q is a possible bottleneck between the two subgroups.
- There are limited interactions among the three teams; more so between the European and Asian teams.
- Member G on the European team is a possible bottleneck, as all communication between the European team and the other teams flows through him.
- If G leaves the European team, it becomes disconnected from the other two teams.

Depending on the nature of the project task allocations and the teams, these observations may not necessarily be bad. However, when collaboration and knowledge sharing are critical to the success of a project, SNA provides a powerful diagnostic tool to managers. SNA can help global project managers in the following ways (Cross et al., 2002a):

- *Promoting effective collaboration within a strategically important group.* As is evident from Figure 13.1, the Asian team has two distinct subgroups within this team. In both the Asian and European teams, it was also observed that certain members were at the periphery and did not connect to most of the members of their respective teams. If these were strategically important teams that needed to function as a single cohesive unit within their boundaries, conducting an SNA would reveal these integration problems.
- Supporting critical junctures in networks that cross functional, hierarchical, or geographic boundaries: Figure 13.1 shows limited interaction between the various groups:
  - The two subgroups within the Asian team show limited interaction, possibly because each represents a different *functional division* within that organization. In large organizations, it is often the case that divisions do not know enough about each other's work and therefore have no idea of how to effectively work together.
  - Physical dispersion of teams across *geographic boundaries* has a similar effect. This is more pronounced with the Asian team; it has very limited interaction with the team from Europe and no interaction with the team from the USA. Language and cultural barriers combined with distance may account for this pattern.
    Although the collaboration across *hierarchical boundaries* is not shown in Figure 13.1, a similar diagram can be created through a survey of top management officials. Such sociograms can show how those in positions of formal authority are embedded within the informal networks, revealing information flows

in and out of this group and how their decisions are influenced by this information. It is conceivable that critical decisions may be biased because the information received by the decision makers comes primarily from a limited part of the organization.

■ *Ensuring integration within groups following strategic restructuring initiatives.* Top executives often resort to restructuring an organization to make it more efficient and effective. Research shows, however, that the performance of an organization does not always improve following such decisions. While this is often attributed to misalignment in the organization's formal structure or failure of leadership, informal networks play an equally important role. In fact, with the trend toward flat organization structures, the rise of cross-functional teams and creation of boundary-less organizations, more and more work occurs through informal networks rather than through formal reporting structures and detailed work processes.

Whatever the cause for lower than desired levels of collaboration, SNA uncovers the patterns, allowing management to begin to diagnose the problem and devise appropriate intervention. This tool becomes highly effective as organizations grow larger and become physically dispersed (imagine three or four levels of hierarchy, 300+ people in two or three different locations around the world). This certainly is the case in global software development projects. Under such circumstances, it becomes very difficult to assess the ways in which work is occurring and decisions are being made without resorting to something similar to SNA.

Tip: Facilitate knowledge sharing and collaboration at specific junctures.

It is not necessary for all members of an organization to be connected to each other through informal interpersonal networks (Cross et al., 2002b); this would not only be cost prohibitive, but would also create an information overload for the members involved. People have a finite amount of time to put into developing and maintaining relationships and, therefore, managers should focus on specific junctures where knowledge sharing and collaboration is desired. In case of problems diagnosed through SNA, techniques such as creating projects jointly staffed by members from different teams, starting new forums for communication such as weekly status meetings or electronic message boards, and financial incentives for the managers of the teams involved can be helpful.

Tip: Watch out for spikes in communication.

Spikes in communication can be early warning indicators for hot spots in your project — where trouble could be potentially brewing. It could be a symptom of the lack of communication or miscommunication between the involved teams — either the required information has not been completely communicated or it has not been properly understood.

13.5 Summary and Conclusions

This chapter discussed drivers and barriers to communication, an activity critical for improving product development performance. Coordination of communication is also significant as coordinated teams have a higher level of performance. Concepts from organization theory, such as coordination dependencies and mechanisms, communication genres and collective mind that help foster improved coordination among collaborating teams, were discussed. Uncontrolled communication can lead to information overload and misinformation. Social network analysis was introduced as a means for tracking communication frequencies for effective management of communication among collaborating groups.

13.6 Discussion Questions

1. What are some of the significant drivers for communication in globally distributed software development projects?
2. List and discuss some of the barriers to communication.
3. How can one achieve better coordination of communication among collaborating teams?
4. What are some of the techniques that help monitor and control communication effectively?

References

Allen, T., *Managing the Flow of Technology: Technology Transfer and the Dissemination of Technological Information within the R&D Organization,* MIT Press, Cambridge, MA, 1984.

Churchill, E. and Halverson, C., "Social networks and social networking," *IEEE Internet Computing,* 9(5): 14–19, 2005.

Cross, R., Parker, A., and Borgatti, S., "Making invisible work visible: using social network analysis to support strategic collaboration," *California Management Review,* 44(2): 25–46, 2002a.

Cross, R., Nohria, N., and Parker, A., "Six myths about informal networks and how to overcome them," *Sloan Management Review,* 43(3): 67–75, 2002b.

Kraut, R. and Streeter, L., "Coordination in software development," *Communications of the ACM,* 38(3): 69–81, 1995.

Malone, T. and Crowston, K., "The interdisciplinary study of coordination," *ACM Computing Surveys,* 26(1): 87–119, March 1994.

McChesney, I. and Gallagher, S., "Communication and co-ordination practices in software engineering projects," *Information and Software Technology,* 46(7), 473–489, 2004.

Scott, J., *Social Network Analysis: A Handbook, second edition,* Sage Publications, Thousand Oaks, CA, 1991.

Sosa, M., Eppinger, S., Pich, M., McKendrick, D., and Stout, S., "Factors that influence technical communication in distributed product development: an empirical study in the telecommunications industry," *IEEE Transactions on Engineering Management,* 49(1): 45–58, February 2002.

Section V

CASE STUDIES

Section V

CASE STUDIES

Chapter 14

GSP 2005

To date, Siemens has executed many software development efforts using distributed teams and understands that there is a large impact of distributing software development on the entire development life cycle, including the management practices (Herbsleb et al., 2005). There are many challenges associated with developing software in a globally distributed setting. Siemens Corporate Research (SCR) is directing its research efforts aimed at developing a better understanding of these challenges and evolve practices for successful management of GSD projects. It has undertaken an experimental applied research project called the Global Studio Project (GSP) that includes the following goals within its scope:

1. Successfully develop the MSLite software system in collaboration with student teams at six universities worldwide. In doing so, document the processes and best practices used, and the issues faced.
2. Collect and analyze data from this project to understand and codify the dynamics of GSD. The specifics of the experimental data to be collected has been established by a team of researchers from SCR, the universities participating in the development of MSLite, Penn State University, the Software Engineering Institute at Carnegie Mellon University, and the Harvard Business School.

The student teams were from: Carnegie Mellon University (CMU), International Institute of Information Technology Bangalore (IIITB), Monmouth University (MU), Technical University of Munich (TUM), Pontifical Catholic University of Rio Grande de Sul (PUCRS) and the University of Limerick (UL).

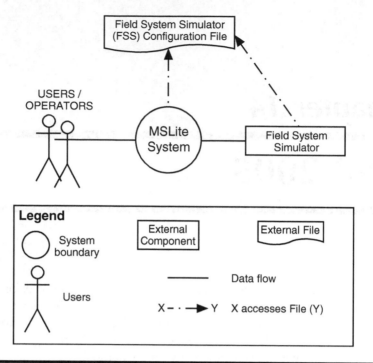

Figure 14.1   Context diagram for MSLite.

14.1   The MSLite Project

The objective of the MSLite project is to develop a unified management station for building automation systems — such as heating ventilation and air conditioning (HVAC), access control, and lighting — that will allow a facility manager to operate such systems. As a practical measure, the building automation systems have been replaced by a home-grown component — the Field System Simulator (FSS), which simulates the building automation domain. Figure 14.1 shows the context of the MSLite system.

A summary of the high-level functional requirements of the MSLite system includes:

1. Manage the field objects (objects in the building automation domain, e.g., HVAC sensors) that are represented in the FSS.
2. Issue commands to the field objects in the FSS to change values of their properties, receiving "Change-of-Value" (COV) events from the FSS to asynchronously update the state of these objects as represented in the user interface (UI).
3. Define logical conditions based on property values of field objects that, when met, trigger reactions and issue commands to field objects.

4. Define alarm conditions akin to the logical conditions that, when met, trigger alarms notifying appropriate users. These alarms then have a life cycle in place that can be managed by users with appropriate privileges.

The MSLite project is structured so as to simulate a hub-and-spoke model, commonly called the "extended workbench" model in Siemens. The hub is the central team at SCR in Princeton orchestrating the effort. Some of its members are student interns. The spokes are the remote teams, consisting entirely of students from different universities at geographically disparate locations from SCR. The central team is responsible for the requirements, software architecture, and some aspects of design, system test, integration, project management, and defining the overarching processes. The remote teams are responsible for design, development, and automated unit tests for well-defined work assignments that correspond to code modules or subsystems defined by the central team during the architecture definition and project planning. The interactions between the central and remote teams are managed by the role of a *supplier manager.* There is a supplier manager for each remote team, and the incumbent of this role is a member of the central team.

Further information on the GSP including a snapshot of the Wiki used by the student teams, is included in the accompanying CD.

14.2 Challenges Faced during First Year of MSLite's Development

The first year of this effort spanned from July 2004 to May 2005. MSLite was organized as sequential time-boxed engineering releases that comprised sets of functionalities that were assumed independent of one another. The development plan was incremental, with additional functionality being added within each build and engineering release. Engineering releases were kept under configuration control and they were made available for system testing within the internal testing group in the central team at SCR. The artifacts to be delivered by each of the remote teams within each release included a statement of work, detailed requirements specification, architectural and design artifacts, unit tests (plans, cases, and reports), and appropriately commented code. All these artifacts were to be specific to the component allocations for a remote team.

While geographically distributed software development presents enormous promise, it also poses challenges, some of which if not managed optimally in a timely manner become insurmountable. The issues faced by MSLite were representative of what Herbsleb and Moitra (2001) categorize as the multiple dimensions of global software development:

- *Strategic issues.* There is no ideal solution to the task of divvying the software into work assignments that will take into account resource availability, the level of technological expertise, and the coupling between software units. The MSLite work allocation scheme in its first year took a much simpler approach and, among other aspects, did not consider the technical skills of the remote teams and dependencies between the architectural elements.

- *Cultural issues.* Culture differs on many critical dimensions such as the need for infrastructure, attitudes toward hierarchy, sense of time, and communication styles (Hofstede, 1997). These differences become barriers to effective communication, as was apparent in the GSP that consisted of six remote teams spanning four continents and five countries.

- *Communication issues.* Software development, particularly in the early stages, requires much communication (Perry et al., 1994). The absence of ongoing conversation leads to surprises from distant sites, and results in misalignment and rework. To substitute informal face-to-face hallway chats, MSLite teams resorted to ad hoc communication mechanisms; there were redundancies in communication imposing an overload on the central team; different communication styles and media were used within the same team at different times, therefore losing out on the consistency of messages. This adversely impacted coordination and control. It became difficult to synchronize the activities of all the teams because of the inability to obtain accurate effort and status information.

- *Knowledge management.* The lack of effective information sharing mechanisms, poorly maintained documentation, and lack of collaboration on artifacts all exacerbate the issue of managing knowledge in a way so as to harness the true potential of GSD. This was evident from the difficulties experienced by the remote teams in understanding the requirements and the architecture. They had not collaborated on the requirements engineering and architecture efforts. From their perspective, the requirements and architecture specifications were too abstract.

- *Project and process management issues.* The lack of synchronization, especially the lack of commonly defined milestones and clear entry and exit criteria across work assignment units, exacerbates the issues inherent to GSD. The remote teams had complete freedom in defining their processes and milestones, which caused difficulties down the road.

■ *Technical issues.* Discrepancies in network capabilities and configurations, incompatible data formats, and different versions of the
same tools are some of the commonly faced technical issues. For
MSLite, each remote team was left to define and set up its own
infrastructure; the development tools available to these teams did
not support concurrent development at multiple sites.

14.3 Approach for the Second Year of MSLite's Development

The issues associated with global development are challenging and the
MSLite project observed most of them during the first year. Operating
primarily with students in academic contexts, it took the central team
some time to experience these issues first-hand and develop the necessary
infrastructure and artifacts for remote development. The next few subsections elaborate the strategy for the second year.

14.3.1 Process

The central team defined the roles and responsibilities for both the central
and remote teams. The central team consists of the following roles (with
some of the characteristic responsibilities for these roles):

■ *Requirements engineer:* maintains the high-level functional requirements, the use case specifications, and the UI specifications; verifies
and validates requirements specifications done by the remote
teams; and maintains traceability between all these artifacts.
■ *Architect:* maintains the system architecture and design; ensures
communication of the specification to the remote teams; verifies and
validates the design specification done by the remote teams (and,
therefore, in the process ensuring the correct understanding of the
architecture); and specifies and maintains the solutions, projects, and
namespaces hierarchy in the selected implementation technology.
■ *Integration engineer* (buildmeister): maintains the code repository
and the automated build environment; maintains and executes
integration test cases; and ensures that the remote teams comply
with the integration process.
■ *Infrastructure manager:* maintains the infrastructure and manages
all infrastructural issues that arise in all the teams.
■ *Wiki administrator:* maintains the wiki templates and structure; and
maintains wiki usage decorum, including verification and validation
of all content on wiki (more on the role of the wiki in the next section).

- *Supplier manager:* manages all interactions with the remote team for which they are assigned; ensures that all communications are maintained over the appropriate mailings; and exercises project managerial and technical compliance control over the remote teams. This role is the primary interface between the remote team and the central team.
- *Quality assurance manager:* creates and maintains the acceptance test cases for each iteration and validates that they are being met; verifies and validates the unit test cases and reports created by the teams; verifies that the important static architectural elements are being reviewed appropriately; and ensures compliance with the defect reporting and tracking process.
- *Process manager:* creates and updates roles and responsibility definitions as and when necessary; defines new processes and maintains existing processes in the processes section of the wiki; and ensures that the central team and the remote teams are complying with the processes defined.
- *Project manager:* maintains and executes the project plan.

The following are the roles for the remote teams and some of their characteristic responsibilities:

- *Developers:* complete all (requirements, design, and development) tasks as defined in the schedule and meet quality objectives; ensure that design decisions are adhered to during development; write and execute automated unit tests; and comply with the integration process. All the remote team members are developers at all times.
- *Team lead:* manages all interactions with the Supplier Manager; and ensures that the team is completing all tasks as specified in the project plan, meeting time, and quality objectives.
- *Requirements engineer:* facilitates team's understanding of all requirements; and ensures that all requirements specification work assigned to the team is being delivered as per schedule.
- *Chief architect:* facilitates team's understanding of the architectural and design specification; and ensures that all specification work assigned to the team is being delivered as per schedule.
- *Quality assurance manager:* responsible for the quality of each commit of code into the repository and for all other artifacts as well; and responsible for attaining the quality metrics defined.
- *Infrastructure manager:* responsible for setting up and maintaining the infrastructure for the team.
- *Process and documentation engineer:* enforces all remote team's role definitions; and enforces disciplined usage of the wiki — will be responsible for all the artifacts delivered by the team on the wiki.

The remote teams decide the incumbents of these roles at the beginning of their engagement. They can change them at any point in time during the project (because they are operating in academic contexts and that requires their exposure to different roles) but update the central team of changes in their team's structure.

The central team has also defined processes that address overarching concerns within the project and the entire organization:

- *Configuration management process:* describes how to use the document and code repository at the central team site.
- *Communication process:* describes the objectives and usage of the various communication media in place, such as the wiki, mailing lists, and conference calls.
- *Design and development process:* defines a road map of the entire design and development process right from point when the central team releases the first draft of the development plan to the point when the remote team delivers the artifacts expected of it and deemed acceptable by their Supplier Manager. This includes negotiation on the contents and the timelines of the development plan, the tasks and artifacts that each remote team must work on during any given iteration, and the criteria for the Supplier Manager to accept the remote team's deliverables.
- *Integration process:* includes the repository structure, the automatic integration environment, and how it works and is to be used by the remote teams. It categorizes changes as isolated or interdependent, and how the remote team developers and the integration manager on the central team should manage changes.
- *Change management process:* defines the process to initiate change requests while publicizing their impact and guaranteeing a certain level of traceability — includes the change management workflow using an automated tool encompassing a voting mechanism that allows the key players to approve a change request assuming "optimistic acceptance of change requests." It supports changes in the requirements, architecture, and design specifications from the central team — aspects that may have impact on the development effort across teams.
- *Defect reporting and tracking process:* categorizes defects as runtime defects, code defects, and document defects and describes the mechanism to submit a defect, assign defects to developers, fixing defects and validating fixed defects using the automated tool.
- *Meetings process:* outlines the structure of the weekly teleconference meetings between the remote teams and the Supplier Manager from the central team. This structure includes templates for the

meeting agenda and minutes to be written by the remote teams. This process also describes what needs to happen before, during, and after the meeting to ensure that each meeting is productive.

■ *Risk management process:* defines the template used for tracking and managing risks affecting the project. All central team and remote team members are expected to add risks to the template, and the central team is expected to use these as a guide and take appropriate actions required for their mitigation.

■ *Team evaluation process:* enumerates how the teams will be evaluated on a weekly basis; and although these evaluations will remain internal to the central team, the two highest performing teams will be acknowledged and rewarded.

14.3.2   Collaboration, Communication, and Knowledge Management

The Achilles' heel for the first year's effort was collaboration and communication; there was no infrastructure that allowed for information and knowledge to be available transparently. The central team is now using a wiki for the project. A wiki is a Web application that not only allows users to add content, as on an Internet forum, but also allows anyone to edit the content. Specifically, the central team decided to use MediaWiki (Figure 14.2) (http://meta.wikimedia.org/wiki/MediaWiki).

The following are the ways in which the wiki is used for collaboration, communication, and knowledge management:

■ *Central artifact repository.* The wiki is the only repository for all project-related artifacts and work assignments to remote teams. The central team's section (entitled "Main Topics") is strictly administered and maintained by the Wiki Administrator. This section is used as the complete, accurate, and up-to-date view of the system being built.

■ *Remote artifact repository.* The wiki is also the only repository for all remote teams' artifacts. The remote teams are encouraged and expected to create their own artifacts and collaborate within the space provided in the "Team Pages" section. Also, the remote teams can use these pages as their workspace for creating artifacts required by the central team before transitioning them to their correct location on the central team's pages. This also ensures complete visibility into everyone's work at any point in time.

■ *Discussions.* Each page on the wiki has corresponding discussion or talk pages. The central team uses these pages to elicit questions, feedback, and issues from the remote teams. These issues are either

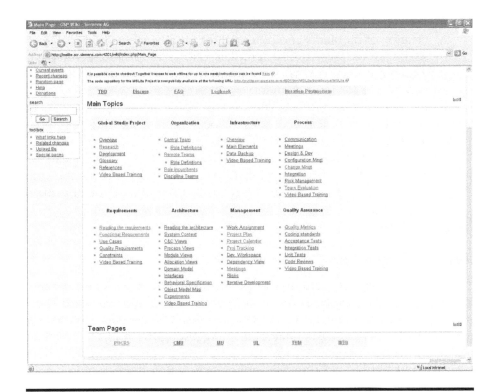

Figure 14.2   The main page of the MSLite Wiki.

addressed immediately by the Supplier Manager or at the weekly
meetings with the remote teams; the remote teams document the
responses or clarifications to these issues. This allows the remote
teams to raise issues as and when they arise, relate them to specific
artifacts on the wiki, and also turn to discussions with other remote
teams for clarifications and guidance, thereby saving the central
team the redundancy of communicating regarding similar issues
with each remote team.

■ *To Be Done (TBD).* When an artifact or a section is incomplete,
this can be easily marked using a predefined "TBD" template.
These show up automatically in the "To Be Done" section, which
is accessible from the main page of the wiki.

■ *Wiki announcements.* When making important or cross-cutting
changes, the central team announces these changes in the "New
& Noteworthy" section on the main page of the wiki. These are
also announced on the mailing lists of all relevant teams. This
feature is used for changes to the wiki itself and not for changes
that influence the requirements, architecture, or design specifications, which are managed under the change management process.

- *Logbook.* The project logbook facilitates open and honest communication of problems and potential for improvements in the project. A simple and easy-to-use template allows all project participants to enumerate problems being faced or areas where they feel there is potential for improvement.
- *Iteration postmortem.* At the end of each iteration, the supplier managers for all teams conduct a post-mortem meeting with their respective team(s) to openly discuss how the iteration was planned and executed and how learning from the first iteration can be applied to the subsequent iterations — these discussions are captured in the section entitled "Iteration Postmortem" on the main page of the wiki.

14.3.3 Requirements

The wiki is the primary medium for specifying requirements specifications. These include the high-level functional requirements, the Use Case specifications, and the UI specifications. The high-level functional requirements are natural language English statements suggesting the primary functionalities of the system available to its user(s). These are grouped into different logical groups based on semantic coherence within these requirements.

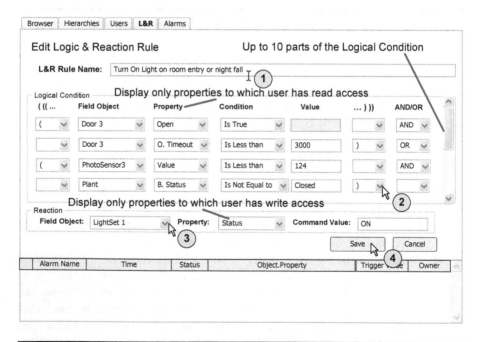

Figure 14.3   An example UI specification.

The Use Case specifications consist of Use Case diagrams in Borland Together segmented into logical packages (based on the groupings in the high-level functional requirements), and Use Case descriptions using the classical Rational Unified Process (RUP) template.

The Use Case steps that are related to functionalities exposed in the UI are hyperlinked to the UI specifications, which are screen mock-ups (made in Microsoft™(MS) Visio) with step markings that denote the sequencing of steps taken by the user on the UI to realize a functionality.

The wiki allows the central team to maintain traceability between these multiple artifacts in an intuitive and usable manner with minimal overhead to the central team. First, the high-level functional requirements are categorized into different groups; each requirement is elaborated into functional specifications; each functional specification is linked to one or more Use Case specifications; steps within a Use Case specification, where appropriate, are in turn linked to elements of the UI specification. Traceability for each high-level functional requirement is also maintained with sequence diagrams and project plan iterations in a traceability matrix (Figure 14.4).

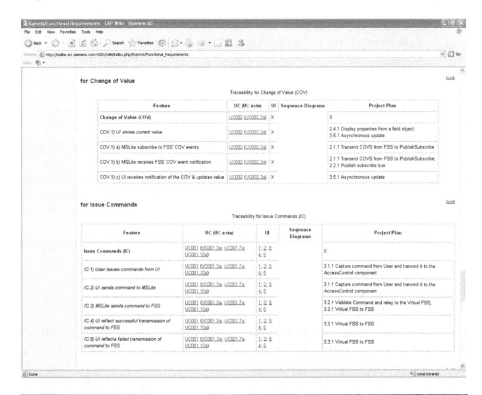

Figure 14.4   Traceability from requirements to project plan.

14.3.4 Architecture and Design

The architecture of the system was identified early on as the centerpiece for success in this project. The central team provides the following different aspects of the architecture (Clements et al., 2002) on the wiki:

- *Component and Connector (C&C) view.* The architectural specification starts with the high-level system context drilling down into the runtime views of the system. This includes the first-level runtime entities in the system (the components and the connectors), and for some of the more important components, a second level of decomposition of the same view.
- *Process view.* The process view is the runtime representation of the processes involved in executing MSLite. The runtime elements show the correspondence between components from the first-level C&C view to processes and how the different processes communicate with one another.
- *Module view.* This is a static view showing the software implementation units (modules) of MSLite and their dependencies.
- *Allocation views.* The deployment view shows a mapping from the software elements from the C&C views to the hardware elements, illustrating how the different subsystems of MSLite are distributed across different machines. The file system view focuses on the structure of the project on the file system that will be used by developers of the project.
- *Interfaces.* These are the publicly visible interfaces of modules describing in detail the parameters and exception conditions.
- *Behavioral specification.* This specification documents how the proposed architecture fulfills the functional requirements. UML 1.5 sequence diagrams have been used to document the behavior based on the module views. The method calls shown in the diagrams are methods in the interfaces of the respective modules.

It is important to note that additional detailed design or rework related to the requirements or the architecture is done in a single place on the wiki.

14.3.5 Technical

Given the importance of a well-integrated infrastructure across multiple sites that span geographical boundaries, the central team has spent considerable energy in creating a pragmatic infrastructural solution. The wiki contains an overview of all the tools and technologies required for the entire duration of the project. It also details the setup required at each of the sites for the project and the usage of the tools.

The central team has chosen open-source solutions for most of its tools because they offer several advantages. These solutions lend themselves better to GSD than some of the commercially available tools; they are available for free, which is a benefit for the remote teams because they are operating in academic contexts; they are available easily and do not require the central team to host them and manage them specially; they also have extensive documentation available that provides adequate guidance on their setup and use.

The central team has obtained the use of the Borland CASE (Computer-Aided Software Engineering) tool suite, which includes the Borland Together Designer and Developer tools that are tightly coupled to the .NET Visual Studio environment and to the .NET platform. Borland has graciously allowed free usage by the students of its tool suite, along with technical training of the central team, which has been video recorded and made available to all remote sites using the wiki.

For some of these infrastructural elements, the central team has put together administration and usage guides on the wiki. Exercises for some of them have also been created — these include exercises on setting up and using the configuration management tool and using the wiki as well. All remote team developers create their own personal pages and team pages on the wiki, which have been structured so as to expose them to features of the wiki they will be called upon to use during the course of the project. The central team has had working sessions that used presentations on the important aspects, such as installing and using the infrastructural elements, process and project management learning from the previous year's effort, and reading the requirements and architectural specifications on the wiki. These working sessions have also been video recorded and made available on the wiki. When remote teams come on board, their initial training exercises include viewing and discussing these video recordings as a team.

14.3.6 Strategic Issues: Planning and Control

Work assignment, project planning, and control are never easy, becoming even more complex when there are geographically dispersed teams. What makes it more difficult is when these teams have different timeframes of engagement and different time commitments during this engagement. The lack of familiarity with the individual members of the remote teams and their specific skill sets further complicates the matter.

14.3.6.1 Work Allocation

The central team has guidelines that it uses to ensure that work allocation is attuned to these complexities of GSD:

■ *Allow teams to become experts in particular functionalities.* Modules are designed and created with high cohesion and low coupling in mind. This reduces the need for remote teams to communicate with each other as they are responsible for a specific module or set of modules that are relatively independent packages of functionality.

■ *Create MSLite using incremental development.* Each iteration results in an executable release of a fraction of the MSLite system. Usually this means that the functionalities are added incrementally in each iteration.

■ *Create MSLite using bottom-up development.* Before developing each module, the modules that it needs as prerequisites should be already developed or under development. The central team has created dependency and timeline views of the system (described later) to achieve this goal.

■ *Avoid requiring teams to learn several technologies.* The central team has created the technology view of the system and assigns work units to teams according to their expertise, thus requiring each remote team to only focus (and therefore specialize) on a core set of technologies rather than work on all the possible technologies during their engagement.

The Design Structure Matrix (DSM) (Browning, 2001) technique has been used to understand and display the dependencies between modules of the system (Figure 14.5).

		1	3	14	4	5	6	15	9	11	16	12	7	10	13	8	2	Number of modules this depends on
Publish Subscribe	1																	0
Command Processing	3																	0
Configuration	14																	0
Value Cache	4	1																1
Data Access	5				1													1
Condition Evaluation	6					1												1
COV Processing	15		1															1
Adapter Manager	9	1	1	1		1		1										5
Property Display	11	1				1			1									3
Alarm Processing	16	1				1			1									3
Alarm Rule Engine	12	1				1	1			1								4
Hierarchy Editor & Display	7					1				1								2
Alarm Display	10					1				1								2
L&R Rule Engine	13	1				1	1		1									4
Rule Editor	8					1						1			1			3
Logon	2					1				1				1	1			4

Number of dependants   6 2 1 1 10 2 1 3 2 2 1 1 1 1 0 0

Legend
1 in bold = uses dependencies
1 regular = regular dependencies

Figure 14.5   The DSM for MSLite modules.

DSM helps in creating a *timeline view* of development for the system — this view denotes the earliest possible period in which a module can be developed right after all its required modules are ready and the latest possible period in which a module can be developed without delaying the development of its dependents, if any.

The *technology view* has also been created, and this provides information about the technologies that each module will require for its implementation. The purpose of this view is to identify how many technologies a development team will have to learn for its work units.

Through multiple views of the development effort, the central team can create an idealized *work assignment view* (Figure 14.6). This view contains:

- Modules assigned to each of the six teams
- Period of time in which a given module must be developed
- Expected functionality at the end of a period based on modules implemented in that period
- Technology that each team must know to implement their modules
- MSLite high-level modules that each team will be involved in implementing
- Length of time (in terms of periods) that teams will need to be involved in the MSLite project
- Time (in terms of periods) available for teams to learn technologies they need to know

14.3.6.2 Project Planning and Control

The central team uses the wiki for project planning and control. Each of the iterations that spans the SDLC has been detailed on the wiki with the following information:

- *Functionality:* the expected (completed) functionality at the end of each iteration
- *Sub-functionalities:* each of the sub-functionalities (primitive functionalities) it would take to complete the main functionality
- *Resources:* teams working on each sub-functionality (this takes into account the multiple different work assignment views created, remote team member skills in all the tools and technologies populated as part of their exercises on the wiki, and the status and level of each remote team's engagement)
- *Delivery date:* for each sub-functionality
- *Description of responsibilities:* includes a high-level description of the tasks; the components, connectors, modules, interfaces, and methods

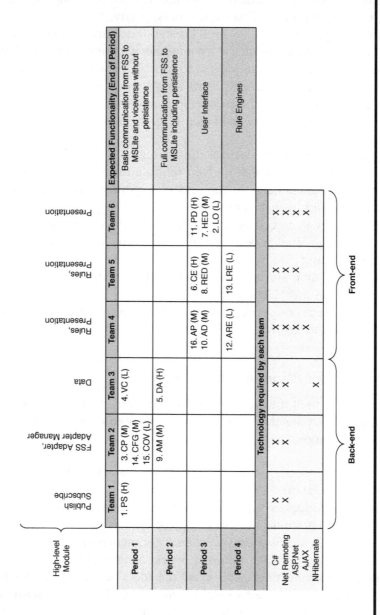

	Team 1 — Publish Subscribe	Team 2 — FSS Adapter, Adapter Manager	Team 3 — Data	Team 4 — Rules, Presentation	Team 5 — Rules, Presentation	Team 6 — Presentation	Expected Functionality (End of Period)
Period 1	1. PS (H)	3. CP (M), 14. CFG (M), 15. COV (L)	4. VC (L)				Basic communication from FSS to MSLite and viceversa without persistence
Period 2		9. AM (M)	5. DA (H)				Full communication from FSS to MSLite including persistence
Period 3				16. AP (M), 10. AD (M)	6. CE (H), 8. RED (M)	11. PD (H), 7. HED (M), 2. LO (L)	User Interface
Period 4				12. ARE (L)	13. LRE (L)		Rule Engines

Technology required by each team

	Team 1	Team 2	Team 3	Team 4	Team 5	Team 6
C#	X	X	X	X	X	X
.Net Remoting	X	X	X	X	X	X
ASP.Net				X		X
AJAX			X			
NHibernate						

Back-end · Front-end

Figure 14.6 Work allocation view for MSLite.

to be developed; the acceptance tests for the sub-functionality; and other miscellaneous information (if relevant) on the technology focus for the sub-functionalities

The project calendar displays the important milestones of the project structured by iteration. The central team has also defined a custom template for project tracking and control. Structured by iterations and further by sub-functionality, this template is used by both the central and remote teams to specify the status of all the prerequisite software engineering tasks required in order to complete their sub-functionality assignments. The template also requires teams to put down the (implementation related) quality metrics (described later) for each of the sub-functionalities assigned to them. The template also shows the status of the acceptance and integration test cases as the deliverables from remote teams are integrated and tested by the central team. The status is maintained not as some percentage indicating the completion of a particular task, but as links to artifacts relevant to the completion of that task. Most of these artifacts are created on the wiki and are organized by high-level modules. For each high-level module, there is a template imposed for defining class diagrams, sequence diagrams, unit test case definitions, code reviews, etc.

With a schedule of weekly meetings between each of the remote teams and their respective supplier manager on the central team, the status of task completion and quality are continuously monitored.

14.3.7 Quality Assurance

There are multiple aspects of quality assurance that are incorporated into project practices and processes:

- *Quality metrics.* These are metrics that have been defined by the central team for deliverables from the remote teams. They have been categorized as defect metrics, review and commenting metrics, process metrics, and overall project metrics. Using a total of 14 metrics spread across these four categories, the teams' deliverables are evaluated by their supplier managers on a weekly basis; and using the team evaluation process mentioned previously, the two highest-performing teams are suitably acknowledged and rewarded on a monthly basis.
- *Coding standards.* The central team has enumerated C# coding standards that are the foundation of the coding guidelines for the development of related artifacts. However, because one of the quality metrics that the remote teams are evaluated against is the number of deviations from the coding standards, they are expected

to either comply with all coding standards or, when the need so arises, update the coding standards using the change management process in consultation with their supplier manager.

- *Acceptance tests cases.* The acceptance test cases are enumerated for each sub-functionality by the Quality Assurance Manager on the central team. These are made available for all sub-functionalities that constitute an iteration before the kick-off of the iteration.

- *Integration tests cases.* Similar to the acceptance test cases, the integration test cases are also defined and maintained by the Quality Assurance Manager for each functionality in an iteration before the beginning of the integration phase for the given iteration.

- *Unit tests and code reviews.* Unit test cases and code reviews are implemented and maintained by the remote teams. Using the template (structured by high-level modules) provided to the remote teams on the wiki, the remote teams document the status of these aspects and have links to the automated unit test classes in the development repository.

14.3.8 Training

Training people on processes, tools, technologies, and about the project in general is an important criterion for success. The ability with which any organization can do so efficiently and effectively is inversely proportional to the degree of geographical dispersion of the team members. Realizing the significance of and the degree of difficulty in achieving this goal, the central team is using a number of different techniques in the second year of this project. Details on every aspect of the project are specified in varying degrees of detail on the wiki using video presentations in most instances. User accounts for the remote team members are created at least a week before the kick-off meeting, and they are requested to start reading through the wiki. The kick-off meeting with any remote team is usually a video-conference, and there is an elaborate checklist that the supplier manager walks through, taking the remote team members on a guided tour of the wiki. Each remote team spends a couple of weeks going through the exercises structured for them to increase their familiarity with the infrastructure, tools, and processes. They then move on to familiarizing themselves with the requirements, architecture, and the project plan. For the teams currently on board, this process has taken, at most, a month before they are up to speed and ready for active development. During this month, the supplier manager helps the remote teams in reinforcing their understanding of the processes and other aspects of the project. So far, the central team has not experienced going back to the drawing board and retraining any given team on any one of these aspects — unless there has been a substantial change in any one of the aspects. In this case, the central team plans time in one of the weekly meetings to dispense all the new and updated information available on the wiki.

14.4 Current Status of the MSLite Development Effort

Currently (as of December 1, 2005), the requirements for MSLite have been baselined. The component and connector, module, deployment and allocation views of the architecture, the high-level domain model of the system, the interface specification (the publicly visible interfaces across components), and the behavioral specification (sequence diagrams across these publicly visible interfaces) are all available on the wiki. These views have been factored into a coherent and manageable project plan. The PUCRS, CMU, and MU teams are on board and engaged in the development of the first iteration. The UL team is being engaged and is currently undergoing its month-long induction and training. The UL team is expected to be involved in the development effort from the second iteration onward.

14.5 Next Steps for MSLite

Looking at the overall goal of efficiently executing geographically distributed projects in a repeatable way, a number of concrete future steps have been identified:

- Include an estimation process and mechanism to be able to better estimate and plan for future iterations.
- Set up the issue tracker, define the issue tracking process, and refine the change management process.
- Understand (and document) the importance of the wiki in the success of the GSD effort, how its usage could be improved, and how it could be scaled up for efficient and effective use in commercial software development projects.
- Gather data using online surveys, the social network analysis, and the automated tool, and perform analyses to identify the issues to focus on and communication patterns that might be of importance in understanding and successfully executing GSD projects.
- Understand and codify how the architecture and its dependencies affect an organization, and vice versa.

References

Browning, T.R., "Applying the design structure matrix to system decomposition and integration problems: a review and new direction," *IEEE Transactions on Engineering Management*, 48(3): 292–306, 2001.

Clements, P., Bachman, F., Bass, L., Garlan, D., Ivers, J., Little, R., Nord, R., and Stafford, J., *Documenting Software Architectures,* Addison-Wesley, Boston, MA, 2002.

Herbsleb, J. and Moitra, D., "Global Software Development," *IEEE Software,* 18(2): 16–20, 2001.

Herbsleb, J., Paulish, D., and Bass, M., "Global software development at Siemens: experience from nine projects," *Proceedings of the 27th International Conference on Software Engineering*, St. Louis, MO, 2005, pp. 524–533.

Hofstede, G., *Cultures and Organizations: Software of the Mind — Intercultural Cooperation and Its Importance for Survival, revised edition,* McGraw-Hill, New York, 1997.

http://meta.wikimedia.org/wiki/MediaWiki

Perry, D.E., Staudenmayer, N.A., and Votta, L.G., "People, organizations, and process improvement," *IEEE Software*, 11(4): 36–45, 1994.

Chapter 15

DPS2000

15.1 Background

Data Processing System 2000 (DPS2000) is a software system used for acquiring and processing meter data from electrical, gas, and water meters. The DPS2000 project was initiated in 1999. The project was previously documented as a Siemens case study (Paulish, 2002). The development was done at four Siemens sites in three countries (Switzerland, Germany, and the United States). The resulting product is currently being successfully sold and distributed. By the usual measures of meeting budget, schedule, quality, and functionality goals, the DPS2000 project was considered successful.

Product development was done iteratively with five initial application packages that were planned for implementation on the DPS2000 platform. An architecture design team was formed, consisting of five engineers with a mixture of domain and architecture design expertise. A chief architect was appointed and the team began the architecture design by analyzing the marketing requirements, developing the conceptual architecture, investigating applicable development technologies, and prototyping. The architecture team consisted of staff from the various development sites who worked in the early phases of the project mainly at the central site. Once development began, the architects worked primarily at their home sites, with frequent meetings that were scheduled at one site when developed subsystems had to be integrated.

15.2 Global Analysis

A global analysis was done for the DPS2000 project as a task within the architecture team. One of the key organizational influencing factors that emerged during the global analysis was that the technical skills necessary to implement the application packages were in short supply within the central organization because prior products had been UNIX based with local user interfaces and the DPS2000 was required to be Windows-based with Web-based user interfaces. The central organization, as frequently happens in Siemens, was an acquired company with a limited technical staff, too small to develop a product platform with the scope of the DPS2000 within the timeframe desired. Thus, a global development was planned to address this influencing factor, such that the required skills would be acquired at three additional Siemens development sites remote from the central site. Also, an additional level of architecture design specification documentation was developed at a lower level than the high-level design. This system design specification concentrated on describing the interfaces between major subsystems of the architecture, and these subsystems were parceled out to the remote software development sites.

Another organizational factor was that management wanted to get the product to market as quickly as possible. Because the market was rapidly changing, it was desired to quickly get some limited features of the product to potential users so that their feedback could be solicited. The strategy planned to address this factor was to develop the product iteratively using time boxing such that scheduled release dates were met even if some features were missing from the release. The DPS2000 project used six- to eight-week development iterations for each engineering release. This iteration duration allowed the development team to provide a reasonable set of features that could be tested and evaluated by the test team.

Many of the practices used on the DPS2000 project are described throughout this book because the project was successful and thus became a studied source of "better practices." One significant process change since this project was executed is the reduction in iteration duration from six to eight weeks to a monthly duration planned as scrum sprints. We have observed that monthly "releases" of development artifacts and code put the project into a development routine and give better visibility into project progress that can be reviewed each month. We do not think the monthly sprints approach is too constraining to a global development project because a development iteration could comprise multiple sprints as long as the iteration duration is on the order of one year or less.

15.3 Design Strategies

Design strategies determine the priorities and constraints of the architecture and help identify potential risks associated with the implementation of the software system. As a result of the DPS2000 global analysis, 24 design strategies were identified that addressed the influencing factors. From these 24 design strategies, six major conclusions were derived and used as guiding principles for the project. One of the six guiding principles was to do multi-site development. This principle is reproduced as described by Paulish (2002) below.

■ *Multi-site development.* The lack of sufficient technical skills within a single location was an influencing factor that was addressed by setting up a multi-site development at four sites within three countries. This put constraints on the design so that components could be more easily distributed for development at multiple locations, and the development environment and tooling was set up for multiple locations.

15.4 DPS2000 Architecture

The DPS2000 architecture was designed such that subsystems could be added at the business logic tier. Furthermore, data acquisition was done by a subsystem that was modified from another Siemens product. Subsystems exchange data through tables in a common database. A summary of the DPS2000 architecture is given in Figure 15.1.

15.5 Project Planning

The DPS2000 software development project was planned as a sequence of incremental engineering releases with increasing functionality. The project schedule was structured such that while in-house testers or users were testing a release, the development team was working on the next release. The release plans were also driven by the dates of industry trade shows, at which time a new release with the latest functionality is required. For DPS2000 project planning, the release dates and iterations were fixed in time, and then functionality for each release was planned into each iteration depending on the bottom-up estimates and testing requirements.

An iterative development process also fits well into a global development project. We found that one of the best means of communication

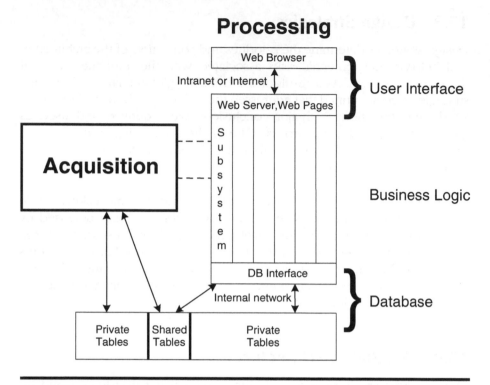

Figure 15.1   Three-tiered DPS2000 architecture. (From Paulish, D., *Architecture-Centric Software Project Management*, **Addison-Wesley, Boston, MA, 2002. With permission.)**

among the teams at the four sites was using the system itself. For example, only after parts of the DPS2000 were prototyped was it possible to fully understand and discuss the requirements. Perhaps this is because the operation of the system itself became a common language for us all. Iterative development also encouraged the developers to quickly learn and start using new technologies because they needed to learn enough to be able to implement even partial functionality.

15.6   Project Management

Each of the four DPS2000 development sites had a local resource manager to manage the team members at that site. There was also an overall DPS2000 project manager and project managers for each software application package development. Thus, there were both project and local site managers responsible for achieving project goals. These managers had to negotiate individual work assignments; for example, if an individual was planned to work on multiple application packages in parallel.

The overall project manager resolved conflicts that could not be handled at a lower level.

The chief architect was responsible for decision making and resolving technical conflicts for the application packages. This was a key role in the project with global authority. In practice, key technical decisions that affected the overall project goals were reviewed with the project and local technical managers before they were implemented.

Each subsystem that was designed and implemented for DPS2000 had a responsible engineer assigned to it. Furthermore, the resources implementing a specific subsystem were collocated at a single site.

Project status tracking was done during weekly teleconferences. Each team member was encouraged to report on their development progress and raise information or issues to be shared with other team members.

The DPS2000 project had approximately 20 software engineers assigned during peak development; thus it was possible for the entire team to report weekly status during weekly teleconferences.

15.7 Lessons Learned

Some DPS2000 team members viewed the development of a system design specification as an unnecessary step that delayed the start of the application packages' implementation. However, newly added development team members working on both the current and new application packages successfully used this specification. It was critical for partitioning work packages across the four development sites. We observed that integration of the various subsystems has gone remarkably smoothly when the subsystem leaders are brought together in one location.

We have had good experiences with the DPS2000 project approach to incremental development. By publishing the URL for the test system physically located in Switzerland, all team members and their management could watch the progress of the development as new features were continualy added. This was a big morale boost for the team, because everyone became aware of the rapid progress that was being made after the high-level design phase was completed and development began. The first engineering release was an implementation of a vertical slice through the architecture. This helped validate the architecture and gave the development team the confidence in and an understanding of the architecture to be able to implement future engineering releases.

Because we put priority on meeting scheduled release dates and traded off functionality and quality as necessary, the development team successfully achieved every release date. This helped build up the credibility of the development team with management because they knew that a new set of functionalities would be ready for validation testing by the dates that were planned and committed to at the beginning of the baselined engineering release cycle. Fortunately, our software quality and system stability remained relatively high throughout the development, so the trade-off between meeting schedule and quality was never seriously challenged.

In the beginning, project meetings were held monthly, rotating among the development sites. Later, meetings were held mainly during major subsystem integrations or when training or detailed design work was necessary to get someone started on a new development task. We had weekly teleconference meetings to track schedule status and to bring up common problems with which developers should be aware. We published the goals of the teleconference in advance, using the techniques we learned to plan and conduct meetings during team-building training.

Two workshops were held with all team members early in the project that, in retrospect, many felt had value to the project. The first was a team-building workshop held at an off-site location in Switzerland. In addition to the usual team-building exercises, specific tasks were addressed, such as developing a standard meeting process for the project. The workshop also included time for individual team members to get to know each other and engage in one-on-one discussions concerning perceptions and differences of opinion.

The second workshop was a multicultural workshop held at the Siemens facility in Princeton, New Jersey. The facilitator of this workshop was trained in the differences among Swiss, German, and American cultures. The response to this workshop was also positive, because the patience of individual team members seemed to grow as they learned more about the different countries' cultures. Development team members grew up in ten different countries, but the workshop primarily focused on the three countries where the development sites were located. One of the outputs of this workshop was to put a larger emphasis on the definitions of the roles and responsibilities of individual team members. This was a result of the realization that certain cultures valued well-defined processes and the position, place, and status of each team member within the project organization. The use of such workshops supports our idea that personal working relationships need to develop among key staff members of the central and remote sites to facilitate communications when things go wrong during the development.

Because software development team members spend large amounts of their time interacting and communicating in meetings, it was important for us to understand the different cultural styles used. Some team members tended to report their progress optimistically, while others were more pessimistic. Some felt uncomfortable or intimidated as different technical approaches were "argued" by proponents. Some contributed to the communications and others did not. What mattered most to management, and what the development team was measured against, was delivering a high-quality product to the market per schedule and budget. Thus, meeting facilitators or team leaders who understood the cultural differences and were able to maximize the outputs of each individual engineer made a good contribution to the project.

Cultural biases on values such as punctuality, perfectionism, work ethic, teamwork, quality, and interaction can often affect project decisions. These biases can either be a strength or a hindrance to project progress. Of course, one of the biggest cultural problems for the global development project manager is holidays. It is difficult to synchronize the work schedules of the central and remote teams, especially if local holidays come up as surprises to the other sites. Time zones present workday communication problems — in this case, a six-hour difference.

Tip: Join frequent traveler programs.

If you are assigned to a global development project it is very likely you will be traveling to some of the remote sites. We think travel and face-to-face communications are necessary for successful global development projects, and encourage project managers to budget sufficient travel money. Nevertheless, you will likely occasionally suffer from jet lag, and may not perform at your peak efficiency when working at remote locations. Thus, join frequent traveler programs and do whatever you can to maximize your personal comfort during such trips and maintain your work efficiency.

15.8 Summary

Despite our best efforts at communicating among the four development sites and our emphasis on design documentation with well-defined interfaces, we experienced that global development was clearly more difficult than single-site development. This was a result of occasional miscommunications caused by different vacations and holidays in the three countries, time zone differences, and occasional network or computer outages. For example, if questions arise for colleagues in Europe during their evening hours while the U.S.-based teams are working, they likely will need to wait until the next day before they can be resolved. To compensate for the unexpected, team members often used the home telephone numbers of their colleagues in the other countries, and the system was rebuilt almost every day in multiple locations using the latest checked source code. We also invested in technical training, team building, and multicultural training for the development team members.

The DPS2000 platform is designed to be very flexible and expandable to handle a wide variety of applications. This was a primary design requirement, because the power distribution industry is rapidly changing as a result of worldwide deregulation. The diversity of our development team members with differing skills and experience helped us achieve a flexible design. For this project, the contributions of a global development team added to the attractiveness of a global product offering.

References

Paulish, D., *Architecture-Centric Software Project Management*, Addison-Wesley, Boston, MA, 2002.

Chapter 16

FS2000

FSI was a highly successful company that provided software solutions for the banking industry. Over time, it noticed a gradual change in this industry's business model. Independent banks, mortgage lenders, investment companies, and insurance providers were gradually merging to form large, integrated financial services networks. Customers could now walk into any financial institution within such a network for a particular financial product and be easily offered other products and services. Once they had an account with one institution, there was no need to open separate accounts with other institutions within the same network. This account served as a single repository for a customer's entire fiscal portfolio, making it possible for them to receive one statement rather than a multitude of statements for each individual financial product.

FSI saw this as a business opportunity for a new software solution — a single financial information system (FS2000) allowing seamless integration and flow of information across the entire enterprise. It formed a research and development (R&D) team of domain experts and software architects to immediately start work on this new product.

16.1 Requirements for the New Enterprise

The domain experts and software engineers working on the team were very familiar with the old banking business model and had their experiences grounded in the stovepipe systems the company had built to serve the needs of independent banks, mortgage lenders, investment companies, and insurance providers. They looked at the new opportunity as one of creating integrated workflows that moved and made customer information available across the enterprise seamlessly. Because each financial institution had variations in the workflows and how they accessed and displayed information, it was important to create flexible and adaptable mechanisms for business process and user interface specifications.

The company did not bring in domain experts with experience with the new business model thinking they had deep knowledge of the domain in house. Barring a few new functions, the project team considered the functional requirements as largely the same; just the nature of how and where this functionality could be accessed needed to be flexible.

Because the team of domain experts and software engineers was fairly small, it was not considered necessary to create any formal requirements and domain model. Informal brainstorming was used as the primary mechanism to drive all the work.

As a result of this organization make-up and work culture, there were a number of consequences. The first and foremost: while the company's vision and the market opportunity were excellent, realization of a flexible, integrated system alone was not sufficient. There were many market segments ranging from small to very large customers; the system necessitated the ability to scale to their needs. Some of the larger customers were highly distributed with offices spanning multiple time zones; the system had to take into account this distribution when deployed in the field. The smaller customers did not want the full capability of the new system; the system required decomposition into components providing flexibility to deploy the system in an incremental fashion. Most customers did not want to take on the responsibility of managing their own systems; the system had to be deployed and managed in a cost-effective manner from the company's own data center. There were a number of business processes that were mission critical for the customers; the system had to ensure their high availability.

The second and more significant drawback was that by not capturing the domain knowledge and the associated requirements, they could not be easily communicated. The impact of this issue was to be felt very shortly; FSI was acquired by MNC, a multinational corporation!

16.2 Scaling the Development Process

MNC saw FSI's strategic initiative as a significant complement to their existing products and services, thus enabling them to provide a total solution for the needs of financial institutions around the world. Moreover, FSI would allow them to gain a significant market share in North America.

Once the acquisition was complete, MNC wanted to expand the scope of FS2000; MNC wanted to internationalize it. It was MNC's impression that the flexibility envisioned in FS2000 would allow them to adapt it for any region around the world.

MNC also brought along with it a global force of software engineers. This, it was thought, would allow them to launch a highly parallel development effort, considerably shrinking the time-to-market. In addition to teams already in place at different locations within the United States, MNC mobilized software development teams from multiple different locations in Norway, Sweden, Germany, the United Kingdom, and India. Requirements were functionally decomposed into modules and distributed around the world for development. Subject matter experts in the United States carried out analysis and design. Development occurred at the remote sites in other countries, and integration of the developed modules took place back in the United States.

However, there was neither a formal set of requirements nor domain models that systematically captured the variability and extensibility within the FS2000 solution. In their absence, the FS2000 project teams created a highly flexible solution that allowed specification of any business process and the display of its associated information on the user interface. The declarative nature of these specifications caused the teams to write an interpreter. As the specifications grew more and more complex, so did the interpreter, ultimately causing the entire framework to become rather costly to test, debug, maintain, and support. The solution also performed poorly.

Meanwhile, the project teams continued to grow to speed up the development process. This created long communication paths between the central location in the United States and its remote development sites. Therefore, on any issue at hand, managers had extreme difficulty achieving a shared understanding among and coordinating the activities of the affected parties.

MNC was eager to move forward and thought it could start an evolution project to capture the domain knowledge and the requirements for FS2000. The captured knowledge could facilitate communication and help with the difficult task of knowledge transfer to its remote teams. This is when MNC ran into another roadblock. To MNC's disappointment, there was very little in the existing documents to give any insight into how FS2000 was put together. It was also discovered that the project team for FS2000 was, in reality, functioning as multiple different mini project teams, each focusing on its areas of expertise with little or no communication among them. This had led each team to consider the enterprise workflow in just its own area, with no thought given to how everything would be integrated into a single FS2000 solution. Worse yet, each of the teams was using its favorite set of technologies to create the workflows.

16.3 The Architecture

While trying to make sense of FS2000, MNC's VP for R&D had an idea: why not start harvesting reusable components from the existing implementation and grow the system one component at a time? A chief architect was appointed and an effort was launched to figure out the smallest configuration of components that could be sold in the market.

The chief architect approached the product management group with this question of what was the smallest saleable configuration. To his surprise, the product management group had never been engaged in the FS2000 project. The sole strategy of this group was to resell the new solution into its existing customer base when it was ready. No attention was given to the needs of smaller customers because FSI, the acquired company, always sold its solutions to large customers. FS2000 was considered as a single monolithic solution and thus the group never considered incremental delivery of the solution by selling its parts.

While disappointed in the news it received from its chief architect, MNC's management was not about to give up. Perhaps by some stroke of luck there would be common assets shared across the entire suite of functionality bundled into FS2000. That could make for a good starting point.

The chief architect plowed along prodding the R&D group to understand the architecture. Each mini-team within the FS2000 virtual R&D team had evolved its part of the solution using its own paradigms and favorite technologies. The best documentation available to the chief architect was a set of PowerPoint slides. Thus, the effort in identifying common assets became an exercise in documenting the architecture.

Not ready to give up just yet, MNC directed its chief architect to complete the architecture documentation to gain insight into an approach to unifying the disparate efforts within the R&D team to achieve a truly integrated FS2000 solution. After several months of hard work, there was more disappointing news: each area of expertise had put together its part of the solution using its own data model. On closer examination, similar concepts were represented differently in each data model. There was no common understanding and agreement on a concept, even as basic as a customer account. MNC now realized it had a tedious problem on hand.

16.4 Restructuring the Organization

MNC observed that there was very little commitment among members of the FS2000 team to collaborate with each other. It turns out that FS2000 was a virtual project with members from different parent organizations representing each of the areas of expertise. They were all serving their respective parent organization's interest, with very little incentive to work toward the unifying vision. Because the vision was never articulated, domain models were never created, and requirements were never captured, they all had a fragmented and incoherent understanding of what FS2000 was about. A different organization structure was needed.

MNC first ensured that the product management group did due diligence in analyzing the market. They defined the products for different market segments along with the minimal configuration of the FS2000 that could be sold. They also defined an incremental evolution of the minimal configuration to a full-scale FS2000 solution.

The company also created an independent strategic architecture group consisting of key domain experts and software architects headed by an R&D manager. This group was chartered to come up with a common, well-documented architecture for the entire family of products within the FS2000 family. This architecture was to identify common assets across this family, and the group was to manage their development.

Separate groups were set up for individual products within the FS2000 family headed by product managers overseeing the analysis and design of their respective product functionality. The functionality was to be decomposed into small, manageable, well-defined components whose development was to be highly parallelized using teams of software engineers from MNC organizations around the world.

The integration of the product components to create solutions for different market segments was the responsibility of the strategic architecture group.

16.5   Achieving Integration

The FS2000 project team was not only fragmented along the areas of specialization, but being new to the object-oriented programming paradigm, led them to many pitfalls. They followed the notion of object decomposition quite well but never aggregated related classes into components with well-defined interfaces, thus hiding these classes from the outside world. This led to extensive coupling among most of the classes, creating a monolithic solution that was both rigid and fragile. A lack of modular code made it difficult to create configurations of components that could be sold in the marketplace as fully functional products.

The newly formed strategic architecture group was challenged by this fragmentation of the FS2000 solution along areas of specialization and its monolithic nature; each area of specialization in itself focused on modules that were rather large even for a single project to manage. It had to ensure that the direction the group chose to end this fragmentation and creating a more manageable modular solution would not only have across-the-board support, but also would be an enabler for creating a shared architectural vision.

The group decided on the standard J2EE platform. This choice was based on multiple reasons. First and foremost, the group thought the use of standards would be welcomed by the different product organizations that previously were engaged in debates over whose architecture was better and spent an inordinate amount of time coming up with the rationale for their choices.

Second, the group thought it best to use the company's energy on its core competency, which was creating solutions for the financial domain and not create technical frameworks for product development that could easily be bought in the market. This would allow the company to focus on innovation and field new products with a shorter time-to-market.

Third, in a highly distributed product development environment leveraging teams from around the world, a standards-based choice would achieve a shared understanding of the architectural vision much more quickly. At least for the aspects of J2EE used in FS2000, face-to-face meetings and costly travel around the globe could potentially be avoided.

Finally, the product teams could use standard J2EE patterns for product design and development. Some legwork would, however, be necessary to ensure a more manageable modular solution.

16.6 Lessons Learned

The most significant issue faced by MNC when it acquired FSI was the absence of well-documented requirements and a domain model. Not having these artifacts created two major problems. First, FSI completely missed the mark on two extremely important quality attributes when modeling a product family — variability and extensibility. While FS2000 was a flexible and adaptable solution, its flexibility and adaptability were limited to the North American market. MNC had a difficult time understanding how it could easily extend the scope of this solution to other international markets. Second, and more importantly from a global development standpoint, it was not clear how to accomplish the difficult task of knowledge transfer to remote teams in the absence of such artifacts.

Also, FS2000 did not have a well-documented architecture. In fact, there was not a single architecture, but disparate architectures for each of the products within the FS2000 family. Moreover, FS2000 lacked a modular design, making it difficult to separate core assets that were common across all products in the product family. It also made it difficult to come up with configurations of components that could result in fully functional solutions for customers ranging from very small to very large financial institutions. It also precluded MNC from having a strategy in which solutions could be built in an incremental fashion through aggregation of components over time. The most significant impact of this on global development was that the lack of architecture documentation made it difficult to disseminate and create a shared architectural vision across remote teams; and the monolithic nature made it not only difficult to distribute the development of FS2000, but also the large size of modules corresponding to different areas of expertise and the dependencies among these modules made it difficult to manage their development.

The organization structure surrounding the research and development effort of FS2000 was also inadequate. The R&D team was a virtual team with no incentive to realize the vision for the new solution. Individual team members were biased toward their parent organization, leading to mini project teams that coalesced around their areas of expertise and creating a stovepipe effect that the FS2000 was supposed to avoid. The matters became even worse as the number of team members working within an area of expertise grew. The communication paths within and across teams became rather long. This made it difficult to coordinate the activities of and achieve shared understanding among the teams.

16.7 Summary

For the case of the FS2000 project, the large size of individual components, the large number of individual domain-specific teams, and the very large overall project size caused complications for global development. Furthermore, the lack of documentation of requirements and architecture caused difficulty in creating a common vision and communicating such a vision to new software engineers who were added to the project after the acquisition of FSI. This case study reinforces our notion that smaller projects are usually better projects. However, the new enterprise requirements require a scalable, highly variable FS2000 product, which leads to complexity. The project team is currently defining a new architecture and exploring ways to refactor existing applications code to divide them into smaller components that can be integrated within a new framework.

Chapter 17

BAS

The Building Automation System (BAS) is a management and control system for monitoring devices within a building or campus of buildings. The BAS is used for managing diverse building automation applications such as heating, ventilation, air conditioning, security, fire, access control, and intrusion.

17.1 Background

The BAS project and earlier management station projects have been previously documented as Siemens case studies by Herbsleb (2005). The development was done at seven Siemens sites in seven countries (Switzerland, Germany, Italy, Australia, Slovakia, India, and the United States).

This case study describes practices used during the inception and elaboration phases of the BAS project. During the inception phase, a small architecture design team was formed, consisting of architects from the various sites. The team worked at a central site in the United States, using a schedule of three weeks working at the central site and then two weeks back at their home office. The architect from Australia relocated to the United States for the duration of the inception phase. The architecture team did the global analysis, analyzed high-level requirements, developed a conceptual architecture, and had an architecture review at the end of the phase. In addition, a project manager performed some schedule and effort estimates to develop the product, based on the conceptual architecture.

During the elaboration phase, the team was expanded to cover product requirements, requirements engineering, architecture design, program management, user interface design, process definition, and prototyping. During this phase, more of a "virtual team" approach was used, wherein team members mainly worked at their home offices and attended meetings that were periodically scheduled at various sites. For example, the program management team met monthly, rotating between the Switzerland and U.S. sites. Staff from the offshore sites, where the majority of the development was anticipated to be done during the construction phase, relocated to the U.S. site where they were engaged in prototyping activities and were "trained" by the central architecture team on the architecture and the business domain.

17.2 Global Analysis

A global analysis was done for the BAS project as a task within the architecture team. One of the key organizational influencing factors that emerged during the global analysis was that the software development staff required to implement the BAS within the time desired was greater than the staff available. Although many development sites were interested in contributing to the BAS, even together the number of software engineers who could work on such management stations was insufficient. This staff shortage was primarily due to the difficulty in freeing up staff who were already working on revenue-producing projects using legacy products. Furthermore, there was an influencing factor of a desired short time-to-market that tended to make the development team size requirements larger as compared to earlier management station development projects. Thus, a project strategy was identified early on that the offshoring of development resources would be necessary.

The BAS required that multiple application disciplines be integrated to run on a single workstation platform. Because these disciplines were implemented as individual competence centers among the company's development sites, this resulted in a project strategy to utilize domain experts from among the distributed company sites. Thus, it was known up-front that staff from multiple Siemens development sites would be needed to implement the BAS.

Many of the practices used on the BAS project are described throughout this book, especially the use of supplier managers to help manage the resources at the remote development sites. Because the project is ongoing, it will not be known for quite some years if the practices used will result in a successful project and a good product. However, many of the practices used during the inception and elaboration phases we consider better practices and they were, in turn, based on practices used in prior projects.

17.3 BAS Architecture

The BAS architecture was designed such that components could be developed by distributed teams and fit within an architecture framework. Applications and migrations to legacy products would be done by the competence centers. Offshore sites will be developed into competence centers over time; but in the early development iterations, they would develop infrastructure-like components to build up the platform. Thus, the resulting architecture was very modular because global development was anticipated from the beginning. Furthermore, architects were asked to keep the component size small. Specifically, the architects were asked to keep the maximum component size to less than about 60 KLOCs of C# code. This was based on the desire to keep the remote component development team sizes small.

A high-level description of the BAS architecture is given in Figure 17.1.

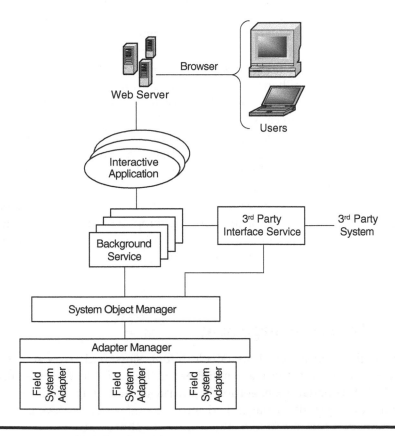

Figure 17.1   BAS high-level architecture.

17.4 Project Planning

Project planning was done using the estimation practices described in Chapter 8. The project manager worked closely with the chief architect to develop code size estimates for each component that was expected to be implemented for the product during the construction phase. The anticipated development project was divided into iterations, and effort estimates and average team sizes were determined for each component. The components were allocated to iterations and to the expected development sites. In-house resources were identified for about half the development tasks needed. The other half were assumed to come from offshore sites, and considerable planning effort went into qualifying those offshore sites and bringing key staff into the central team during the early phases such that they could become leaders of the remote component development teams.

There was considerable effort put into exploring reuse candidates for acquiring rather than building some of the components needed. These investigations brought up many questions concerning functional and technology fit; but because of the large shortfall of available resources, every effort was made to find suitable components to be reused or slightly modified for reuse rather than building everything from scratch.

Also, due to the large shortfall of available development resources, multiple offshore sources were pursued. Although it was well recognized that adding additional development sites created complexity for managing the project, it was felt that using two offshoring companies would help minimize political risk and provide additional flexibility if and when large numbers of developers were required.

With both of the offshore sites and a third internal site, pilot efforts were initiated in advance of full-scale development. These pilots helped debug the global development processes to be used during the construction phase. The sprint goals were identified for each month during the four-month pilot period.

17.5 Project Management

Each of the anticipated BAS development sites had a local resource manager to manage the team members at that site. There was also an overall BAS program manager leading a program management team. The central development manager had supplier managers working for him who managed the interface to the remote offshore sites.

The chief architect was responsible for technical decision making and resolving technical conflicts. This was a key role in the project with global responsibility. There was also a chief requirements engineer responsible for modeling and analyzing requirements that originated from a marketing team that generated stakeholder requests across the various application disciplines.

Each BAS component assigned to a remote development team for the pilots also had a focus team consisting of a central requirements engineer, a central architect, and the supplier manager for that site. This focus team defined the sprint goals for the remote component development team but the remote team did the planning to meet the sprint goal.

Project status tracking was done during monthly program review meetings that alternated between the U.S. and Swiss sites. The review meetings were scheduled for multiple days and included status and informational meetings with top management and team-building social events.

17.6 Lessons Learned

Many of the lessons learned on the BAS project had to do with communications among the distributed team members. Early on, the architecture team used three weeks at the central site and then two weeks at their home office schedule. This worked relatively well, and the team was able to organize collaborative type tasks (e.g., design meetings) and work-alone type tasks (e.g., writing the architecture description) into these timeframes. Each team member of this small architecture design team had a place to sit and work at the central site and a dedicated conference room for design meetings. Thus, the maximum physical distance between the team members during the three-week on-site time period was probably less than 15 meters; and as a consequence, there was a high degree of communication among the team members. Furthermore, when at the central site, team members would periodically meet for dinner, when the local staff would host the remote staff at various restaurants in the area. The architecture team was led by a chief architect who would facilitate work assignments and determine what design decisions were made versus which issues remained open. We have observed that architecture design work is never ending and that time boxing is required to effectively make design decisions (Paulish, 2002). An effective chief architect knows when to cut off discussion and make a design decision and when to encourage discussion for further consideration of alternate designs.

A project manager worked with the architecture team and developed estimates of the development effort and schedule. It became apparent early on that the scope of the desired product was such that the BAS project was likely to be bigger than earlier projects that the organization had undertaken. The project manager used the marketing requirements, the architecture description, cost estimation tools, and historic size, schedule, and effort data from earlier projects to develop these SWAG estimates for the product development cost and schedule.

Later on, when the project team was expanded to include activities such as requirements engineering, test planning, process definition, integration planning, prototyping, and user interface design, the teams were set up as functional organizations consisting of staff from the various development sites. Thus, the teams became geographically distributed and had relatively more communication, coordination, and efficiency problems as compared to the earlier three-weeks-on, two-weeks-off approach. During this time, team meetings were held periodically and rotated among the various development sites. It was observed that general productivity was not as good as compared to the small team sitting within 15 meters of each other during the three-week time periods at the central site. Rotating the meetings at various sites meant that some of the members were jet-lagged, and they struggled with physical issues that affected their degree of alertness, patience, etc. Because the team meetings extended over multiple days, visiting team members would often try to schedule the trip for one week. Depending on the schedule, this often meant weekend travel, which impacted family time for team members with spouses and children. To avoid this loss of family time, some team members would get off a transcontinental flight and go directly to their meeting. In some cases, loss of sleep would make such meetings physically difficult.

After some time, it was recognized that collocation of team members was necessary to enhance the communications among the team members working on such collaborative early phase activities. However, relocating staff to a central site was complicated due to financial constraints and personal constraints of key team members. The other issue resulting from highly distributed teams is that when team members were at their home offices, they would often get called on to help out on prior legacy products. Thus, not only were these staff members remote from the central site, but they would often become part-time to the BAS project. After some time it was decided to collocate key team members at a central site, but the project schedule was disturbed as candidate lists were created and individual discussions were held concerning the relocation of staff to foreign countries. From this case study and others, we believe that certain early phase software engineering tasks that are highly collaborative, such as architecture design, require a collocated small team similar to we had earlier during the schedule of three weeks on working at the central site.

Because we had two Siemens software companies providing offshore resources in Slovakia and India, it was easy to observe the differences in practices used by these suppliers. We required that key people from the remote sites work at the central site during the early phases so that they would be "trained" to lead the component development teams back at their home site during the construction phase. We observed the value of such collocation and did not resent the additional costs associated with relocating someone from a low-cost country to the United States. What was different between the two supplier companies was the amount of support they gave the staff working at foreign sites. One supplier relocated not only the engineer, but also his family for the six months of this "training" assignment. Thus, with his family nearby, there was less need to return to the home site. The other supplier relocated just the engineer, with his family remaining at home. This was not as good a practice as viewed by the central site members because the engineer was often returning home for holidays and family visits. In the worst case, this situation would degrade to the three-weeks-on, two-weeks-off approach that was used by the initial architecture team. Such relocation approaches depend on the individual situations and type of work, but we considered the relocation of families for six months or more as a better practice for this project.

As with the GSP, we did a Social Network Analysis (SNA) (see Chapter 13) on this project. Social Network Analysis looks at the communications patterns between team members across all the sites of the project. The input to the SNA is an organization chart with the names and work locations for each team member. A Web-based survey is set up for each team member to describe his communications with the project team. The survey takes about ten minutes per team member to complete, so it is a relatively lightweight data collection approach. The results of the analysis are network diagrams showing the communications connectivity among the team members. Although the BAS SNA results were not much different than other distributed projects, it became clear that additional and more efficient communications among team members within a site and between sites would benefit the project. One key observation was that only about half of the staff assigned to the project and appearing on the project organization chart were working full-time on the project. The combination of part-time and remote staff creates difficulties for a central site project manager to plan work and execute the project to plan.

Tip: Beware of virtual teams.

Certain early phase activities such as architecture design require a large amount of communications among the team members to complete the work. Such teams are typically small but are made up of experts with different specialized skills. Thus, exchange of information among the team members is necessary to incorporate the diverse skills. When such teams are not collocated, it creates longer communication paths, and either the productivity of the team or the quality of the output of the team can be negatively affected. Furthermore, such experts are valuable sources of information to the organization, often with many years of experience. When such experts are physically located at a remote site within their home organization, they will often be interrupted with questions from staff working on legacy products. Thus, virtual teams are generally not amenable to achieving time-boxed, intense, early phase work where expertise and experience are shared by communication among the team members.

17.7 Summary

Although the BAS project is ongoing and it is difficult to determine whether or not it will be successful, a number of better practices can be observed concerning communications among team members within a large, widely distributed project team. Certain early phase activities such as architecture design must be done at one site to enable rich communications among the team members. Time boxing must be used to force decision making and demonstrate project progress. Part-time resource allocations in key project roles can be detrimental to project progress, especially when they are sitting remote from the central team.

References

Herbsleb, J., Paulish, D., and Bass, M., "Global software development at Siemens: experience from nine projects," *Proceedings of the International Conference on Software Engineering (ICSE 2005)*, 2005, pp. 524–533.

Paulish, D., *Architecture-Centric Software Project Management*, Addison-Wesley, Boston, MA, 2002.

Section VI

CONCLUDING
REMARKS

Chapter 18

Conclusions

Software development is inherently complex. For more than a decade, studies performed by the Standish Group have been reporting that a large percentage of software projects fail or do not meet their budget, schedule, and functionality goals (Johnson, 2000). Distributing software development across multiple sites in different countries and time zones adds further to this complexity.

This chapter summarizes the issues that surround globally distributed software projects. The core beliefs described throughout this book are summarized to illustrate how one can successfully develop software using geographically distributed teams. Readers are encouraged to capture and describe their own best practices, and the importance of experimentation in this area of software engineering is emphasized.

18.1 Issues in Globally Distributed Development

The economics of software development are pushing business organizations to a globally distributed approach. Lower paid software engineers living and working in certain parts of the world are being included in distributed projects as a way to get products to market more cheaply or to get more products to market more quickly. Communications resources and technologies such as the Internet are enabling collaboration among distributed software engineers through electronic means. As discussed in the opening chapter of the book, some of the major business drivers for globally distributed software development include (Carmel, 1999):

- Limited trained workforce in technologies that are required to build today's complex systems
- Availability of low-cost software engineers in countries such as India, Brazil, China, and in eastern Europe
- Possibility for "follow the sun" development with engineers working in different time zones
- Advances in communications and software development infrastructure and technologies

Although there are strong business reasons to distribute software development, software project managers now have people working for them in foreign countries whom they have never met, and they do not have the opportunity to "look over their shoulders" to check on the quality of their work or the progress of development. Gone are the days when a software project manager could "manage by walking around (MBWA)." Furthermore, because remote staff is cheaper and relatively plentiful, today's software project managers are probably managing larger projects than they are used to. Bigger projects with more staff involved, large lists of features to be developed, and short-time-to-market goals increase project complexity and the associated risks with achieving a successful implementation.

As pointed out throughout the book, there are many potential pitfalls facing the software project manager involved with global development (Mockus and Herbsleb, 2001):

- Interdependencies among work items and difficulties of coordination among different distributed development sites may arise if the architecture of the system does not promote the assignment of relatively independent modules or work packages to remote sites.
- Coordination becomes an issue because of process non-uniformities: for example, variances in the definition of a unit test may cause mismatched expectations and conflict, a slip in schedule at one site may affect other sites, but it is often not communicated early enough, or the differences in time zones may lead to more frequent work handoffs as in follow-the-sun development.
- Building a "shared mental model" of the product to be developed is more complicated across multiple sites. This takes longer to communicate and formulate a common understanding because remote teams understand it mainly through specifications, e-mail, and telephone discussions. The possibilities to drop in on the chief architect where he sits, ask some questions, see a product demo, etc. are limited for remote developers such that a shared vision is more difficult to formulate.

- There are infrastructural differences in different development locations, including network connectivity, software development environments, test and build labs, and change and version management tools and processes.

Potentially, the largest pitfalls are issues related to communication across sites because project participants have diverse and different depths of technical, cultural, and domain backgrounds. They are less likely to have participated previously in the same projects, have experience with different development processes, were educated differently, come from different cultures, and speak different native languages. In addition, the participants are much less likely to have unplanned contact with other sites due to the absence of face-to-face, hallway, or lunchtime conversations.

18.2 Recipe for Success

There are a number of critical success factors described in this book that we believe are key to the success of GSD projects. While most of these factors are also important to collocated projects, their business case and necessity is stronger for GSD projects. The implementation of these factors should be seen as an investment in quality and risk mitigation. One should, however, be aware that this investment has a much higher return over a long-term partnership with a supplier.

We refer to these critical success factors in general terms as:

- *Reduce ambiguity.* Software problems are inherently uncertain and ambiguous. A lot of uncertainty and ambiguity in software projects gets resolved through informal communication, which is easier if collaborating teams are collocated. GSD projects require much thought and work to establish conventions for how remote teams work together and communicate so that they extract the intended meaning from project artifacts.
- *Maximize stability.* Instability in aspects of projects has the same detrimental effect as ambiguity. Change requests, and especially late change requests, are risky and should be monitored and managed carefully. They can dramatically slow down GSD projects; therefore, we recommend taking the time to create stable artifacts such as those for requirements and architecture even if it means delaying initiation of the construction phase of the product.
- *Understand dependencies.* Interdependencies among tasks assigned to remote teams determine the coordination needs for these teams.

It is, therefore, critical to understand these dependencies for planning and execution of the project. For example, if two tasks are highly interdependent, it is preferable to allocate these to a collocated team or teams in close proximity to each other, with considerable overlap in working time and some history of having worked together.

- *Facilitate coordination.* When teams work on interdependent tasks, they need to coordinate. Therefore, they must be able to do so commensurate with their needs. Communication is one way that teams can coordinate, but they can also coordinate via processes, management practices, and product line architectures, to name a few. These choices can be viewed as a trade-off between overhead and risk. Investing in process improvement, automation, and guidance of development should be not neglected.

- *Balance flexibility and rigidity.* Remote teams have different backgrounds, domain knowledge, language, cultures, and organization practices. The development process should be flexible enough to accommodate these differences. At the same time, certain aspects of the process should be well defined as they provide project manager visibility into the progress of the remote teams in the absence of the luxury to manage by walking around.

We have defined a phase-based iterative process framework that operationalizes the best practices codified in these critical success factors. Early phase activities such as developing a requirements model and describing the architecture are critical to provide understanding and divide the work packages for remote teams. These early phase activities are performed by small collocated teams that include some key members of the anticipated remote development sites. Without having good documentation of product requirements and its structure, we do not see how remote teams will be able to successfully implement the product.

Our research and experience also indicates that some tasks can be distributed and some are better done using a collocated team. For example, early phase activities such as architecture design require large amounts of interaction among team members and should not be distributed. Once an architecture is defined and work packages can be identified that are relatively loosely coupled to each other, distributed development teams can work on such tasks.

Breaking down a complex project into iterations with monthly sprints helps the global project manager gain visibility into the development progress and helps focus the distributed teams into achieving coordinated one-month goals. The development results of one month are tested during the next month while the development teams continue with fleshing out vertical slices of the product with ever-increasing functionality.

We recommend keeping teams smaller than ten members as this is the right size for agile development. This requires that the architects be given constraints so that within the architecture component sizes are not too large, such that a remote development team can implement a component in less than about ten staff-years of effort.

The communications for large, complex distributed projects quickly grows out of control unless some assistance is provided in the form of rules for how teams must communicate with each other and infrastructure support. For example, we recommend restricting e-mail to communicate information that is transient in nature; but for complex issues with information that may need persisting over a long time for the benefit of the project, discussion forums are preferred. Much thought must go into creating a sound knowledge management strategy. Collaborative tools such as the wiki could be considered for managing the content.

Distributed teams become more productive as they work together over time. Thus, offshoring should be viewed as a long-term strategy in which the remote supplier develops into a competence center. We do not recommend doing distributed development for the sole purpose of short-term cost reduction. While it may be possible to achieve, in our experience we have not seen any such cost reduction over the short term.

Despite all the excellent specifications that a central team writes, we believe it is still difficult for remote teams to understand everything they read, especially if they are not native speakers in the project working language. Furthermore, even well-planned projects experience changes to plan as they progress and issue resolution is more difficult when working with strangers. Thus, we recommend significant travel in the early phases of the project, face-to-face communication, and the exchange of staff members for extended periods of time among the distributed sites.

18.3 Sharing Best Practices

Our work and this book are attempts to encourage the sharing of best practices on global software development. As a result of the small amount of publicly available information on global development, we feel like we embrace even "better" practices that is, practices that have worked well at least once for some project that can be documented for others to try on another project. The basic problem is that each project is unique and there is a wide diversity of software development project types, domains, sizes, and processes used. Thus, there is no guarantee that a practice used successfully on one project will even be a good practice on another project.

Nevertheless, we do not believe that the discipline of software engineering will be improved without widespread sharing of best practices and case studies. Handbooks of best practices, rules of thumb, and organizational patterns and antipatterns are the tools that a project manager uses to include others' experiences into his own and plan successful projects.

Another way to advance the state-of-the-practice in software engineering is through experimentation. We have been fortunate to do so with Carnegie Mellon University, Harvard Business School, International Institute of Information Technology Bangalore, Monmouth University, Penn State University, Technical University of Munich, University of Limerick, and the Pontifical Catholic University of Rio Grande de Sul. This joint Global Studio Project has progressed over multiple years, and it is large enough using student development teams from five nations across four continents such that a rich set of cultural, organizational, and technical issues can be studied. Although the use of student teams will not exactly match the industrial environment, it is a useful simulation. For example, graduate students participating in the project as part of a capstone course will receive a grade for the course rather than a salary and bonus. Nevertheless, there is the opportunity to be rewarded for good work. Also, many of today's software engineering graduate students have some amount of industrial experience; thus, their skills profiles are not that much different from the staff at our low-cost supplier companies.

The biggest advantage of this experimental project is that there is no business risk associated with a failed project. Thus, the research team can learn from both successes and failures. Promising technologies, tools, and processes can be experimentally applied, whereas an industrial project would tend to minimize risk and not attempt brand-new approaches. No industrial software project manager wants his or her project to be experimental.

We have instrumented this project to collect large amounts of quantitative and qualitative data as the iterations progress. This data is made available to software engineering researchers. In this way, we can get a better understanding of what works and what does not work for global software development.

18.4 Summary and Conclusions

The world is certainly getting flatter (Friedman, 2005), especially for software engineers. It is not our intent to analyze all the political and economic issues associated with global software development. There is significant evidence that globalization is a non-stoppable trend and, as a consequence, GSD is a necessity. Our goal, therefore, is to understand how global software development projects can achieve successful outcomes. We believe the better practices and rules of thumb we have suggested can also benefit larger complex collocated projects. If you are a software engineer, then in the reality of today's business world, the chances are very good that you will be collaborating with colleagues in other countries. It is best to get ready, and we hope you are enriched by the experiences of working with foreign engineers. We hope that you enjoy this part of your work life and take time to savor the German beers, Swiss chocolates, Indian chai, Peking duck, American barbecue, Polish sausage, and other pleasures while making lifelong friendships with engineers who grew up in countries other than your own.

We hope that you will find useful the suggestions, tips, and practices we have described for global software development. The biggest reward for any software engineer is to see the products he worked on developing being used by others. Engineers engaged in global projects will likely have the opportunity for world travel and will learn to work with people from different backgrounds and cultures. As you attempt to manage complexity and overcome all the risks associated with a successful development, we believe you will have fun working on such distributed projects. We wish you good luck on your next global software development project.

References

Carmel, E., *Global Software Teams: Collaborating Across Borders and Time Zones,* Prentice Hall, Upper Saddle River, NJ, 1999.

Friedman, T., *The World is Flat: A Brief History of the Twenty-First Century,* Farrar, Straus and Giroux, 2005.

Johnson, J., "Turning chaos into success," *Software Magazine,* 19(3): 30–39, Dec. 1999/Jan. 2000.

Mockus, A. and Herbsleb, J., "Challenges of global software development," *Proceedings of the Seventh International Software Metrics Symposium,* April 4–6, 2001, London, England, pp. 182–184.

Index

Q

Index